Toxic Sludge Is Good for You
Lies, Damn Lies and the Public Relations Industry

BY

John C. Stauber
AND
Sheldon Rampton

Common Courage Press
MONROE, MAINE

First edition, twelfth printing

Common Courage Press
Box 702
Monroe, Maine 04951
Phone: (207) 525-0900
Fax: (207) 525-3068

Typeset by Strong Silent Type, Madison, Wisconsin
Cover by Dan Perkins
Cartoons by Dan Perkins and Kirk Anderson

Printed in Canada

Library of Congress Cataloging-In-Publication Data

Stauber, John C. (John Clyde), 1953–
    Toxic sludge is good for you : lies, damn lies and the public rela-tions industry / John Stauber and Sheldon Rampton.
        p.   cm.
    Includes index.
    ISBN 1-56751-061-2. -- ISBN 1-56751-060-4 (pbk.)
    1. Public relations--Corporations--United States. 2. Industrial publicity--United States--Corrupt practices.   3. Corporations--Corrupt practices--United States.   4. Public relations firms--Corrupt practices--United States.   I. Rampton, Sheldon, 1957-   II. Title.
HD59.6.76S72   1995
659.2'09723--dc20   95–21185
                                                                    CIP

D0454278

CONTENTS

Acknowledgments

We are especially grateful to investigative journalist Joel Bleifuss. Joel's extensive writings, which appeared under his byline in *PR Watch* and *In These Times,* have been incorporated in these chapters: "Poisoning the Grassroots," "Silencing Spring" and "All the News That's Fit to Print."

Others whose research or writings have been incorporated in this book are Keith Ashdown, Jill Cashen, Ronnie Cummins, Rob Inerfeld and Peter Montague. Thanks to Liz Chilsen for permission to use portions from *Friends In Deed* in "The Torturers' Lobby." Thanks also for permission to incorporate material by Sheldon Rampton published previously in *Z Magazine* under the title, "Colombia: The Bosnia In Our Own Backyard."

We wish to express our gratitude to the staffs and boards of the following nonprofit foundations: CS Fund, Educational Foundation of America, Foundation for Deep Ecology, HKH Foundation, Ottinger Foundation, Florence and John Schumann Foundation, Stern Family Fund and Town Creek Foundation.

The following friends have provided support, ideas, encouragement and inspiration: Grant Abert, Greg Bates, Elva Barnes, Audrey Bedwell, Laura Berger, Eileen Cyncor, Mark Dowie, Carol Bernstein Ferry, William H. Ferry, Wade Greene, Cherrie Ivey, Linda Jameson, Kevin McCauley, Robert McChesney, Joe Mendelson, David Merritt, Alida Messinger, Dan Perkins, Renee Rampton, Scott Robbe, Debra Schwarze, Flic Shooter, John H. Stauber, Martin Teitel, Nancy Ward, Ken Whyte, Walda Wood and Winifred Woodmansee.

Torches of Liberty

by Mark Dowie

On the surface it seemed like an ordinary publicity stunt for "female emancipation," the pre-Depression equivalent of women's liberation. A contingent of New York debutantes marched down Fifth Avenue in the 1929 Easter Parade, each openly lighting and smoking cigarettes. It was the first time in the memory of most Americans that any woman who wasn't a prostitute had been seen smoking in public.

It was dubbed the "torches of liberty contingent" by Edward Bernays, its brilliant behind-the-scenes organizer. Bernays, a nephew of Sigmund Freud, later admitted that he had been paid a tidy sum to orchestrate the march by George Washington Hill, president of the American Tobacco Company. But long before the public learned who had engineered the parade, it had achieved its goal of breaking the taboo against female smoking. Within months, in fact, the politest of American ladies were puffing in public and sales of Hill's Lucky Strikes were soaring.

The event is still hailed in public relations lore as a "triumph." Some people consider it *the* coup that launched a whole new, distinctively American industry.

Most of us are aware of public relations. "That's just a lot of PR," we say, with smug confidence that we have pierced the veil of hype around us rather than be taken in by some anonymous huckster. But few outside the public relations industry know how well PR really works, and fewer still realize how often we are persuaded by it. Nor do many of us know how much of our "news" and other information originates from the desks of public relations practitioners. "The best PR is never noticed," says the proud unwritten slogan of the trade.

The sad truth, which this book amply documents, is that PR executives are today mediating public communications as never before. "Flacks" are no longer mere authors of press memos, "video news releases" and pre-packaged articles used by lazy reporters and editors. Nor are they simply "builders of bridges into prosperity . . . in a fly-by-night, flim-flam business," as theatrical publicist Ben Sonnenberg once described his chosen profession. That too we now accept about PR. But the intricate practice of relating to the public has evolved even further and requires the kind of close examination that John Stauber and Sheldon Rampton provide.

PR has become a communications medium in its own right, an industry designed to alter perception, reshape reality and manufacture consent. It is run by a fraternity carefully organized so that only insiders can observe their peers at work. Veteran PR professionals can read the front page of almost any newspaper in the country, or watch a segment of broadcast news and identify which of their peers "placed," "handled" or "massaged" a specific story—even which executives arranged the "placement," managed the "spin" or wrote the CEO's quotes. But can you or I? Or do we assume, as we are supposed to, that some dogged reporter, trained and determined to be the objective "eyes and ears of the public," set out to research, investigate and report his or her findings as accurately as possible?

This book is of particular interest to me as a journalist, not only because I spend so much of my time on the phone with "communications directors," "public information officers" and "community relations liaisons," but also because about a third of America's currently practicing PR men and women began their careers as journalists, where they learned how to investigate people and institutions, how newsrooms work and how to write a compelling and informative story. In a strange way many of them still *are* journalists. Academicians who study media now estimate that about 40% of all "news" flows virtually unedited from the public relations offices, prompting a prominent PR exec to boast that "the best PR ends up looking like news."

Also disconcerting is the fact that the 150,000 PR practitioners in the US outnumber the country's 130,000 reporters (and with the media downsizing its newsrooms, the gap is widening). Furthermore, some of the country's best journalism schools now send more than half their graduates directly into public relations (an almost traitorous career choice to traditionalists like myself who instruct students how to handle PR executives and circumvent the barriers they erect between the truth and the story they want told about their clients).

With media becoming dependent on PR for more and more of its content, public relations executives have become inordinately powerful. Even the most energetic reporters know that they have to be somewhat deferential in the presence of a powerful publicist. No one on a national beat can afford to get on the wrong side of a Frank Mankiewicz or a Harold Burson knowing that their firms (Hill & Knowlton and Burson-Marsteller) together represent a third of the most quotable sources in the country.

❖ ❖ ❖

People often equate public relations with the advertising industry, and in fact almost every major Madison Avenue agency, from J. Walter Thompson to Young & Rubicam, owns or is paired with a large PR firm. But PR firms carry out activities that are often considerably more secretive and sinister than designing clever slogans and video imagery. The modern "account" managed by a PR/advertising giant can now package a global campaign that includes a strategic blend of "paid media" (advertising) and "free media" (public relations). Add to that some of the other standard services offered by most PR firms—including "crisis management," industrial espionage, organized censorship and infiltration of civic and political groups—and you have a formidable combination of persuasive techniques available to large corporations and anyone else who can afford to hire the services of a PR firm. You know you're looking at propaganda when you open your newspaper and notice an ad for General Electric, but you're less likely to notice the rest of the mix— the story about GE that appears on page one, which may well have been placed by the same firm that placed the ad, and may in addition have deployed a private investigator to infiltrate and subvert the efforts of an activist organization attempting to combat GE's environmental practices. The independence of the press, already challenged by the influence of Madison Avenue, is now being further compromised by the interdependence of advertising and PR.

Corporations use the term "integrated communications" to describe this massive institutional meld, and its consequences are profound. The methods of modern advertising, steeped in subliminal psychology and imagery aimed at the subconscious, have proven themselves effective at selling cars, mouthwash and cigarettes. Today similar methods are used almost reflexively to promote and protect ideas, policies, candidates, ideologies, tyrants and hazardous products. As propaganda, once the honorable purview of speechwriters, editorialists and orators, bypasses the conscious mind and is targeted at the subconscious, the consequences for culture, democracy and public health are staggering to contemplate.

As Stauber and Rampton clearly demonstrate in chapter after chapter of this book, a single public relations professional with access to media, a basic understanding of mass psychology and a fistful of dollars can unleash in society forces that make permanent winners out of otherwise-evident losers—whether they be products, politicians, corporations or ideas. This is an awesome power we give to an industry that gravitates to wealth, offers surplus power and influence to those who need it least, and operates largely beyond public view.

It is critical that consumers of media in democratic societies understand the origin of information and the process by which it is mediated, particularly when they are being deceived. Thus it is essential that they understand public relations. By offering between-the-lines analysis of PR's role in some of the most important stories of our time, this book leaves its readers with a much better sense of what is genuine. By deconstructing the modern triumphs of PR, it also shows how objective inquiry becomes subsumed by manufactured information, which either changes the public's perception of an event or the outcome of the event itself. In such an environment, facts cannot survive, nor can truth prevail.

Mark Dowie, a former publisher and editor of Mother Jones *magazine, is the recipient of 14 major journalism awards, including an unprecedented three National Magazine awards.*

CHAPTER ONE

BURNING BOOKS
BEFORE THEY'RE PRINTED

Who kills a Man kills a reasonable creature, God's Image; but he who
destroys a good Book, kills reason itself, kills the Image of God.

JOHN MILTON
Areopagitica

"All documents . . . are confidential," warned the September 7,
1990 memo from Betsy Gullickson, senior vice-president at the giant
Ketchum public relations firm. "Make sure that everything—even
notes to yourself—are so stamped. . . . Remember that we have a
shredder; give documents to Lynette for shredding. All conversations
are confidential, too. Please be careful talking in the halls, in eleva-
tors, in restaurants, etc. All suppliers must sign confidentiality agree-
ments. If you are faxing documents to the client, another office or
to anyone else, call them to let them know that a fax is coming. If
you are expecting a fax, you or your Account Coordinator should
stand by the machine and wait for it. We don't want those documents lying around for anybody to pick up."[1]

Gullickson, a 1969 graduate of Northwestern University's prestigious Medill School of Journalism,[2] understood perfectly the need
for secrecy. If word leaked out, the media might have had a field
day with Ketchum's plan to scuttle a groundbreaking environmental book even before it went to press.

The stakes were high for Ketchum's client, the California Raisin
Advisory Board (CALRAB), the business association of California
raisin growers. In 1986, CALRAB had scored big with a series of

clever TV commercials using the "California Dancing Raisins." The
singing, dancing raisins, animated through a technique known as
"claymation," were so popular that they had transcended their TV-
commercial origins. Fan mail addressed to the Raisins was forwarded
to Ketchum, along with phone inquiries from the media and public
clamoring for live public performances. Ketchum obligingly supplied
live, costumed characters dressed as the Raisins, who performed at
the White House Easter Egg Roll and Christmas Tree Lighting, Macy's
Thanksgiving Day Parade, and "A Claymation Christmas Celebration"
on the CBS television network.

In the summer of 1988, the Raisins were sent out on a 27-city
national tour, beginning in New York and ending in Los Angeles.
Along the way, they performed in hotel lobbies, children's hospitals
and convalescent centers and supermarkets. In several cities, they
were greeted by the mayor and given keys to the city. They visited
historic landmarks, singing and dancing their version of "I Heard It
Through the Grapevine." They performed at a charity benefit hon-
oring singer Ray Charles and his claymation counterpart, "Raisin Ray."
Over 3,000 people joined the California Dancing Raisins Fan Club,
and a research poll found that the Raisins were second in popular-
ity only to comedian Bill Cosby.[3]

For CALRAB, of course, the real payoff came in raisin sales, which
had risen 17 percent since the Dancing Raisins were first introduced.
Behind the scenes, however, trouble was brewing, and Gullickson's
secret memo outlined Ketchum's plan to "manage the crisis."

The "crisis" was a science writer named David Steinman. In 1985
while working for the *LA Weekly,* Steinman had written a story about
fish contaminated from toxic waste dumped near his home in the
Santa Monica Bay area, and was shocked when a test of his own
blood showed astronomical levels of both DDT and PCBs. Steinman
had read the research linking these chemicals to higher rates of
cancer and other diseases, and started "wondering how many other
poisons were in the food I ate. It started me asking why government officials, who had known about the dumping for years, had
withheld the information for so long." In his search for the answers
to these questions, Steinman began a five-year investigation, using
the Freedom of Information Act to obtain obscure government
research reports. Based on this research, he had written a book, titled
Diet for a Poisoned Planet, scheduled for publication in 1990.

Steinman's investigation had uncovered evidence showing that
hundreds of toxic carcinogens and other contaminants, mostly

pesticides, are found routinely in US foods from raisins to yogurt to beef. For example, government inspectors found "raisins had 110 industrial chemical and pesticide residues in sixteen samples." *Diet for a Poisoned Planet* recommends that people avoid any but organically-grown raisins raised without pesticides.[4]

By compiling this information in book form, *Diet for a Poisoned Planet* enables readers to make safer food choices. But before shoppers can use the information, they must first hear about the book, through media reviews and interviews with the author during a publicity campaign in the weeks after the book is published. And the California Raisin Advisory Board wanted to make sure that Steinman's book was dead on arrival.

PR firms, of course, are the experts at organizing publicity campaigns. So who better to launch an *anti*-publicity campaign, to convince journalists to ignore Steinman and his book?

For Spies' Eyes Only

Our copy of Betsy Gullickson's memo came from an employee of Ketchum PR. Despite the risk of being fired, conscience drove this corporate whistleblower to reveal Ketchum's campaign aimed at concealing the possible health risks from high pesticide levels in California raisins and other foods.

"I find it very discouraging when I read in the paper that cancer among children has increased dramatically, and they don't know why," our source explained. "I believe that people have the right to know about the little Dancing Raisins and the possibility that they might be harming children. There is a new censorship in this country, based on nothing but dollars and cents."

According to the 1994 *O'Dwyer's Directory of PR Firms,* Ketchum is the sixth largest public relations company in the United States, receiving net fees of over $50 million per year. Headquartered in New York City, Ketchum represents a number of corporate food clients, including Dole Foods, Wendy's, the Potato Board, Oscar Mayer Foods, Miller Brewing, Kikkoman, H.J. Heinz, the Beef Industry Council, the California Almond Board, and the California Raisin Advisory Board.[5] In addition to writing press releases and organizing news conferences, Ketchum aggressively markets its services in "crisis management," a growing specialty within the PR industry. In a profile written for *O'Dwyer's PR Services Report,* Ketchum boasted of its experience handling PR problems ranging "from toxic waste crises to low-level nuclear wastes, from community relations at Superfund sites to scientific meetings where issues like toxicology of pesticides are reviewed."[6]

Gullickson's PR expertise is in "food marketing strategic counsel,"[7] and Steinman's book is the type of "crisis" that she was hired to manage. Her memo outlined a plan to assign "broad areas of responsibility," such as "intelligence/information gathering," to specific Ketchum employees and to Gary Obenauf of CALRAB. Months before the publication of *Diet for a Poisoned Planet,* Ketchum sought to "obtain [a] copy of [the] book galleys or manuscript and publisher's tour schedule." Gullickson recommended that spokespeople "conduct one-on-one briefings/interviews with the trade and general consumer media in the markets most acutely interested in the issue. . . . The [Ketchum] agency is currently attempting to get a tour schedule so that we can 'shadow' Steinman's appearances; best scenario: we will have our spokesman in town prior to or in conjunction with Steinman's appearances."[8]

To get this information, Ketchum used an informant involved with the book's marketing campaign to tell them when and on which talk shows Steinman was booked. "They called up each and every talk show," explained our source inside Ketchum. A "list of media to receive low-key phone inquiries regarding the Steinman book" included specific journalists at the *New York Times,* the Larry King Show, and the *Washington Post.* The callers from Ketchum argued that it would be unfair to allow Steinman on the show without the other side of the issue, or tried to depict him as an "off-the-wall extremist without credibility."

Ketchum wasn't the only PR firm working to cripple Steinman's book publicity efforts. Jean Rainey of Edelman Public Relations contacted the *Today Show,* providing anti-Steinman material and offering to make available "the president of the American Dietetic Association" to counter Steinman. Apparently she succeeded in bouncing him from the program. *Today* interviewed Steinman, but never aired the segment.[9]

Government Moves to Suppress

Gullickson's memo also suggested possible "external ambassadors" who might be recruited into the campaign, including Republican California Governor Pete Wilson and Democratic Party fundraiser Tony Coelho. Thanks to a pesticide industry front group with deep Republican connections, the stealth campaign against Steinman's book even reached into the White House and other arms of the US government.

Elizabeth M. Whelan is a prominent anti-environmentalist who heads the American Council on Science and Health (ACSH), a group funded largely by the chemical industry. The ACSH is also a client of Ketchum PR. On July 12, 1990, Whelan wrote a letter to then-White House Chief of Staff John Sununu warning that Steinman and others "who specialize in terrifying consumers" were "threatening the US standard of living and, indeed, may pose a future threat to national security." Whelan's letter was copied to the heads of the government's Food and Drug Administration, Department of Agriculture, Department of Health and Human Services, Environmental Protection Agency, and the Surgeon General. Whelan also contacted her friend, former Surgeon General C. Everett Koop, whom she calls a "close colleague."[10] Dr. Koop joined the attack against Steinman's book, calling it "trash" in a statement mailed nationwide.[11]

In September 1990, before Steinman's book was published, the USDA initiated its anti-book campaign through the Agriculture Extension Service. The federally-funded effort was led by government employees Kenneth Hall, Bonnie Poli, Cynthia Garman-Squier and Janet Poley. According to a government memo, the Department of Agriculture group felt that "communications with the media by concerned parties have been effective in minimizing potential public concern about issues in the book." Attached to the memo is a "confidential analysis" of Steinman's book written by the National Food Processors Association, a food and pesticide trade group. The memo warns recipients that this information is "for internal use and should not be released" to the news media.[12]

Dr. William Marcus, who was then a senior science advisor to the US Environmental Protection Agency, wrote the introduction to *Diet for a Poisoned Planet.* Marcus' views were his own, but they greatly angered Whelan. She asked White House Chief of Staff Sununu to personally investigate the matter, and exerted pressure to have the introduction removed from the book. Marcus refused, and was later fired from the EPA.[13] Government policy has now been changed to prohibit officials from writing book forwards.

Deciding What You'll Swallow

You are probably going to eat some food today. It is possible, in fact, that you are in the process of eating *right now.*

You have the right to eat. You have the right to eat wholesome foods. You have the right to read, even while you are eating. You have the right to read *about* the foods you are about to eat. Neither

Ketchum Public Relations nor the White House has any right to interfere with your access to good food or good reading materials.

You have never voted for a politician who campaigned on a pledge that he would work to limit your access to information about the food you eat. You never voted for Ketchum PR, and, if you are like most people, you've never even *heard* of them. You never gave your consent for them to become involved in your life, and in return, they have never bothered to *ask* for your consent. After all, they're not working for *you*. They're working for the California Raisin Advisory Board.

One of the most cherished freedoms in a democracy is the right to freely participate in the "marketplace of ideas." We value this freedom because without it, all our other freedoms are impossible to defend. In a democracy every idea, no matter how absurd or offensive, is allowed to compete freely for our attention and acceptance. Turn on the TV, and you'll find plenty of absurd and offensive examples of this principle in action. On the Sunday public affairs shows you'll find Republicans, Democrats, Republicans who love too much, and Democrats who love Republicans. On "A Current Affair" or "Oprah Winfrey," you'll find self-proclaimed werewolves, worshippers of Madonna, and doomsday prophets from the lunatic fringes of American society.

Unfortunately, what you *won't* find can kill you.

Diet for a Poisoned Planet is a serious, important contribution to the public debate over health, the environment, and food safety. It fell victim to a PR campaign designed to prevent it from ever *reaching* the "marketplace of ideas." And it isn't alone. Here are some other examples:

- In 1992, John Robbins was promoting his book, *May All Be Fed*, which advocates a strict vegetarian diet. He became the target of an anti-book campaign by Morgan & Myers PR, working on behalf of the world's largest milk promotion group, the National Dairy Board. Based in Jefferson, Wisconsin, Morgan & Myers is the nation's 42nd largest PR firm, with about sixty employees and a 1993 net fee intake of $3.7 million. Within its field of specialization—representing agribusiness interests—Morgan & Myers ranks fifth in the United States. Its clients include Kraft, the Philip Morris subsidiary that buys and sells most of America's cheese; Upjohn, a major producer of antibiotics used on livestock; and Sandoz, a manufacturer of atrazine herbicide, a carcinogen that contaminates thousands of water wells.[14]

THIS MODERN WORLD

by Tom Tomorrow

As with Ketchum's California Raisins campaign, Morgan & Myers used behind-the-scenes contacts to undermine Robbins' publicity tour, thereby limiting his book's public exposure and readership. A Morgan & Myers memo of September 17, 1992, states that "M&M currently is monitoring coverage of Robbins' media tour," to counter his advice that readers cut back their consumption of dairy products. The memo was widely distributed to key dairy industry contacts. It contained the schedule of Robbins' book tour and provided this tactical warning: "Do not issue any news release or statement. Doing so only calls attention to his message. . . . Ideally, any response should come from a third party, uninvolved in the dairy industry."[15]

- The September 22, 1981, *Washington Post* reported that "a single telephone call from a DuPont public relations man to the Book-of-the-Month Club financially doomed an unflattering history of the

DuPont family and its businesses." The book by author Gerard Colby Zilg, titled *DuPont: Behind the Nylon Curtain,* was a "relentlessly critical" exposé of the business and personal affairs of the wealthy DuPont family. After a copy of the manuscript found its way into the hands of the DuPonts, they deployed PR representative Harold G. Brown Jr., who phoned the Book-of-the-Month Club editor to say that several people at DuPont considered the book "scurrilous" and "actionable."

The Book-of-the-Month Club had already contracted with Prentice-Hall, the publisher, to feature *DuPont* as a November selection of its Fortune Book Club, but a few days after Brown's phone call the club called Prentice-Hall to back out of the deal. Apparently intimidated by the implied threat of a DuPont lawsuit, Prentice-Hall made no effort to enforce its contract with the Book-of-the-Month Club or to seek money damages. Instead, the publisher reduced the book's press run from 15,000 to 10,000 copies, and cut its advertising budget from $15,000 to $5,500, even though the book was getting favorable reviews in major publications. The *Los Angeles Times,* for example, called it "a vastly readable book and . . . a very important one." Peter Grenquist, president of Prentice-Hall's trade book division, ordered the book's editor, Bram Cavin, not to discuss the matter with the author. In October, three months later, conscience finally drove Cavin to disobey Grenquist's order and inform the author of the phone call from DuPont. Cavin was later fired for being "unproductive." [16]

- PR firms also campaigned against the book *Beyond Beef,* by activist Jeremy Rifkin. *Beyond Beef* recommends that people stop eating beef for ethical, health and environmental reasons. Its message has been loudly denounced by both the Beef Council and the National Dairy Board, clients of Ketchum and Morgan & Myers, respectively. Rifkin's enemies hired an infiltrator to pose as a volunteer in his office. The spy—Seymour "Bud" Vestermark, whose infiltrations of other organizations are detailed in chapter 5 of this book—obtained Rifkin's book tour itinerary, after which all hell broke loose. [17]

In *The War Against The Greens,* author David Helvarg reports that Rifkin's spring 1992 national book tour "had to be canceled after it was repeatedly sabotaged. Melinda Mullin, *Beyond Beef*'s publicist at Dutton Books, says . . . radio and TV producers who'd scheduled Rifkin's appearance began receiving calls from a woman claiming to be Mullin cancelling or misrepresenting Rifkin's plans. Finally, Mullin had to begin using a code name with the producers. Liz Einbinder, a San Francisco-based radio producer who had had *Beyond Beef* on her desk for several weeks, was surprised to receive angry calls and an anonymous package denouncing Rifkin within hours of placing her first call to Mullin. This led to speculation that Dutton's New York phones might be tapped." [18]

Making the World Safe from Democracy

The public relations or "PR" industry did not even exist prior to the twentieth century, but it has grown steadily and appears poised for even more dramatic growth in the future. No one knows exactly how much money is spent each year in the United States on public relations, but $10 billion is considered a conservative estimate. "Publicity" was once the work of carnival hawkers and penny-ante hustlers smoking cheap cigars and wearing cheap suits. Today's PR professionals are recruited from the ranks of former journalists, retired politicians and eager-beaver college graduates anxious to rise in the corporate world. They hobnob internationally with corporate CEOs, senators and US presidents. They use sophisticated psychology, opinion polling and complex computer databases so refined that they can pinpoint the prevailing "psychographics" of individual city neighborhoods. Press agents used to rely on news releases and publicity stunts to attract attention for their clients. In today's electronic age, the PR industry uses 800-numbers and telemarketing, advanced databases, computer bulletin boards, simultaneous multi-location fax transmission and "video news releases"—entire news stories, written, filmed and produced by PR firms and transmitted by satellite feed to hundreds of TV stations around the world. Video news releases are designed to be indistinguishable from genuine news, and are typically used as "story segments" on TV news shows without any attribution or disclaimer indicating that they are in fact subtle paid advertisements. "Most of what you see on TV is, in effect, a canned PR product. Most of what you read in the paper and see on television is not news," says a senior vice-president with Gray & Company public relations. [19]

The PR industry also orchestrates many of the so-called "grassroots citizen campaigns" that lobby Washington, state and local governments. Unlike genuine grassroots movements, however, these industry-generated "astroturf" movements are controlled by the corporate interests that pay their bills. On behalf of the Philip Morris tobacco company, for example, Burson-Marsteller (the world's largest PR firm) created the "National Smokers Alliance" to mobilize smokers into a grassroots lobby for "smokers' rights." Deceptive PR has become so cynical that sometimes it staggers belief. To fight former Attorney General Ed Meese's Pornography Commission, *Playboy* and *Penthouse* magazines had Gray & Company PR create a front group called "Americans for Constitutional Freedom," to "assist in countering the idea that those who opposed the commission's efforts were motivated only by financial self-interest" or were "somehow 'pro-pornography.' " [20] To defeat environmentalists, PR firms have created green-sounding front groups such as "The Global Climate Coalition" and the "British Columbia Forest Alliance."

In defense of these activities, the PR industry claims that it is simply participating in the democratic process and and contributing to public debate. In reality, the industry carefully conceals most of its activities from public view. This invisibility is part of a deliberate strategy for manipulating public opinion and government policy. "Persuasion, by its definition, is subtle," says another PR exec. "The best PR ends up looking like news. You never know when a PR agency is being effective; you'll just find your views slowly shifting." [21]

Today's PR industry is related to democracy in the same way that prostitution is related to sex. When practiced voluntarily for love, both can exemplify human communications at its best. When they are bought and sold, however, they are transformed into something hidden and sordid. There is nothing wrong with many of the *techniques* used by the PR industry—lobbying, grassroots organizing, using the news media to put ideas before the public. As individuals, we not only have the *right* to engage in these activities, we have a *responsibility* to participate in the decisions that shape our society and our lives. Ordinary citizens have the right to organize for social change—better working conditions, health care, fair prices for family farmers, safe food, freedom from toxins, social justice, a humane foreign policy. But ordinary citizens cannot afford the multi-million-dollar campaigns that PR firms undertake on behalf of their special interest clients, usually large corporations, business associations and governments. Raw money enables the PR industry to mobilize private detectives, attorneys, broadcast faxes, satellite feeds, sophisticated information systems and other expensive, high-tech resources to out-maneuver, overpower and outlast true citizen reformers.

Talking Back to the Flacks

Although the public relations industry is a twentieth-century phenom-enon, the art of influencing opinion has a long history, dating in fact to the days of ancient Athens, the first recorded western democracy. Aristotle's *Rhetoric* remains one of the most insightful books ever written on the subject. Aristotle argues that rhetoric is an "art" as opposed to the sciences, which are governed by logic. The sciences deal with measurable quantities, known facts, and principles of proof based on propositions which can definitely be labeled "true" or "false." In social life, however, people are often confronted with situations in which many of the facts are unknown and unknow-able. In addition, competing sectors within society have conflicting interests. It is often impossible to say for sure whether a proposition is "true" or "false," and scientific logic is incapable of evaluating statements whose degree of truth can only be approximated using concepts like "maybe," "probably," or "probably not." Instead of logic, therefore, people turn to *rhetoric,* the art of communication and persuasion.

Aristotle recognized that rhetoric could be used to mislead as well as to enlighten the public. Persuasive speakers could lead their audi-ence into unwise choices. For this reason, he argued that rhetoric should be widely taught and understood, so that the wise members of society would be able to contend effectively with the rhetoric of the unwise. Society would be best served if the public could choose from a range of contending arguments, and if people were trained in the skills necessary to recognize manipulative uses of rhetoric.

Aristotle's analysis is over 2,300 years old, but it offers the best solution that we have found to the problem of democracy in our own age—the age of public relations. Today's opinion manipulation industry is a powerful giant, but like Goliath, it is a giant with a fatal weakness. When the public is educated about its techniques, it often loses its ability to mislead and manipulate. In Nevada, for example, Don Williams, president of Altamira Communications and widely known as a Nevada "political king maker," attempted in 1992 to per-suade the state to serve as a national storage site for nuclear waste. When the nuclear industry's PR activities were exposed in Nevada newspapers, public opinion turned decisively *against* the plan.[22]

The founders of the American revolution argued that the price of freedom is eternal vigilance. "Every man ought to exercise the faculties of his mind, and think and examine for himself, that he may be the less likely to be imposed on, and that he may form as accurate an opinion as possible of the measures of his ruler," wrote one farmer who campaigned against the British. Christopher Gadsen, another American revolutionary, argued that it was easier to stop the work of "crafty, dissembling, insinuating men" *before* rather than *after* they "carry their point against you."[23] The price of democracy is the same today as it was in the days of Samuel Adams and Thomas Jefferson, and the PR industry is a haven for many of the "crafty, dissembling men" we need to guard against.

The PR industry is a little like the title character in the 1933 Claude Rains movie, *The Invisible Man*. Rains plays an evil scientist who attempts to rule the world, committing crimes such as robbery and murder and using his invisibility to evade detection. *The Invisible Man* was an early special effects film, using hidden wires and other tricks to make ashtrays, guns, and other objects float in mid-air as though they were manipulated by an invisible hand.

Instead of ashtrays and guns, the PR industry seeks to manipulate public opinion and government policy. But it can only manipulate while it remains invisible.

We like to think of this book as the literary equivalent of a nice, big can of fluorescent orange spray paint. We are spray-painting the Invisible Man in order to make him visible again. We want the public at large to recognize the skilled propagandists of industry and government who are affecting public opinion and determining public policies, while remaining (they hope) out of public view.

In a democracy, everyone needs to know who is really in charge, who makes the decisions, and in whose interest. Democracies function best without Invisible Men.

CHAPTER TWO

THE ART of the HUSTLE
ANd the SCIENCE of PROPAGANdA

A state is bound to be more dangerous if it is not governed openly
by the people, but secretly by political forces that are not widely
known or understood.

ANDREI SAKHAROV

In 1836 legendary showman P.T. Barnum began his career by buying an old Negro slave woman named Joice Heth and exhibiting her
to the public as "George Washington's childhood nursemaid."

Joice Heth claimed to be 160 years old. Was she for real? The
man who coined the phrase, "there's a sucker born every minute,"
kept the public guessing through a clever series of forged letters to
the editors of New York newspapers. Written by Barnum himself
and signed by various fake names, some of the letters denounced
Barnum as a fraud. In other letters, also written by Barnum, he
praised himself as a great man who was performing a service by
giving the public a chance to see George Washington's "mammy."
The letters succeeded in stirring up controversy. Joice Heth was discussed in news reports and editorial columns, and the public turned
out in droves to see for themselves. Barnum collected as much as
$1500 per week from New Yorkers who came to see the pipe-smok-
ing old Negro woman.

When Joice Heth died, doctors performed an autopsy and estimated her true age at around eighty. Barnum handled the situation
like the PR pro that he was. He said he was shocked, *deeply* shocked,
at the way this woman had deceived him.[1]

Barnum knew that in his publicity for "the greatest show on earth," it didn't matter whether people called him a scoundrel or a saint. The important thing was that the newspapers spelled his name right, and that they mentioned him often. He was one of the first people to manipulate the news for fun and profit.

The 1830s marked the beginnings of what we now call the "mass media" with the rise of "penny presses" such as the *New York Sun* which used low newsstand prices to draw in a large readership. Because of their larger circulation, they were able to charge enough for ads that advertisers, rather than readers, became their main source of income. This change also gave advertisers more power to influence the news and editorial sections. Newspapers offered "free puff stories" to paying advertisers—a practice which is widely denied but still common today, especially in the business, food and automobile sections of newspapers.[2]

This transformation deepened as the years progressed. According to James Melvin Lee's *History of American Journalism,* it was possible by the end of the 19th century "to insert at a higher cost almost any advertisement disguised as a bit of news. Sometimes these paid reading notices of advertisers were distinguished by star or dagger, but more frequently there was no sign to indicate to the readers that the account had been bought and paid for and was not a regular news item."[3]

By disguising paid notices as "news," companies tried to bypass readers' innate skepticism toward advertising. Then, as now, readers understood that advertisements were "propaganda," and they were more likely to believe a story if it seemed to come from an independent reporter.

The First Flacks

Before the public relations industry existed, companies employed "press agents" to feed advertisements and publicity to newspapers. Many early press agents worked for circuses, Broadway shows and other entertainment enterprises. Often they were recruited from the ranks of underpaid reporters anxious for a way to earn more money. They used flattery, pleading and, of course, payments of money to grease the wheels for their clients' publicity. They were colorful, scheming, desperate men, drifters and con artists with bad reputations, constantly scrounging for clients and begging for favors.[4] In 1911, writer Will Irwin described them as "the only group of men proud of being called liars."[5]

Like P.T. Barnum, the early press agents were more interested in generating publicity for their clients than in building "images" or "reputations." The railroads, utility companies and big businesses like Standard Oil were just starting to learn that their profit margins could be affected by the public's opinion of them. When a reporter suggested that the New York Central Railroad should adjust its train schedules to accommodate the public, New York Central President William Vanderbilt angrily replied, "The public be damned!" His remark provoked public outrage, and attacks by the New York legislature forced him to sell off part of his railroad holdings.[6]

At the turn of the century, social movements rose up to challenge the power of big business: the Grange movement, the Socialist Party, the Greenbackers, the Populists and Progressives. The labor movement was growing, and radical agitators were urging exploited farmers to "raise less corn and more hell." President Teddy Roosevelt coined the word "muckrakers" to describe the growing number of journalists who were dedicating themselves to exposing the corruption of business and government.[7] William Randolph Hearst's newspapers attacked privilege, monopoly, corporate power, and the "plunderbund" of banks and trusts. The public-be-damned attitude of "robber barons" like Vanderbilt turned public opinion against the railroads, prompting Congress and state legislatures to enact over 2,000 laws affecting the industry between 1908 and 1913.[8]

Ivy Lee was one of the first consultants to offer the service of corporate image-building. According to PR industry historian Scott Cutlip, Lee worked for J.P. Morgan's International Harvester Company to stave off antitrust action and later for the Pennsylvania Railroad, which hired him in 1906 to "take 'offensive' measures as it were, to place our 'case' before the public."[9] This led in turn to work as personal representative of railroad magnate E.H. Harriman. In 1914, Lee was hired as counsel to John D. Rockefeller, Jr. The Rockefeller family had become widely hated because of the ruthless, monopolistic business tactics of their company, Standard Oil. Lee is widely credited (incorrectly, according to T.J. Ross, his former business partner) for advising John Sr. to soften his image as a cold, sinister tycoon by carrying a pocketful of dimes to give away to children whenever he was seen in public.[10]

Lee invented the public relations specialty that is today known as "crisis management": helping clients put the best possible "spin" on a bad situation. At the time he went to work for the railroads, accidents were common, and the railroad companies dealt with the situation by withholding information and using bribes such as free railroad passes to suppress reports of accidents and their costs in lives and property. Lee had worked previously as a newspaper reporter, and knew that this approach often invited suspicion and bad publicity. As an alternative, he proposed an "open policy" of providing information to the press. Shortly after he went to work for the Pennsylvania Railroad, a wreck occurred. Instead of trying to suppress the story, Lee invited reporters to travel to the scene at the railroad's expense and set up facilities to assist them once they got there. Company executives thought Lee was crazy, but they changed their minds after they discovered that his "open" strategy won them more favorable coverage than the old approach.[11]

To advertise his policy of openness, Lee distributed a "Declaration of Principles" to newspapers across the country which is often quoted today in public relations textbooks:

> This is not a secret press bureau. All our work is done in the open. We aim to supply news. This is not an advertising agency; if you think any of our matter ought properly to go to your business office, do not use it. Our matter is accurate. Further details on any subject treated will be supplied promptly, and any editor will be assisted most cheerfully in verifying directly any statement of fact. . . . In brief, our plan is, frankly, and openly, on behalf of business concerns and public institutions, to supply to the press and public of the United States prompt and accurate information concerning subjects which it is of value and interest to the public to know about.[12]

According to Cutlip, Lee's approach to PR was not limited to putting "the most favorable light" on corporate activities. He saw himself as a counselor who studied public opinion and advised companies how to "shape their affairs" so that "when placed before the public they will be approved." His standard prescription was, "Set your house in order, then tell the public you have done so."[13]

In practice, however, Cutlip admits, this "two-way street" approach to public relations was limited by the fact that Lee's clients were engaged in activities that the public would never be likely to approve. In fact, Lee's first job for the Rockefellers was to counter bad publicity following their brutal union-busting tactics in the Ludlow Massacre, in which Colorado state militia and company guards used machine guns to fire on a tent colony of striking mine workers, killing women and children. Lee responded with a series of pro-Rockefeller bulletins titled "The Struggle in Colorado for Industrial Freedom." According to Ray Hiebert, Lee's biographer, "most of the bulletins contained matter which on the surface was true but which presented the facts in such a way as to give a total picture that was false." [14]

The Great War

The fledgling publicity industry got a big boost with World War I. Ivy Lee and many other industry pioneers joined the US government's campaign to mobilize public opinion in support of the war effort. The Committee on Public Information, led by George Creel, used posters, billboards, advertising, exhibits, pamphlets and newspapers to promote the "war to end all wars"—to "make the world safe for democracy."

In a history of the war effort titled *Mobilizing Civilian America,* Harold Tobin and Percy Bidwell describe the committee's work as "perhaps the most effective job of large-scale war propaganda which the world had ever witnessed." The committee "bombarded the public unceasingly with enthusiastic reports on the nation's colossal war effort and with contrasts of our war aims and those of our allies, with the war aims of the Central Powers. Dissenting voices were stilled, either by agreement with the press or by the persuasive action of the agents of the Department of Justice." [15] The committee enrolled 75,000 civic leaders as "Four-Minute Men" to deliver war messages to people in churches, theaters and civic groups. Ivy Lee's publicity program for the Red Cross helped it grow from 486,000 to 20 million members and raise $400 million by the time the war ended. The Creel Committee also used the time-tested tactic of feeding wartime hysteria with fantastic atrocity stories depicting the Germans as beasts and Huns. [16]

The war demonstrated the power of propaganda and helped build the reputations of Creel Committee members, who returned to civilian life and offered their services to help business in the transition from a wartime to a peacetime economy. They applied and refined the publicity methods they had learned during the war.

The postwar years saw Ivy Lee's firm defending the Rockefellers again, in a private war between coal mine owners and striking mine workers in West Virginia. Nearly 400,000 miners had gone out on strike to protest dangerous working conditions, low wages, and other abuses such as payment of wages in "company scrip" that could only be used in overpriced company stores. The coal companies hired armed Pinkerton detectives. President Warren G. Harding sent in federal troops. The governor of West Virginia declared martial law. Logan County's corrupt sheriff, Don Chafin, used money from the coal companies to hire "deputy sheriff" strikebreakers. The resulting battles left at least 70 miners dead.

Lee worked to clean up the reputation of the coal companies by publishing bulletins titled *The Miner's Lamp* and *Coal Facts*. The bulletins ran stories praising the charitable works of mine owners, and a "first-hand sketch of Sheriff Don Chafin" which "reveals different traits than the public has been given to understand." They attacked the union's method of organizing and collecting dues, and claimed that "company stores protect mine workers' pocketbooks." [17]

These activities notwithstanding, Ivy Lee was the most widely sought-after advisor of his day to companies seeking to improve their public image. Many historians and industry insiders consider Lee the "father of public relations," an honor he would probably hold without challenge if his reputation had not been tainted by scandal near the end of his career. In 1933, shortly after Adolf Hitler's rise to power, Lee's firm went to work for the German Dye Trust to advise them on ways to improve German-American relations, leading to charges that he was a Nazi propagandist. The *New York Mirror* ran a story in July 1934 headlined: "Rockefeller Aide Nazi Mastermind." In November of that year, with the scandal still hanging over his head, Lee died of a brain tumor. An obituary in the *Jewish Daily Forward* described him as "an agent of the Nazi government." [18]

Bernays and the "Engineering of Consent"

Ivy Lee's fall from grace enabled another early PR practitioner, Edward Bernays, to claim credit for founding the field of public relations. In his history of the PR industry, Scott Cutlip describes Bernays as "perhaps public relations' most fabulous and fascinating individual, a man who was bright, articulate to excess, and most of all, an innovative thinker and philosopher of this vocation that was in its infancy when he opened his office in New York in June 1919." Much of Bernays's reputation today stems from his persistent public relations campaign to build his own reputation as "America's No. 1 Publicist." During his active years, many of his peers in the industry were offended by Bernays' constant self-promotion. According to Cutlip, "Bernays was a brilliant person who had a spectacular career, but, to use an old-fashioned word, he was a braggart." [19]

Born in Vienna, Bernays was a nephew of Sigmund Freud, the "father of psychoanalysis," and his public relations efforts helped popularize Freud's theories in the United States. Bernays also pioneered the PR industry's use of psychology and other social sciences to design its public persuasion campaigns. "If we understand the mechanism and motives of the group mind, it is now possible to control and regiment the masses according to our will without their knowing it," Bernays argued.[20] He called this scientific technique of opinion molding the "engineering of consent."[21]

One of Bernays's favorite techniques for manipulating public opinion was the indirect use of "third party authorities" to plead for his clients' causes. "If you can influence the leaders, either with or without their conscious cooperation, you automatically influence the group which they sway," he said. In order to promote sales of bacon, for example, he conducted a survey of physicians and reported their recommendation that people eat hearty breakfasts. He sent the results of the survey to 5,000 physicians, along with publicity touting bacon and eggs as a hearty breakfast.[22] His clients included President Calvin Coolidge, Procter & Gamble, CBS, General Electric and Dodge Motors. Beyond his contributions to these famous and powerful clients, Bernays revolutionized public relations by combining traditional press agentry with the techniques of psychology and sociology to create what one author called "the science of ballyhoo."[23]

"When a person would first meet Bernays," noted writer Scott Cutlip, "it would not be long until Uncle Sigmund would be brought into the conversation. His relationship with Freud was always in the forefront of his thinking and his counseling." According to Irwin Ross, another writer, "Bernays liked to think of himself as a kind of psychoanalyst to troubled corporations." In the early 1920s, Bernays arranged for the US publication of an English-language translation of Freud's *General Introduction to Psychoanalysis.* In addition to publicizing Freud's ideas, Bernays used his association with Freud to establish his own reputation as a thinker and theorist—a reputation which was further enhanced when Bernays authored several landmark books of his own, most notably *Crystallizing Public Opinion* and *Propaganda.*[24]

Bernays defined the profession of "counsel on public relations" as a "practicing social scientist" whose "competence is like that of the industrial engineer, the management engineer, or the investment counselor in their respective fields."[25] To assist clients, PR counselors used "understanding of the behavioral sciences and applying them —sociology, social psychology, anthropology, history, etc."[26]

This definition of PR was worlds apart from the old days of press agents and circus handbills. In *Propaganda,* his most important book, Bernays argued that the scientific manipulation of public opinion was necessary to overcome chaos and conflict in society: "The conscious and intelligent manipulation of the organized habits and opinions of the masses is an important element in democratic society. Those who manipulate this unseen mechanism of society constitute an invisible government which is the true ruling power of our country. . . . We are governed, our minds are molded, our tastes formed, our ideas suggested, largely by men we have never heard of. This is a logical result of the way in which our democratic society is organized. Vast numbers of human beings must cooperate in this manner if they are to live together as a smoothly functioning society. . . . In almost every act of our daily lives, whether in the sphere of politics or business, in our social conduct or our ethical thinking, we are dominated by the relatively small number of persons . . . who understand the mental processes and social patterns of the masses. It is they who pull the wires which control the public mind."[27]

Compared to Ivy Lee's claim that "all our work is done in the open," Bernays was audaciously blunt about the secret, manipulative nature of public relations work. His celebration of propaganda helped define public relations, but it didn't win the industry many friends. In a letter to President Franklin Roosevelt, Supreme Court Justice Felix Frankfurter described Bernays and Lee as "professional poisoners of the public mind, exploiters of foolishness, fanaticism and self-interest."[28] And history itself showed the flaw in Bernays' claim that "manipulation of the masses" is natural and necessary in a democratic society. The fascist rise to power in Germany demonstrated that propaganda could be used to subvert democracy as easily as it could be used to "resolve conflict."

In his autobiography, Bernays recalls a dinner at his home in 1933 where "Karl von Weigand, foreign correspondent of the Hearst newspapers, an old hand at interpreting Europe and just returned from Germany, was telling us about Goebbels and his propaganda plans to consolidate Nazi power. Goebbels had shown Weigand his propaganda library, the best Weigand had ever seen. Goebbels, said Weigand, was using my book *Crystallizing Public Opinion* as a basis for his destructive campaign against the Jews of Germany. This shocked me. . . . Obviously the attack on the Jews of Germany was no emotional outburst of the Nazis, but a deliberate, planned campaign."[29]

CHAPTER THREE

Smokers' Hacks

I'll tell you why I like the cigarette business. It costs a penny to make.
Sell it for a dollar. It's addictive. And there's fantastic brand loyalty.

WARREN BUFFETT
once R.J. Reynolds's largest shareholder

One of the PR industry's first major clients was the tobacco industry. In the early twentieth century, the tobacco companies used PR's
psychological marketing skills to first hook women and then children on their drug. Edward Bernays, Ivy Lee and John Hill all worked
on PR for tobacco, pioneering techniques that today remain the PR
industry's stock in trade: third party advocacy, subliminal message
reinforcement, junk science, phony front groups, advocacy advertising, and buying favorable news reporting with advertising dollars.

Prior to World War I, smoking cigarettes was considered unre-
fined for women and effeminate for men, who either smoked cig-
ars or stuck to tobacco of the chewing variety. The war brought
cigarettes into vogue for men, and during the Roaring Twenties, the
American Tobacco Company turned to PR to develop a vast new
market—American women—for sales of its Lucky Strike brand. The
company first hired adman A.D. Lasker, who portrayed Lucky Strikes
as a healthy cigarette by concocting surveys using spurious data to
claim that doctors preferred Luckies as the "less irritating" brand.
Lasker also developed an advertising campaign featuring female Metropolitan opera stars, their soprano voices somehow unaffected by
smoking, giving testimonials such as "Cigarettes Are Kind to Your
Throat" and "I Protect My Precious Voice With Lucky Strikes." [1]

Edward Bernays was hired by Liggett & Myers, the maker of
Chesterfields. To spoof their rivals at American Tobacco, Bernays

created an organization called the "Tobacco Society for Voice Culture" to "establish a home for singers and actors whose voices have cracked under the strain of their cigarette testimonials." The satire was successful enough that American Tobacco President George Washington Hill hired Bernays away from Ligget & Myers. Some time later, Bernays learned that Hill had also hired Ivy Lee's PR firm a year earlier. When Bernays asked Hill about this, he replied, "If I have both of you, my competitors can't get either of you." [2]

To persuade women that cigarette smoking could help them stay beautiful, Bernays developed a campaign based on the slogan, "Reach for a Lucky Instead of a Sweet." The campaign played on women's worries about their weight and increased Lucky sales threefold in just twelve months. (The message, "cigarettes keep you thin," reverberates today in the brand name Virginia Slims.) [3]

But smoking remained a taboo for "respectable" women, and Bernays turned to psychoanalyst A.A. Brill for advice. Brill provided a classic Freudian analysis:

> Some women regard cigarettes as symbols of freedom. . . . Smoking is a sublimation of oral eroticism; holding a cigarette in the mouth excites the oral zone. It is perfectly normal for women to want to smoke cigarettes. Further the first women who smoked probably had an excess of masculine components and adopted the habit as a masculine act. But today the emancipation of women has suppressed many of the feminine desires. More women now do the same work as men do. . . . Cigarettes, which are equated with men, become torches of freedom. [4]

Brill's analysis inspired Bernays to stage a legendary publicity event that is still taught as a model in PR schools. To sell cigarettes as a symbol of women's liberation, he arranged for attractive debutantes to march in New York's prominent Easter parade, each waving a lit cigarette and proclaiming it a "torch of liberty." Bernays made sure that publicity photos of his smoking models appeared world-wide. [5]

Decades of saturation cigarette advertising and promotion continued into the 1950s via billboards, magazines, movies, TV and radio. Thanks to Bernays and other early pioneers of public relations, cigarettes built a marketing juggernaut upon an unshakable identification with sex, youth, vitality and freedom. The work for the tobacco industry, in turn, earned PR widespread credibility and launched the rise of today's multi-billion dollar public relations industry.

The Truth Hurts

In the early 1950s, the first scientific studies documenting tobacco's role in cancer and other fatal illnesses began to appear. In 1952, *Reader's Digest* ran an influential article titled, "Cancer by the Carton." A 1953 report by Dr. Ernst L. Wynder heralded to the scientific community a definitive link between cigarette smoking and cancer. Over the next two years, dozens of articles appeared in the *New York Times* and other major public publications: *Good Housekeeping*, the *New Yorker, Look, Woman's Home Companion*. Sales of cigarettes went into an unusual, sudden decline.[6]

The tobacco czars were in a panic. Internal memos from the industry-funded Tobacco Institute refer to the PR fallout from this scientific discovery as the "1954 emergency." Fighting desperately for its economic life, the tobacco industry launched what must be considered the costliest, longest-running and most successful PR "crisis management" campaign in history. In the words of the industry itself, the campaign was aimed at "promoting cigarettes and protecting them from these and other attacks," by "creating doubt about the health charge without actually denying it, and advocating the public's right to smoke, without actually urging them to take up the practice."[7]

For help, the tobacco industry turned to John Hill, the founder of the PR megafirm, Hill & Knowlton. Hill designed a brilliant and expensive campaign that the tobacco industry is still using today in its fight to save itself from public rejection and governmental action. Hill is remembered today as a shrewd but ethical businessman. In a letter, he once stated, "It is not the work of public relations . . . to outsmart the American public by helping management build profits." Yet Hill's work to save tobacco in the 1950s is such an egregious example of "outsmarting the American public . . . to build profits" that Hill & Knowlton is still in court today answering criminal charges.[8] The company's role is described as follows in a 1993 lawsuit, *State of Mississippi vs. the Tobacco Cartel*:

> As a result of these efforts, the Tobacco Institute Research Committee (TIRC), an entity later known as The Council for Tobacco Research (CTR), was formed.
>
> The Tobacco Industry Research Committee immediately ran a full-page promotion in more than 400 newspapers aimed at an estimated 43 million Americans . . . entitled "A Frank Statement to Cigarette Smokers." . . . In this advertisement, the participating tobacco companies recognized their "special responsibility" to the public, and promised to learn the facts about smoking and health. The participating tobacco companies promised to sponsor independent research.

. . . The participating tobacco companies also promised to cooperate closely with public health officials. . . .

After thus beginning to lull the public into a false sense of security concerning smoking and health, the Tobacco Industry Research Committee continued to act as a front for tobacco industry interests. Despite the initial public statements and posturing, and the repeated assertions that they were committed to full disclosure and vitally concerned, the TIRC did not make the public health a primary concern. . . . In fact, there was a coordinated, industry-wide strategy designed actively to mislead and confuse the public about the true dangers associated with smoking cigarettes. Rather than work for the good of the public health as it had promised, and sponsor independent research, the tobacco companies and consultants, acting through the tobacco trade association, refuted, undermined, and neutralized information coming from the scientific and medical community.[9]

Smoke and Mirrors

To improve its credibility, the TIRC hired Dr. Clarence Little as director. Previously, Little had served as managing director of the American Society for the Control of Cancer, forerunner to today's American Cancer Society.[10] Little promised that if research did discover a direct relationship between smoking and cancer, "the next job tackled will be to determine how to eliminate the danger from tobacco." This pretense of honest concern from a respected figure worked its expected magic. Opinion research by Hill & Knowlton showed that only 9% of the newspapers expressing opinions on the TIRC were unfavorable, whereas 65% were favorable without reservation.[11]

There is no question that the tobacco industry knew what scientists were learning about tobacco. The TIRC maintained a library with cross-indexed medical and scientific papers from 2,500 medical journals, as well as press clippings, government reports and other documents. TIRC employees culled this library for scientific data with inconclusive or contrary results regarding tobacco and the harm to human health. These were compiled into a carefully selected 18-page booklet, titled "A Scientific Perspective on the Cigarette Controversy," which was mailed to over 200,000 people, including doctors, members of Congress and the news media.

During the 1950s, tobacco companies more than doubled their advertising budgets, going from $76 million in 1953 to $122 million in 1957. The TIRC spent another $948,151 in 1954 alone, of which one-fourth went to Hill & Knowlton, another fourth went to pay for media ads, and most of the remainder went to administrative costs.

Despite TIRC's promise to "sponsor independent research," only $80,000, or less than 10% of the total budget for the year, actually went to scientific projects.[12]

In 1963 the TIRC changed its name to the Council for Tobacco Research. In addition to this "scientific" council, Hill & Knowlton helped set up a separate PR and lobbying organization, the Tobacco Institute. Formed in 1958, the Tobacco Institute grew by 1990 into what the *Public Relations Journal* described as one of the "most formidable public relations/lobbying machines in history," spending an estimated $20 million a year and employing 120 PR professionals to fight the combined forces of the Surgeon General of the United States, the National Cancer Institute, the American Cancer Society, the American Heart Association and the American Lung Association.[13]

The tobacco industry's PR strategy has been described by the American Cancer Society as "a delaying action to mislead the public into believing that no change in smoking habits is indicated from existing statistical and pathological evidence."[14] In the 1990s, medical studies estimated that 400,000 of the 50 million smokers in the United States were dying each year from tobacco-related diseases, and that smoking was likely to be a contributing factor in the deaths of half the smokers in the country.[15] Tobacco opponents lobbied for public education and strict new regulations to prevent youthful addiction and to protect the public's right to a smoke-free environment. But despite smoking's bad press, tobacco profits have continued to soar, and the industry is opening new, unregulated mega-markets in Asia, Eastern Europe and the Third World.[16] Even in the US, most attempts at serious federal or state regulation or taxation are swatted down by tobacco's skilled army of highly paid lobbyists.

Snatching Victory from the Ashes

One way the cigarette industry intends to keep winning is by escalating to unprecedented levels its use of front groups such as the "National Smokers Alliance," an ambitious and well-funded "grassroots" campaign developed by Burson-Marsteller PR with millions of dollars from Philip Morris.

The National Smokers Alliance (NSA) is a state-of-the-art campaign that uses full-page newspaper ads, direct telemarketing, paid canvassers, free 800 numbers and newsletters to bring thousands of smokers into its ranks each week. By 1995 NSA claimed a membership of 3 million smokers. The campaign's goal is to rile up and mobilize a committed cadre of foot soldiers in a grassroots army directed by Philip Morris's political operatives at Burson-Marsteller. Philip Morris knows that to win politically it has to "turn out the troops," people who can emotionally battle on its behalf. The NSA is a sophisticated, camouflaged campaign that organizes tobacco's victims to protect tobacco's profits.

In the past, the tobacco industry attempted, not too convincingly, to distance itself from pro-smoking forces. The Tobacco Institute's Brennan Dawson told the *Congressional Quarterly* in 1990, "If we were to fund smokers' rights groups and bring them to Washington, wouldn't they then be viewed as an arm of the tobacco industry?"

Apparently desperate times require more obvious measures. In 1994, *National Journal* writer Peter Stone observed that NSA "is increasingly looking like a subsidiary of Burson-Marsteller," and noted that the PR firm "used its grassroots lobbying unit, the Advocacy Communications Team, to start building membership in the group last year." Thomas Humber, a Burson-Marsteller vice-president, is president and CEO of the NSA. Burson executives Kenneth Rietz and Pierre Salinger are active, as is Peter G. Kelly, a prominent Democrat with the firm of Black, Manafort, Stone & Kelly, which is owned by Burson-Marsteller.[17]

How does the NSA recruit smoking's victims into becoming its advocates? Through a combination of high-tech direct marketing techniques and old fashioned "feet in the street" community organizing. Like every good grassroots group, the National Smokers Alliance has a folksy but strident newsletter for its membership, called *The NSA Voice*. According to its June 1994 issue, the NSA pays hundreds of young activists to sign up members in bars and bowling alleys in cities around the country. Eric Schippers, in charge of the membership drive, reported that "during only the first two months of activity, the Chicago campaign put 180 recruiters on the street and enlisted more than 40,000 members."

Many NSA members are first recruited via full-page ads with 800 numbers that exhort puffers to stand up for their rights. Everyone who calls receives the NSA newsletter free for three months, along with 10 membership recruitment cards and stickers to place in stores and restaurants that say, "I am a smoker and have spent \$_____ in your establishment." NSA members who sign up another ten people at \$10 each can win a free NSA t-shirt. The committed and informed pro-smoking advocate can also call a free 800 number to order more sign-up cards and stickers, or get the latest marching orders regarding which bureaucrats or politicians need nudging from Marlboro's masses. One recent NSA mailing, sent first class to hundreds of thousands of smokers, urged them to write letters to the Occupational Safety and Health Administration (OSHA) to defeat new regulations that would "ban smoking in any site where work is conducted."

Burson-Marsteller's propagandists have even coined a clever play on words that questions the patriotism of anti-smokers by calling them "anti Americans." NSA's newsletter advises, "If 'Anti' America is pushing a discriminatory smoking ban in your workplace, speak up," and "check the laws in your state with regard to the protection of individual rights." [18]

Bringing in the Sheaves

In recent years California has been the front line of the tobacco wars and the state where the industry has suffered its worst setbacks. In 1988 the cigarette companies spent more than $20 million in a failed effort to defeat a major anti-smoking initiative. Since then health activists have passed hundreds of local smoking bans. As a result, California has seen a 27% decrease in cigarette consumption, the most success of any state in reducing tobacco's deadly toll.[19]

Philip Morris is fighting back through a California PR firm called the Dolphin Group. Dolphin CEO Lee Stitzenberger used a half-million dollars from Philip Morris to set up a front group called "Californians for Statewide Smoking Restrictions." Using this deceptive name, NSA members gathered signatures to put a referendum on the California ballot in November 1994, which the Dolphin Group promoted with billboards reading, "Yes on 188—Tough Statewide Smoking Restrictions—The Right Choice." [20]

In reality, Proposition 188 was a *pro*-tobacco referendum which, if passed, would have undermined 270 existing local anti-smoking ordinances in California cities, as well as the state's new statewide smoke-free workplace law.[21] Anti-smoking groups charged that many of the people who signed petitions in favor of the referendum were led to believe that they were supporting a measure to protect non-smokers and youths. After the public learned about the funding source behind "Californians for Statewide Smoking Restrictions," opinion turned decisively against the referendum and it was voted down. "The $25 million smokescreen the tobacco industry created to dupe Californians into voting for Proposition 188 has cleared, and the voters have spoken," declared the American Cancer Society.[22]

The tobacco industry's PR campaign is not really about swaying public opinion, a battle which the industry has already lost. Even half of smokers favor stricter government regulation of their deadly habit.[23] The industry's goal is not to win good PR, but to avoid losing political and legal battles. This survivalist strategy has served the cigarette industry well for forty years. At a PR seminar in May 1994, Tom Lauria, the chief lobbyist for the Tobacco Institute, pointed out that tobacco sales continue to grow worldwide. He dismissed tobacco critics as simply a "political correctness craze" and ridiculed predictions of tobacco's demise, saying that the media has been preparing smoking's obituary for decades. Tobacco may be fighting for its life, but Lauria reminded the assembled PR practitioners that his industry has been fighting and winning that battle for a long time.[24]

Hazy Ethics

Sixteen thousand PR practitioners (including Harold Burson and Lee Stitzenberger) belong to the Public Relations Society of America (PRSA) and pledge to abide by its seventeen-point "Code of Professional Standards." The code states that a PRSA member "shall conduct his or her professional life in accord with the public interest."

PR legend Edward Bernays, who designed the "torches of liberty" parade that made smoking socially acceptable for American women, later said if he'd known of the dangers of tobacco he would have refused the account. "When the profession of public relations was first outlined," Bernays stated, "it was envisioned as other professions functioned: that is, as an art applied to a science, in this case social science, and in which the primary motivation was the public interest and not pecuniary motivation. . . . No reputable public relations organization would today accept a cigarette account, since their cancer-causing effects have been proven."[25]

These ethical qualms in his later years made Bernays a minority voice within the public relations industry. In 1994, an informal survey of 38 PR firms revealed that only nine would decline a contract to represent the tobacco industry.[26]

Bernays, a nonsmoker, lived to be 103 years old, passing away in March 1995. His final years were spent fruitlessly appealing to the PRSA to police its own ranks. "Under present conditions, an unethical person can sign the code of PRSA, become a member, practice unethically—untouched by any legal sanctions," Bernays observed. "In law and medicine, such an individual is subject to disbarment from the profession. . . . There are no standards. . . . This sad situation makes it possible for anyone, regardless of education or ethics, to use the term 'public relations' to describe his or her function."[27]

CHAPTER FOUR

Spinning the Atom

Once a bright hope shared by all mankind, including myself, the rash proliferation of nuclear power plants is now one of the ugliest clouds hanging over America. . . . Proliferation of capabilities to produce nuclear weapons of mass destruction is reaching terrifying proportions. And now, the prospect of the reprocessing or recycling of nuclear wastes from scores of atomic power plants is close upon us.

DR. DAVID LILIENTHAL
physicist and first chairman
of the US Atomic Energy Commission

As part of Edward Bernays' incessant effort to create a "professional" image for public relations, he proposed creating an informal social forum where public relations professionals could mingle and share ideas with top leaders in business and government. To get the group started, he organized a dinner at his home in January 1938, with university professors, journalists, business leaders, and other PR professionals as invited guests. He followed up by sending a memo about the dinner to *Time* magazine, which ran a story in its January 24 issue: "Around a dinner table in Manhattan frequently gather some 20 of the top propagandists in the US. This unpublicized high-powered group calls itself the Council on Public Opinion. Chairman is the Nation's No. 1 publicist, dark Machiavellian Edward L. Bernays. . . . This small group might be the seat of a sinister super-government were it not that no two members of the Council on Public Opinion completely agree on anything very important." [1]

Indeed, disagreements quickly led to a shakeup within the group. The self-serving reference to Bernays as "the Nation's No. 1 publicist" offended Hill & Knowlton founder John Hill, who complained that Bernays' press release had depicted him as "sitting at the feet of the master to learn public relations." Hill organized a monthly dinner and social forum of his own, to which Bernays was not invited. At a meeting hosted by the PR director of Bethlehem Steel, a member joked that after "our pilgrimage to Bethlehem" they should call themselves "the Wisemen." The name stuck, and the Wisemen have been meeting ever since, an elite group of high-level practitioners who regularly discuss social, economic and political trends.

Near the end of World War II, the US government turned to the Wisemen for advice on how to handle publicity aspects of the top-secret Manhattan Project to develop the atomic bomb. With government security men guarding the doors, the Wisemen met with Major General Leslie Groves, chief of the Manhattan Project, at the University Club in New York City. Groves briefed them on the atomic development and asked for advice on how to handle PR for the first tests in New Mexico. At their suggestion, the War Department invited *New York Times* reporter Bill Lawrence to observe the tests and to be the "pool reporter" relaying information from the bombings of Japan to other reporters the Army had assembled in Manila.[2]

The end of the war left the US with a new set of public relations concerns related to the bomb. The US monopoly on nuclear weapons quickly evaporated as the Soviet Union developed bombs of its own. By 1952, both countries had graduated from A-bombs to H-bombs, yielding more than 15,000 times the destructive power of the explosion that obliterated Hiroshima. As US-Soviet hostilities hardened, the public was left to consider the horrifying potential that atomic power had unleashed—the prospect that the next "world war" could involve bombs capable of destroying whole cities in a war that even then people realized no one would win.[3]

Atoms for Peace

In 1953, President Dwight Eisenhower delivered his now-famous "Atoms for Peace" speech to the United Nations. Using a swords-into-plowshares approach borrowed from the Bible, he pledged that "peaceful power from atomic energy is no dream of the future. That capability, already proved, is here—now, today," ready to "provide abundant electrical energy in the power-starved areas of the world. . . . The US pledges . . . to help solve the fearful atomic dilemma—to devote its entire heart and mind to find the way by which the miraculous inventiveness of man shall not be dedicated to his death, but consecrated to his life."[4]

Eisenhower's speech marked the beginning of a public relations campaign to transform the image of nuclear technology. Previously, its sole proven use had been for the purpose of designing destructive weapons. Now the US Atomic Energy Commission (AEC) promised that nuclear generators would make electricity "too cheap to meter." The government's monopoly on ownership of nuclear materials was abolished, and private companies were invited to participate in the commercial development of atomic energy.[5] The US promised to share atomic energy technology with underdeveloped nations. The atom's image as a magical source of unlimited energy was promoted using educational films, brochures and experts who promised that a lump of uranium the size of a pea could unleash enough energy to drive a car to the moon and back.[6] Less than a year following his "Atoms for Peace" speech, Eisenhower appeared on national television to personally lead a publicity stunt on Labor Day of 1954. Waving a "magic wand," he electronically signalled a radio-controlled bulldozer to begin breaking ground at the small Pennsylvania town of Shippingport, marking the start of construction on the country's first commercial nuclear power plant.[7]

Once again, however, image and reality were worlds apart. Although scientists had already demonstrated the possibility of using nuclear reactors to generate electricity, the technology had little support among US utility companies, who saw nuclear generators as expensive and unnecessary. In fact, the cost per kilowatt of electricity generated by the Shippingport reactor was ten times higher than the prevailing cost of power; federal subsidies were necessary to make it commercially competitive with conventional coal-powered reactors.[8] The true purpose of Shippingport was symbolic; it sent a message that the atom *could* be harnessed for peaceful uses.

In 1950, David Lilienthal had resigned as AEC chairman. He became increasingly disillusioned with the "many instances of the way in which public relations techniques—the not-so-hidden persuader—have been used to promote the appropriation of funds for the peaceful Atom." He criticized the "elaborate ritual" of providing nuclear technology to underdeveloped countries: "Even as a propaganda move it was self-defeating and naïve. A great many of these countries need and could use doctors and medicine, storage batteries, plows and fertilizers and seed—and good *elementary* scientific instruction. Only the desire to prove somehow that atoms were for peace could justify the absurdity of a separate program, not in the foreign aid part of the State Department but in the AEC."[9]

By 1962, nuclear power was still more expensive than energy generated by conventional means, but the AEC and private companies such as Westinghouse, Union Carbide and General Electric had spent billions of dollars in research and development, and they were anxious to see a return on their investment. With great fanfare, GE announced in 1962 that it had contracted to build a nuclear plant at Oyster Creek, New Jersey, for $91 million, entirely *without* federal subsidy. In reality, however, the Oyster Creek reactor was a "loss leader." General Electric built it at a bargain-basement price, accepting a loss on the deal so it could position itself to dominate the reactor market. The ploy worked. The mystique of high-tech atomic power proved hypnotic, and orders for new reactors began rolling in from utility companies convinced that they needed nuclear power to remain on the cutting edge of "America's energy future." As the orders came in, GE discreetly jacked up its prices, until utility companies were actually paying *more* for the privilege of "buying into the future" than if they had stayed with conventional generators.[10]

Damage Control

As the rhetoric of power "too cheap to meter" faded, the AEC and nuclear advocates spoke instead of someday producing atomic electricity that would be "competitive in cost" to coal, gas or hydroelectric power. This goal was never achieved in practice. But even if nuclear power *could* be produced at a competitive price, the technology had another major problem: safety.

At a conventional power plant, an accident or sabotage might kill a few dozen people—a couple of hundred in a worst-case scenario. By contrast, a 1957 study by the Brookhaven National Laboratory estimated that a "worst case" accident at a small, 150-megawatt nuclear reactor 30 miles upwind of a major city would kill 3,400 people, injure another 43,000, and cause $7 billion in property damage. An accident at a larger, 1,000-megawatt reactor could kill as many as 45,000 people, cause property damage of nearly $300 billion, and radioactively contaminate an area the size of the state of Pennsylvania. These estimates stunned the AEC steering committee which had commissioned the study. In an internal memorandum, steering committee member S. Allan Lough wrote that "Great care should be exercised . . . to avoid establishing and/or reinforcing the popular notion that reactors are unsafe. Though this is a public information or promotional problem that the AEC now faces with less than desirable success, I feel that by calculating the consequences of hypothetical accidents, the AEC should not place itself in the position of making the location of reactors near urban areas nearly indefensible." The steering committee decided to withhold publication of the Brookhaven study, and when word of its existence leaked out, the AEC responded by saying only that it had never been completed.[11]

In fact, the industry had already seen a series of catastrophic incidents, most of which were successfully kept out of the press. As the years unrolled, new accidents kept happening:

- In Kyshtym in the Soviet Union, a massive radioactive explosion at a high-level waste dump in 1957 rendered an area of over 70 square miles permanently uninhabitable.[12]

- At the SL-1 test reactor in Idaho, an exploding fuel rod killed three reactor operators and saturated the reactor building with radiation. Three weeks after the January 3, 1961, accident, the hands and heads of the three victims were still so hot with radiation that they had to be severed from their bodies and buried separately as radioactive waste.[13]

- On October 5, 1966, a partial meltdown at the 300-megawatt Enrico Fermi I fast-breeder reactor at Monroe, Michigan prompted utility officials to seriously consider the possibility of trying to evacuate Detroit, 40 miles to the north. News of the accident was successfully withheld from the public until the early 1970s, when John G. Fuller, one of the engineers who witnessed the meltdown, published a book titled *We Almost Lost Detroit*.[14]

- In 1975, fire damaged electric cables and safety systems at the Tennessee Valley Authority's Browns Ferry complex in Alabama. The fire triggered near panic in the plant's control room and started a process that could, if allowed to continue, have led to a meltdown.[15]

Containment Failure

Despite aggressive publicity efforts, the "peaceful atom" was never able to overcome its association with the nuclear weapons industry. The movement against nuclear power originated with the campaign against above-ground bomb testing, which educated citizens about the health and environmental dangers posed by radiation. Environmental concerns also fed the first local opposition to the building of nuclear power stations, when the Sierra Club in 1961 opposed construction of the Bodega Head plant near San Francisco on a site that was not only part of a local nature reserve, but also on an earthquake fault.[16] The activism of the 1960s led naturally to growing protests linking nuclear power to nuclear bombs, and by the late 1970s, "no-nuke" groups were active throughout the United States, lobbying and developing information programs which criticized the nuclear industry on environmental, scientific and economic grounds.

In response, electrical utilities stepped up their PR campaigns. A 1978 survey of business-funded educational materials in US public schools showed that "more than any industry group, the electric utilities provide extensive multi-media materials on energy issues. . . . These energy education efforts notably target the elementary grade levels through the use of films, comic books, cartoon graphics or simple phrasing. This emphasis on the lower grades seems aimed at cultivating a future constituency in support of the electric power industry in general and nuclear power in particular." The educational cartoon books included titles such as *The Atom, Electricity, and You,* distributed by the Commonwealth Edison Company; *For A Mature Audience Only,* published by Westinghouse; and *Mickey Mouse and Goofy Explore Energy,* produced by Exxon.[17]

The PR campaign attempted to portray nuclear power as not only safe, but environmentally cleaner than other power sources. In *The Story of Electricity,* published in 1975 by the Florida Power and Light Corporation, comic-book characters promised that "nuclear plants are clean, odorless and generate electricity economically . . . and most important, help *conserve fossil fuels!*" Another comic book titled *The Battle for Survival—The War Against Environmental Pollution,* published by Virginia Electric and Power, claimed that "nuclear generating stations are just about the cleanest and most desirable neighbor that any community can have . . . and our power company is a leader in constructing these new plants!"[18]

Despite decades of efforts to generate favorable publicity, the nuclear industry was strikingly unprepared to handle the image crisis that erupted in Pennsylvania on March 28, 1979, when control systems failed at the Three-Mile Island facility. According to Robert Dilenschneider, the Hill & Knowlton PR executive who was brought in to manage the crisis, "the miscommunication at Three-Mile Island was the most monumental I have ever witnessed in business, and itself caused a crisis of epic proportions."[19] By way of bad luck, public alarm was heightened by the ominously coincidental similarity of events at Three-Mile Island to the plot of a recently-released Hollywood movie, *The China Syndrome,* which portrayed a utility company more concerned with corporate profits and coverups than with serious safety problems. Metropolitan Edison, the company managing Three-Mile Island for parent company General Public Utilities, seemed to be reading from the same script as the movie in its initial response to the discovery that its reactor was overheating.

The first rule of effective public relations in a crisis is to announce the bad news as completely and quickly as possible. Metropolitan Edison broke this rule in the first day of the crisis by attempting to evade the facts and downplay the extent of radiation released from the ailing reactor.[20] Worse yet, Met Ed's public-relations staff gave out contradictory and inaccurate information. "There have been no recordings of any significant levels of radiation, and none are expected outside the plant," said Met Ed's chief spokesman, Don Curry. Shortly after this statement was released, Pennsylvania's Department of Environmental Resources sent a helicopter over the plant with a geiger counter and detected radiation. Company officials backpedaled and said they didn't know *how much* radiation had been released. Later that afternoon, they changed their position again and said the release was minor. Company vice-president Jack Herbein became the perfect target for skeptical journalists, talking in technical jargon and losing his temper with reporters. When someone asked what might happen if the hydrogen bubble inside the reactor came in contact with a spark, he answered that the result could be "spontaneous energetic disassembly" of the reactor. When reporters asked him to explain the difference between "spontaneous energetic disassembly" and an explosion, he angrily refused to answer further questions.[21]

Alarmed by the utility company's refusal or inability to explain what was happening inside the plant, Pennsylvania Governor Richard Thornburgh suggested that pregnant women and children leave an area within a five-mile radius of the plant. Panic followed. Forty-nine percent of the population living within fifteen miles of the plant—144,000 people—packed up and fled. "The photographs in the press were appalling," Dilenschneider recalled. "They resembled refugee lines in World War II. People were living off bottled water and canned food. There was an exodus. They packed their cars and their campers with everything they could, and jammed the highways: babies bundled in blankets, kids with scarves wrapped across their faces to limit their exposure to the 'radiation,' and pregnant women in sheer panic about the future they might be facing."[22]

Following the accident, opinion polls registered a sharp drop in public support for nuclear power, and the nuclear industry responded with a multi-million-dollar media blitz. Teams of utility executives spread across the country to hold press conferences and appear on TV talk shows. Pro-nuclear advertisements were placed in magazines aimed at women readers. Videotapes of experts discussing technical aspects of nuclear power were distributed free to TV stations, and information packets were sent to the print media. An industry-funded Nuclear Energy Education Day was organized on October 18, 1979, with over 1,000 sponsored events, including a brunch for congressional wives in Washington and a joggers' mass relay race in California. When Jane Fonda and Tom Hayden went on an anti-nuclear speaking tour, the industry sent out two nuclear engineers as a "truth squad" to follow them and refute their arguments.[23]

In reality, however, the nuclear power industry was in decline even before Three-Mile Island. Between 1970 and 1980, the price for building a new reactor had quintupled. The nuclear industry complained that legal challenges and delays from anti-nuclear citizens were responsible for many of the cost increases. Rising costs led utility companies to cancel their plans to build new reactors. The last order for a nuclear power plant was placed in 1978. In 1984 at least half a dozen nuclear power plants under construction were cancelled as the industry realized that it was cheaper to let them sit unused and incomplete than to try to finish and operate them.[24] The 1985 meltdown of the Russian nuclear plant at Chernobyl, which spewed radioactive contamination over Europe and around the globe, seemed to mark the final nail in the coffin of an already dying technology, born of hype and deception.

Waste Not Want Not

The radioactive waste from nuclear power plants contains the deadliest substances known. It consists mostly of spent fuel which, although it is no longer suitable for generating power, will remain radioactive and lethal for over 100,000 years. At the government's Hanford, Washington, test reactor in the late 1940s, engineers used remote-controlled machinery to remove radioactive waste, put it into heavy containers, and bury it in the ground near Hanford. This crude method has remained the basic model for disposal ever since, despite promises by experts that "science will find a way" to dispose of it safely.

Since the late 1950s, deep underground geologic disposal has been proposed as a means to isolate the used highly radioactive fuel for the thousands of years necessary. Several exploratory efforts to locate repository sites in salt beds buried deep beneath Ohio, Michigan and New York were halted when state and local officials discovered the work being done by the AEC and objected. By the 1980s, growing quantities of nuclear waste had become the ultimate hot potato. Everyone, including critics of the industry, agreed that the stuff needed to be stored *somewhere*, but nobody wanted it anywhere near where *they* lived.

In 1986, the Department of Energy announced that it had narrowed the locations under consideration to three sites in Nevada, Texas and Washington state. The governors of all three states responded immediately with lawsuits challenging the decision. In 1987, Texas and Washington were eliminated from consideration, leaving Yucca Mountain, Nevada, as the only remaining candidate. Located about 100 miles north of Las Vegas, Yucca Mountain is a barren ridge of compressed volcanic ash. Government scientists stated that nuclear waste could be buried there in underground tunnels with minimal risks to public health or the environment, but Nevada residents remained unconvinced. Surveys showed that Nevadans opposed the Yucca Mountain repository by a 4-to-1 margin.[25]

In January 1991, the American Nuclear Energy Council (ANEC) began funding the "Nevada Initiative" in an effort to change public opinion. Designers of the Nevada Initiative included Kent Oram, a key advisor to Nevada Governor Bob Miller; Ed Allison, a longtime Nevada Republican political operative; and Don Williams, a political campaign consultant and lobbyist who had worked for numerous state politicians from both parties. Using military jargon, the plan proposed a series of TV ads to provide "air cover" for the repository plan. Local reporters were to be hired to present the "industry's side of the story" to their peers. Kent Oram trained scientists from the Department of Energy to act as a "scientific truth response team" to reply to critics of the repository. The goal of the campaign, according to the plan, was to "reduce the public's concerns over safety. Once public sentiment swings, the next phase of the campaign will focus on the merits of nuclear energy. . . . With our 'campaign committee' of Nevada political insiders, our strategic response teams, the advertising program and the polls that will provide us a road map along the way, we believe that as each move is made, one or more of the targeted adversaries will begin to surface, move our way, fight us and then, eventually dialogue with the industry. It is through this strategic game of chess that the campaign will ultimately prevail and move to checkmate anti-nuclear forces in Nevada."

The planners warned, however, that the campaign "has a formidable goal. It took Nevadans a lifetime to build up fears and resentments regarding nuclear energy. Countering the amount of free press against nuclear, such as accidents at Three-Mile Island and Chernobyl, hazardous leaks and various other plant problems, along with science fiction movies, would literally cost tens of millions of dollars in terms of column inches and air time in Nevada alone. Across the country, the cost would run into the billions."[26]

In October 1991, the Nevada Initiative began its first massive barrage of "air cover" ads. Narrated by Ron Vitto, a popular former sportscaster, the ads attempted to demonstrate the safety of transporting high level nuclear waste. One advertisement showed a truck and trailer bearing a cask of nuclear waste being rammed at high speed by a train to show that nuclear waste casks could safely survive such a collision. Other ads featured DOE scientists explaining that nuclear waste would not explode, or claiming that living near a nuclear power plant would not cause cancer.[27]

"Nevada political officials at all levels have been extremely aggressive in opposition to the project," explained a letter dated October 25, 1991, from Florida Power President Allen J. Keesler to other members of the Edison Electric Institute, a US association of electrical utility companies. "They have effectively frustrated DOE's efforts to move forward. . . . Sustained progress on the Yucca Mountain program can only be achieved by developing a cooperative environment in Nevada." To fund the PR campaign, Keesler asked each utility engaged in nuclear energy production to pay a "special assessment . . . collected through a special billing included with EEI's dues." Keesler's letter closed by reminding recipients that "this document is *Confidential*. You can understand the sensitivity associated with it becoming public."[28]

In November, three weeks into the advertising campaign, industry-funded pollsters conducted a survey and reported that although 72.4% of Nevada residents had seen the ads, the results were "not encouraging":

> Fewer than 15 percent of the respondents who had seen the ads said the ads made them more supportive of the repository, while 32 percent said the messages made them less supportive. Despite the barrage of pro-repository messages, almost three-quarters of the respondents (73.8%) said they would oppose the repository if they were to vote on whether it should be built—almost exactly the same proportion as before the ad campaign. . . . Almost half (48.5%) of the

respondents who had seen the advertisements said they did not believe the ads, . . . while 3.3 percent felt insulted by the ads . . . and 11.8 percent disagreed with the ads for a variety of reasons. . . . These three categories of negative comments make up 63.6 percent of the recorded responses.[29]

A few weeks later, the campaign hit another, even worse snag. One of the nuclear utility executives who had received Allen Keesler's "confidential" letter decided to leak it to anti-nuclear forces, along with other key documents detailing the industry's PR strategy. The documents proved highly embarrassing. In televised testimony before the Nevada Commission on Nuclear Projects, ANEC vice-president Ed Davis had claimed that the purpose of the advertising campaign was strictly "to inform and educate the public." Newspapers and television coverage contrasted his statement with the campaign's internal documents, which talked of bringing pressure on the state of Nevada to cooperate with the program, and hiring local reporters to present the "industry's side of the stories" and "convince the public that nuclear energy is safe."

Nevadans reacted with outrage. Newspapers and television coverage featured scathing attacks by state officials that continued for weeks. Nevada Senator Richard Bryan demanded an explanation from Energy Secretary James Watkins regarding the role of his department in the PR campaign. Governor Bob Miller wrote the governors of other states with nuclear power plants, challenging the propriety of using utility ratepayer funds to persuade Nevadans that they ought to accept nuclear wastes that no other state wanted.[30]

The PR campaign's death throes are captured in a report titled "The Nevada Initiative: A Risk Communication Fiasco" by James Flynn, Paul Slovic and C.K. Mertz, employees of an opinion polling firm named Decision Research:

> Perhaps the most devastating rejoinders to the ANEC campaign came from a pair of Las Vegas disk jockeys who began to parody each of the new TV ads. The main character in their satiric skits bore the mock name "Ron Ditto," whose simple-minded pronouncements were heaped with ridicule: "Hi! This is Ron Ditto, your formerly respected sportscaster, trading in your respect for much-needed dollars."
>
> Local businesses joined in. A TV advertisement showed the disk jockeys in a huge pair of overalls as a two-headed mutant, "Yucca Mountain Man," in a commercial for a Las Vegas auto dealership. A restaurant extolled the quality of the tomatoes in its salad bar by putting one through the same tests that nuclear waste casks were subjected to in the ANEC ads: After the tomato survives being run into a

cement wall, hit by a speeding train and dropped from a high tower, "You can be sure that it's one high-quality tomato."

The ANEC campaign, faced with disbelief, ridicule, and little measurable influence on public opinion, was discontinued. . . . By that time, the campaign's credibility had been damaged considerably. A survey conducted in June 1992 by researchers from Arizona State University and the University of Nevada, Las Vegas showed that after seeing the ads only 3.3 percent of respondents reported an increased level of trust in the repository program while almost 41 percent were *less* trusting and the remainder were unchanged.[31]

In April 1991 former Secretary of Energy James Watkins created a task force to "analyze the critical institutional question of how the Department of Energy (DOE) might strengthen public trust and confidence in the civilian radioactive waste management program." After two years of public meetings and hearing formal presentations from more than 100 organization representatives, the task force concluded that "distrust [in DOE's activities] is not irrational." Moreover, "this distrust will continue for a long time, will require sustained commitments from successive Secretaries of Energy to overcome, and will demand that DOE act in ways that are unnecessary for organizations that have sustained trust and confidence."

During the task force hearings, participants made repeated references to the public relations tactics of the nuclear industry. DOE found itself in the unfortunate position of being blamed for these activities as well as their own. The huge sums of money paid to PR operatives of the nuclear industry had left a legacy that was not only unsuccessful in molding public opinion, but permanently harmful to the industry's image.

Nukem

The combination of public opposition and management problems within the Department of Energy led to repeated postponements of the anticipated completion date for the Yucca Mountain repository. On average, in fact, every year the date was pushed back by *two* years, making for what the Decision Research team described as "an extremely slow moving program. . . . Combined with funding shortfalls, questions about the ability to meet regulatory requirements, and a history of inadequate management of the scientific work, the program often appears on the verge of collapse."[32]

With the date for completion of a permanent storage site postponed until sometime in the 21st century, the industry has been forced to fall back on a "temporary" plan—storing spent fuel locally in the yards of power plants across the country. A strategy for dealing with this latest embarrassment is outlined in an industry-published article titled, "The Public Relations Behind Nuclear Waste." It begins: "So . . . the necessity of keeping spent fuel in dry casks and in the yards of power plants is adding yet one more blemish on the face of the nuclear industry, *is it?* Not when good PR is used. Many utilities across the United States are finding that public relations campaigns, when launched well in advance of dry cask installation, are turning potentially negative situations into positive ones. . . . Make no mistake about it. All the public relations in the world will never cause the public to greet radioactive waste with open arms. But for those utilities running out of pool space, a smart PR program will make them better equipped to temper the tempest and to get the public thinking about waste in a more scientific way." [33]

The article appeared in the March 1995 issue of the *Nukem Market Report,* published by Nukem, Inc., of Stamford, Connecticut. Described by the *New York Times* as "unfortunately named," Nukem, Inc., is a subsidiary of the German corporation, Nukem GmbH. Apparently in German, the name doesn't carry quite the same negative connotations as it does in English. Evidently aware that its name is a bit of a PR problem, the American subsidiary has tried various typographical strategies to encourage people to place the emphasis on the second syllable when pronouncing Nukem—sometimes spelling it, for example, with the "k" or the last three letters capitalized, i.e., "NuKem" or "NuKEM."

Nukem GmbH designs and operates waste treatment systems for the chemical and nuclear power industries. In December 1987, the company's nuclear shipping unit temporarily lost its license after it was disclosed that some 2,000 barrels of nuclear waste had been illegally shipped into West Germany from Belgium and stored without proper identification. The company was investigated following charges by German politician Volker Hauff that Nukem had sold fissionable materials to Libya and Pakistan in violation of the Nuclear Nonproliferation Treaty. The charges were never proven, but the scandal led to the suspension of top Nukem executives Karl-Gerhard Hackstein and Peter Jelinek-Fink. [34] Like its parent corporation, American Nukem is engaged in the business of "environmental waste management," but its primary activity is buying and mining uranium for sale to nuclear power plants.

According to the *Nukem Market Report,* "honesty, openness and cooperation" are the PR tools with which utility companies can persuade "their next-door neighbors, local government and business leaders, and environmentalists" to tolerate nuclear waste. As an example of "openness," it advises utility companies to conduct plant tours, meet with local elected officials, and communicate their point of view to plant employees, since "neighbors tend to ask plant workers for the 'inside scoop' on what's really going on." The Nukem strategy also attempts to enlist "moderate" anti-nuclear groups in support of selected goals of local power companies. In Michigan, for example, the Consumers Power Company "made a presentation to the moderate group, West Michigan Environmental Action Council" and succeeded in persuading the council to focus "more on getting the material out of the state of Michigan and to Yucca Mountain . . . rather than bemoaning the fact that '*The waste is here.*' "

As an example of "cooperation," Nukem praises the Baltimore Gas & Electric Company for paying its employees to "donate" one hour each week for public service activities in their community. "As a result, BG&E employees serve in senior positions in local volunteer fire companies and have 'adopted' a total of three elementary schools for mentoring and tutoring programs. Over 100 employees are coordinating about 50 charities, including the United Way, Multiple Sclerosis, Muscular Dystrophy, and March of Dimes fundraising drives." By cultivating a caring, community-minded image, BG&E has been able to limit opposition to its dry cask proposal. The key, says BG&E Public Information Officer Karl Neddenien, is to build this image early: "As long as ten years before a utility even *thinks* about a dry storage facility, it had better have developed a good community image."[35]

These innocuous-sounding activities are state-of-the-art PR, reflecting the industry's sophisticated understanding of the techniques necessary to sway public opinion in today's cynical world. During the 50 years since the detonation of the first atom bomb, public opinion has steadily become more suspicious of nuclear power, despite the work of the powerful, well-funded nuclear lobby. The failed Yucca Mountain campaign in Nevada is one of many examples showing that the powers-that-be in today's society need more than "air cover"—advertising and manipulation of the mass media—to win public acceptance. Troops are also needed to fight the "ground war" for public opinion. In order to fight that war, the PR industry has studied the tactics of grassroots democracy used by environmentalists and other citizen activists, and it has begun to adapt and use those tactics for its own purposes.

CHAPTER FIVE

Spies for Hire

"The military is a role model for the business world."
ROBERT DILENSCHNEIDER
ex-CEO of Hill & Knowlton Public Relations

"Bud" looked the part of a B movie detective: a huge, hulking man in his late 50's, pushing 270 pounds, with pale skin, a military haircut, sweaty palms and fidgety manners. He almost always wore the same cheap dark blue suit and carried a large leather briefcase.[1]

For years Bud was a frequent visitor to the offices and events of nonprofit public advocacy groups, particularly those involved in environmental, food safety and animal welfare issues. Sometimes he said he was a freelance writer, sometimes just a concerned citizen.

One day Bud showed up at a press conference organized by the Beyond Beef campaign to persuade consumers that they should eat less meat for health and environmental reasons. A reporter thought he recognized Bud and went over to say hello. "How are you doing?" the reporter asked. "Are you still working for McDonald's?"

"I don't know what you're talking about," Bud said, fidgeting.

"Sure," the reporter said, perplexed. "We've met before. You used to work for McDonald's."

"You have me confused with someone else," Bud said, shifting nervously.[2]

The incident raised suspicions, and members of the Beyond Beef campaign decided they ought to learn a little bit more about Bud. A Beyond Beef staffer followed Bud leaving their headquarters and tailed him to the office of the secretive PR/public affairs firm of Mongoven, Biscoe and Duchin (MBD). When activists inquired, company president Jack Mongoven denied that Bud was an employee, but an

MBD secretary admitted that Bud often visited the office. Inquiring messages left on Bud's home phone machine went unanswered.

Public Policy and Private Eyes

Movements for social and political reform have often become targets of surveillance. In the early days of the labor movement, businesses used private detective agencies to infiltrate trade unions. In the 1920s and during the Cold War, the government spied on Communists and suspected "fellow travelers." In the 1960s, the FBI and local police investigated civil rights demonstrators and anti-war protesters. The Watergate scandal leading to the resignation of President Nixon began when White House staff members organized illegal espionage of Nixon's political opponents. Revelations of these activities provoked public outrage and led Congress to pass laws restricting the government's right to spy on law-abiding citizens.

In the private sector, however, spying is relatively unrestricted. The federal civil rights act, for instance, applies mainly to government action. "What's amazing about private surveillance is that there is no legal protection against it," says Philadelphia lawyer David Kairys.[3]

"Public police are accountable," says sociologist Gary T. Marx. "They have to, in principle, make a case for their actions in open court, and the accused has a right to challenge and oppose evidence. Also, they're restrained by the exclusionary rule and the entrapment doctrine, but private systems of justice don't have to contend with those. We've always thought of big brother in government as a threat to liberty, but the framers of the Constitution didn't pay much attention to private groups, because there weren't large corporations at the time. With the rise of multinationals, there is a powerful third force."[4]

In fact, government agencies sometimes encourage the private sector in activities that the government itself is forbidden from carrying out. In 1987, for example, administrators of US government research agencies met with a lobbyist for the private biomedical researchers to develop a strategy for fighting the growing animal rights campaign against animal testing. "The stakes are enormous," stated a memo circulated at the meeting by Frederick K. Goodwin, one of the participating federal officials. The memo went on to outline a strategy for keeping the government behind the scenes while encouraging private groups to undermine the animal rights movement: "Wherever feasible, the research institutions should leave the 'out front' activities to the other groups. . . . Agencies should find some acceptable way to provide funding for some of these efforts and technical support for others." Interviewed later, Goodwin explained the reasoning behind his strategy: "We're not allowed to lobby. There's a law against it. [But] all federal agencies have linkages to various advocacy groups interested in the business of that agency."[5]

The public relations industry has developed a lucrative side business scrutinizing the thoughts and actions of citizen activists, using paid spies who are often recruited from government, military or private security backgrounds. Take, for example, "Bud," the mole inside the Beyond Beef campaign. Bud's real name was Seymour D. Vestermark, Jr. Before becoming a PR spy, he began his career path as an Army analyst for the Department of Defense, writing reports such as *Vulnerabilities of Social Structure: Studies of the Social Dimensions of Nuclear Attack,* which laid out "approaches for determining the likely social effects of nuclear attack" in order to plan for post-war "reorganization" and "shorter-term and longer-term recovery."[6] He went on to work in the executive office of the president of the United States, staffing a task force on "political assassinations and collective violence." On March 27, 1976, he was mentioned briefly in a *New York Times* article describing a State Department conference on "international terrorism."[7] In 1978, he co-authored a book titled *Controlling Crime in the School,* to help high school principals grapple with problems such as "how to use intelligence information for good public relations," "the dilemma created by the bomb threat," "the proper use of surveillance photography," "extremists and their unfolding scenarios," "developing mass arrest procedures" and "why kids hate cops."[8]

Flacks and Spooks at the Watergate Hotel

In addition to domestic espionage, the PR industry has been linked repeatedly to overseas spying, often lending its overseas offices to serve as CIA front groups. Some of those links are explored in *The Power House,* Susan B. Trento's critical biography of PR executive Robert Keith Gray. Trento reports that the giant Hill & Knowlton firm "decided to open overseas offices . . . on the advice of friends, including then-CIA director Allen W. Dulles." According to Hill & Knowlton executive Robert T. Crowley, "Hill & Knowlton's overseas offices were perfect 'cover' for the ever-expanding CIA. Unlike other cover jobs, being a public relations specialist did not require technical training for CIA officers." George Worden, another company executive, said he "used to kid at Hill & Knowlton about our office in Kuala Lumpur, because nobody would tell me what it did, and I swore it had to be a CIA front."[9]

Another PR firm with CIA links, Robert R. Mullen & Co., played a key role in the Watergate scandal. A report on the scandal by Howard Baker, the Republican vice-chairman for the Watergate committee, states that Mullen & Co. "maintained a relationship with the Central Intelligence Agency since its incorporation in 1959. It provided cover for an agent in Europe and an agent in the Far East at the time of the Watergate break-in." [10] In addition to fronting for the CIA, Mullen provided public relations services for clients including the Mormon Church, General Foods, and the US Department of Health, Education and Welfare.

In 1971, the Mullen firm was purchased by Robert F. Bennett, the son of Wallace Bennett, Utah's conservative Republican senator. Robert Bennett figures prominently in a lengthy analysis of the Watergate affair by J. Anthony Lukas published in the January 4, 1976, *New York Times Magazine.* "Robert Foster Bennett is one of the most intriguing figures in the Watergate saga," Lukas writes. "Through his political ally, Chuck Colson, he maintained close relations with the Committee to Re-elect the President. . . . And in early 1971, through Colson's good offices, he purchased Robert R. Mullen & Company, a Washington public-relations firm which served as a CIA front in Stockholm, Singapore, Amsterdam and Mexico City, provided cover for some CIA activities in this country, and hired a whole platoon of 'former' CIA men—among them Howard Hunt." [11]

The day after Hunt's "retirement" from the CIA on April 30, 1970, he went to work for the Mullen Co. As the presidential election campaign was gearing up, Colson called Bennett in July 1971 and arranged to have Hunt "moonlight" for the White House. The Mullen Co.'s offices were located at 1700 Pennsylvania Ave., directly across the street from the offices of the Committee to Re-elect the President at 1701 Pennsylvania, and the Nixon campaign planned many of its dirty tricks, including the Watergate burglary, in Hunt's office at the Mullen Co. [12]

The day after Hunt's accomplices were arrested at the Watergate hotel, a Mullen Co. attorney helped the burglars make bail. Subsequent investigations showed other connections between the Mullen firm and the Watergate conspiracy, including a series of phone calls from Hunt's office to Donald Segretti, who was later convicted for directing a campaign of political espionage and sabotage against the Democrats. In fact, several prominent journalists investigating the Watergate affair, including Lukas, came to the conclusion that Mullen CEO Robert Bennett was "Deep Throat," the mysterious secret informant who leaked Watergate information to *Washington Post* journalists Bob Woodward and Carl Bernstein. According to Senator Howard Baker's Watergate report, "Bennett was feeding stories to Bob Woodward who was 'suitably grateful'; . . . he was making no attribution to Bennett; and . . . he was protecting Bennett and Mullen and Company. According to Watergate defendant Chuck Colson, Bennett was the key figure in the CIA's efforts to cover up its own role in Watergate and to blame the whole thing on the White House."[13] By positioning himself as an information source rather than a target of the Watergate investigation, Bennett survived the scandal with his reputation intact, and in 1992 Utah voters elected him to his father's old seat in the US Senate.

The Nestlé Crunch

In 1977, a church-based group of activists became concerned about the Swiss-based Nestlé corporation and its deadly practice of selling infant formula to women in Third World countries. To stimulate sales, Nestlé gave away free infant formula to hospitals along with "educational materials" instructing women to use the formula to feed their newborns. Use of the free formula interrupted women's lactation process, preventing their breasts from producing enough milk and obliging them to buy formula once the samples ran out. In the Third World, many people lack access to clean water, and poor people often cannot afford to buy sufficient formula. Women who were induced to use Nestlé formula in place of breast milk often had no choice but to dilute the formula with contaminated water, leading to diarrhea, dehydration and death among Third World infants.

Activists opposed to this practice originally planned a six-month publicity campaign around the issue, but Nestlé's hostile response backfired and prompted a protracted boycott of the company's products. Eventually over 700 churches and activist groups world-wide joined the boycott.[14]

After three years of a losing confrontation, Nestlé tried a different approach beginning in 1980 with the formation of the Nestlé Coordination Center for Nutrition (NCCN). Nestlé's chief strategists were Rafael Pagan and Jack Mongoven. Before entering the private sector, Pagan had been a military careerist whose work included political and economic briefings at the White House, a tour of duty at the Pentagon, and various missions to Latin America. Mongoven was a journalist before turning to political work as a Republican party organizer, followed by work in the communications office of the

Nixon and Ford administrations. Although Mongoven did not have a military background, he had studied military strategy and found it useful in planning political campaigns. He and Pagan bonded on their first day together when Mongoven listed the "nine principles" of German military theorist Carl von Clausewitz during a strategy planning meeting. In developing their campaign, they also turned to Sun Tzu's classic theoretical work, *The Art of War*.

Pagan and Mongoven conducted an in-depth analysis of the coalition supporting the boycott and developed a "divide and conquer" strategy. Some of the boycott's strongest support came from teachers, represented by the National Education Association, so NCCN courted support for Nestlé from the American Federation of Teachers, a smaller, more conservative rival union.To counter the churches involved in the boycott, they needed to find a strong church that would take their side. The United Methodists were supporting the boycott, but through negotiations and piecemeal concessions, Nestlé gradually succeeded in winning them over. Finally, NCCN helped establish the Nestlé Infant Formula Audit Commission (NIFAC), an "independent" group chaired by former US Secretary of State Edmund S. Muskie for the purpose of "monitoring" Nestlé's compliance with the World Health Organization's policies on marketing of breast-milk substitutes. Although NIFAC was organized by Nestlé, NCCN carefully selected educators, clergy and scientists— including boycott supporters—whose service on the commission would create a perception of legitimacy, objectivity and fairness.

It took years, but this strategy of appeasement and image manipulation gradually dampened the fires of outrage. In January 1984, the International Nestlé Boycott Committee announced that they were ending the boycott.[15] In 1989, Nestlé's infant-formula marketing practices prompted renewed concern, but this time the company was ready. They hired Ogilvy and Mather Public Relations to develop a strategy, called "proactive neutralization," which included plans to monitor Nestlé's critics, an analysis of various church leaders and organizations to gauge how strongly they would support the boycott, and suggestions for winning over wavering boycott supporters. John Kelly, a BBC reporter who discovered the Ogilvy and Mather plan, described it as "an open and shut case of a spy plan."[16]

The end of the bitterly-fought Nestlé boycott left Rafael Pagan and Jack Mongoven with reputations as PR miracle workers, and a database of information about activist organizations. During the Nestlé campaign, they had developed dossiers on groups such the International Organization of Consumer Unions and the Pesticide Action Network, along with clergy and labor unions. In 1985, they left Nestlé to form their own PR firm, Pagan International, offering their expertise and strategic advice to defense contractors as well as the chemicals, pharmaceuticals and foods industries.[17] Pagan's clients quickly grew to include Union Carbide, Shell Oil, Ciba-Geigy Corp., Chevron and the Government of Puerto Rico.[18]

In 1987, the firm suffered an embarrassing setback when someone leaked to the press its "Neptune Strategy" for helping Shell Oil counter a boycott against its business dealings in South Africa. Activists were pressuring Shell and other companies to pull out of South Africa as part of a campaign against the country's racist apartheid system. Instead of divesting its South African holdings, the Neptune Strategy advised Shell to "develop a task force" of South Africans, church leaders, US activists and executives to issue a statement about the company's role in helping South Africa prepare for life after apartheid and to develop "post-apartheid plans" that "will ensure the continuation and growth of the Shell companies in the United States and South Africa."

To implement this plan, Pagan International organized and subsidized a front group composed of black clergy called the Coalition on Southern Africa (COSA). Launched with great fanfare in September 1987, COSA talked of ambitious plans to develop black-black business links between South Africa and the United States, promote education and training of South African blacks, and pressure for an end to apartheid. In reality, COSA was a paper front group with no resources to carry out these goals. According to Donna Katzin, a leader in the Shell boycott, COSA reflected a deliberate attempt to "divide and weaken the position of the religious community with regard to South Africa." She noted that immediately after COSA was created, companies with South African operations began to point to COSA to show that not all US church groups backed disinvestment.[19]

Public disclosure of the Neptune Strategy prompted Shell to cancel its account with Pagan International, and company revenues plunged. Jack Mongoven left to form his own firm in partnership with other key Pagan executives, including Ronald Duchin and Alvin Biscoe. Lawsuits followed, with Mongoven, Biscoe and Duchin complaining that Pagan owed them money, and Pagan accusing them of deliberately undermining the firm by leaking the Neptune Strategy to the press. Pagan went down in bankruptcy, but the new firm of Mongoven, Biscoe & Duchin (MBD) has prospered.[20]

MBD Unplugged

Like Pagan International, MBD specializes in providing "public policy intelligence." Its services do not come cheap. Regular clients pay a retainer ranging from $3,500 to $9,000 per month. In addition, Mongoven, Biscoe & Duchin sometimes produces special reports, such as a 1989 analysis of the Natural Resources Defense Council, one of the country's leading mainstream environmental organizations. Corporations interested in obtaining the report paid $1,500 per copy.[21]

The company refuses to name its clients, but an internal MBD document says they "are almost all members of the Fortune 100 and six are members of the Fortune top 20."[22] Known clients include Monsanto, DuPont, Philip Morris and Shell Oil. Mike Miles, the former CEO of Philip Morris, had a particular affinity for MBD's cold-war style. According to PR executive Robert Dilenschneider, Miles "has a voracious appetite for intelligence, and he's very much aware of the other side's intelligence-gathering efforts. He's so careful that he has his company's travel people glue stickers on airline ticket jackets cautioning his executives not to talk shop while en route!"[23]

MBD tries to get on the mailing list of as many organizations as possible. Its employees read activist newsletters and other publications to keep tabs on controversial issues that may affect its clients. Those interests have expanded vastly beyond the food safety issues that concerned Pagan and Mongoven during the Nestlé boycott. According to MBD documents, they include: "acid rain, clean air, clean water, hazardous and toxic wastes, nuclear energy, recycling, South Africa, the United Nations, developments in Eastern Europe, dioxin, organic farming, pesticides, biotechnology, vegetarianism, consumer groups, product safety, endangered species, oil spills." Information related to all of these topics is sifted and reviewed by company analysts, then distilled into reports and memos.[24]

MBD's promotional brochure says the purpose of this research is to maintain "extensive files on organizations and their leadership," particularly "environmental and consumer groups, churches and other organizations which seek changes in public policy." A typical dossier on an organization includes its historical background, biographical information on key personnel, funding sources, relationships with other organizations, publications, and a "characterization" of the organization aimed at assessing the potential for coopting or marginalizing the organization's impact on public policy debates.[25]

To gather information, MBD also uses covert operatives like "Bud" Vestermark and Kara Zeigler. Kara spies both in person and over the phone, falsely representing herself as "a writer for *Z Magazine*"[26] or a friend-of-a-friend.[27] Sometimes she will correctly identify herself as representing "MBD, a public affairs company," without elaborating on the real reasons behind her call.

In one single day, Kara placed calls to an aide to US Senator Russ Feingold (D–Wisconsin); Dr. Michael Hansen of Consumers Union, the publisher of *Consumer Reports* magazine; and Wisconsin dairy farmer Francis Goodman. She was calling as part of a frenetic MBD campaign to gather "intelligence" about groups opposed to the use of recombinant bovine growth hormone (rBGH), a controversial new genetically-engineered drug being injected into dairy cows.

The Mutations Industry

Monsanto, the developer of rBGH, is one of the world's largest transnational corporations, manufacturing a wide range of chemicals, drugs and other high-tech products—many of which are dangerous or lethal. Monsanto was the manufacturer of most of the world's PCBs—persistent chemicals used in electrical equipment which have been shown to cause cancer and birth defects. It is also the world's largest producer of herbicides, including products contaminated with dioxin. In the area of consumer products, Monsanto produces the Ortho line of lawn chemicals, as well as NutraSweet,™ a sugar substitute whose safety has been challenged by safe food activists.

Bovine growth hormone is the flagship product in Monsanto's attempt to claim leadership in the fledgling biotechnology industry. Designed to replicate a hormone that occurs naturally in cows, rBGH can increase milk production by up to 25 percent when injected into dairy cows. Monsanto spent hundreds of millions of dollars developing rBGH for commercial use, and has hyped the synthetic hormone as a miracle technology that will increase milk production and lower food costs to consumers.

In 1985, Monsanto Chief Executive Richard J. Mahoney estimated the potential market for rBGH at $1 billion a year once the hormone received approval from the Food and Drug Administration. The stakes for the biotechnology industry as a whole were even higher. Other chemical and drug giants such as Eli Lilly, American Cyanamid, W.R. Grace, Upjohn and Calgene also had major investments in biotech development and were poised to follow Monsanto's lead by introducing their own genetically-altered fruits, vegetables and farm animals—"frankenfoods" such as genetically-engineered cows from Bristol-Myers Squibb that produce human mother's milk protein; potatoes that kill pests by producing their own insecticide; slow-ripening tomatoes; virus-resistant squash; herbicide-tolerant cotton and soybean plants; growth hormone for pigs; and meat from cloned cattle.

Beginning in 1986, however, rBGH faced organized international resistance spearheaded by Jeremy Rifkin's Foundation on Economic Trends. The issue attracted other rBGH opponents including the Consumers Union, the Humane Society of the US, Food and Water, Inc., and grassroots farmer organizations. Critics of the hormone raised a number of serious questions about its safety and alleged benefits:

- Monsanto's own tests showed increased levels of mastitis, a painful udder infection, in cows injected with rBGH. According to food safety experts, increased mastitis would force farmers to use more antibiotics, which would then be more likely to contaminate the cows' milk. Milk from treated cows would also spoil faster because it contains more bacteria and has a higher "somatic cell count." (Translated from scientific jargon into layman's language, this means that rBGH-induced milk contains "more pus.")[28]

- Dr. Richard Burroughs worked for the FDA from 1985 to 1988, analyzing test data supplied by Monsanto and the other companies engaged in developing rBGH. His analysis convinced him that the companies were manipulating data. In 1989, Burroughs was fired after he went to Congress accusing his superiors of covering up this information.[29]

- Cows treated with rBGH need to consume more protein, often in the form of "rendered animal protein" derived from the carcasses of cows and other dead animals. Cows consuming animal byproducts are susceptible to bovine spongiform encephalopathy, also known as "mad cow disease." This disease has plagued England for a decade, and some doctors worry that it could migrate from cows to humans as a fatal dementia called CJD.[30]

- Increased milk production from rBGH hardly seemed like a blessing to dairy farmers struggling for survival in an already glutted market. And rBGH came with extra costs. Small dairy farmers, reeling from high production costs and low market prices, worried that the hormone threatened their livelihood, already threatened by competition from huge farm conglomerates.[31]

In response to this opposition, Monsanto and its corporate allies pulled out all the stops. They hired a who's-who list of heavy-hitting

PR firms and lobbyists, including Hill & Knowlton; Burson-Marsteller; Edelman; Jerry Dryer & Associates; Manning, Selvage & Lee; Morgan & Myers; Porter/Novelli; Covington & Burling; King & Spalding; and Foreman & Heidepreim. The PR effort included presentations to dairy farmers and veterinarians, lobbying of state legislators and the distribution of thousands of brochures, videotapes and other pro-rBGH materials to the press and the general public. The Animal Health Institute, based in Alexandria, Virginia, coordinated the PR campaign. During the three years from 1988 to 1991 alone, the Animal Health Institute spent over $900,000 on rBGH promotion.

Activists caught a glimpse of one PR firm's methodology for doing "opposition research" in November 1990. The Consumers Union, publisher of *Consumer Reports* magazine, was preparing a highly critical report on rBGH when a woman claiming to be a scheduler for ABC-TV's *Nightline* contacted Michael Hansen, the report's author, and requested a preview of his findings. The woman said *Nightline* was interested in Hansen's research for a show they were considering on the rBGH controversy, and asked Hansen to fax her his curriculum vita. Somewhat suspicious, Hansen phoned a friend at ABC to follow up on the *Nightline* call. His friend, David Sostman, who worked in the tape library at ABC News, discovered that no one on the *Nightline* staff had contacted Hansen. Intrigued, Sostman tracked the mystery caller. "The bottom line was they said they were calling from ABC but the fax number they gave came from [PR firm] Burson-Marsteller's office," he said.[32]

As part of its public relations campaign, the pro-rBGH coalition used polling and focus groups to determine public attitudes toward dairy foods from hormone-treated cows. The results were discouraging. Surveys showed widespread consumer doubts about the industry's claim that rBGH milk would be identical to milk from untreated cows. A large majority, particularly parents with children under 18, reported a fear that ill effects caused by rBGH would be discovered in the future.

In late 1989, media coverage of rBGH intensified, and per capita consumption of milk began to decline. The pro-rBGH Dairy Coalition responded by setting up consumer telephone hotlines and designated over 250 "regional experts," including doctors, nutritionists and animal scientists, to act as media contacts. The coalition prepared "educational resource kits" for distribution to over 5,000 targeted recipients, including dairy retailers, state and national trade associations, national and state consumer media, and members of the

National Association of Science Writers. The PR campaign lined up supporters from the American Academy of Pediatrics and the National Institutes of Health. It arranged for the American Medical Association to publish an article and an editorial (written by scientists who had received research grants from Monsanto) claiming that all available scientific evidence showed rBGH was safe.

The National Dairy Promotion and Research Board, a quasi-governmental agency, also bought into the campaign. In theory, the National Dairy Board is supposed to promote the interests of dairy farmers. Its $75 million annual budget comes from farmers in the form of mandatory deductions from milk sales. Publicly, the Dairy Board declared its "neutrality" on the rBGH issue. However, internal documents obtained through the Freedom of Information Act revealed that the Board was working in coalition with Monsanto.

Secret Agents

In November 1991, a farm advocacy group called Rural Vermont issued a report based on information obtained from a dairy scientist at the University of Vermont, one of the state universities around the country engaged in testing rBGH research sponsored by Monsanto. Contrary to Monsanto's claims of rBGH safety, the scientist's data showed an unusually high rate of deformed calves born to rBGH-treated cows. University officials reacted with outrage. University PR spokesperson Nicola Marro insisted in an interview that the Rural Vermont report was merely the first wave of a national, well-coordinated campaign against rBGH organized by Jeremy Rifkin. How did Marro know that this campaign was being planned? "Monsanto had a mole in Rifkin's meeting," Marro said.[33]

A little research quickly confirmed the truth of Marro's boast. In October 1990, Rifkin's organization had participated in a conference in Washington, DC, to oppose rBGH. One of the participants at the meeting was a woman who identified herself as Diane Moser, an intern working for the "Maryland Citizens Consumer Council." As conference participants racked their brains to guess who might have been the "mole," several people immediately thought of her. Moser had brought a book to the meeting and avoided small talk. "She said she represented housewives concerned about BGH," recalled Andrew Christianson, a Vermont state representative who had been at the DC meeting. "I had suspicions immediately. I've never seen anyone with a paperback coming to a meeting like that. It's usually pretty serious activists."[34]

An investigation quickly showed that the "Maryland Citizens Consumer Council" did not exist, and sleuthing by activists revealed that Moser was an employee of Burson-Marsteller. A reporter called Timothy Brosnahan, general manager for B-M's Washington office. "I know Diane, but I have no idea what she does in her spare time," Brosnahan said.[35] Further investigation linked another member of the nonexistent Maryland Citizens Consumer Council to Burson-Marsteller—Laurie Ross (a.k.a. "Lisa Ellis"), who, like Diane Moser, worked under the supervision of B-M vice-president Sheila Raviv. In response to reporters' questions, Raviv—who has since been promoted to CEO of B-M's Washington office—behaved like a model spymaster, disavowing any knowledge of the operation.[36]

Kaufman PR, the National Dairy Board's PR agency from 1990–91, spied on another anti-rBGH meeting, this time in New York City in January of 1990. After the event, organizers discovered that Monsanto PR coordinator Larry O'Neil had successfully contacted New York media in advance of the conference to convince them it would not be newsworthy. A check of National Dairy Board records through the Freedom of Information Act showed that several of the conference attendees were PR spies. Four days before the meeting, Kaufman PR had signed a subcontract agreement with the Direct Impact Co., an Alexandria, Virginia, PR firm that specializes in "grassroots lobbying." The agreement called for Direct Impact to recruit "between six and eight residents of New York to attend the event, monitor developments, ask questions, and provide other support as appropriate. Each attendee must be able to articulate the basic [pro-rBGH] arguments on the issue and cite one or more substantive reasons for supporting the Dairy Board's position."[37]

The purpose of the covert operation was apparently to minimize news coverage of the conference, and to "spin" the coverage by planting "housewives" in the audience who would appear to favor injecting milk cows with bovine growth hormone.

The Kaufman/Direct Impact covert action was less than subtle. "When a woman said she was a typical housewife and then made highly technical statements, you knew she hadn't gleaned her information from *Better Homes and Gardens*. It was kind of a B-grade spy routine," said conference organizer Dave Carter.[38]

Going to the Dogs

The ubiquitous Seymour ("Bud") Vestermark spied on anti-rBGH groups and also infiltrated a number of animals rights organizations

in the late 1980s. His name appeared as senior contributing editor
on a newsletter titled the *Animal Rights Reporter,* published by
Perceptions Press. The *Animal Rights Reporter* claimed to be an
"objective analysis of the animal rights movement." In reality, it
offered persistently negative reporting on animal rights groups and
advice on undermining the movement. Animal rights activists who
saw the newsletter were shocked to find that it contained details
about their organizations that could only have been known by their
own members.[39]

Fund for Animals staffer Heidi Prescott recalls someone pointing
Vestermark out to her and warning that he was a spy when she first
began attending rallies in 1989. "It was kind of common knowledge
among people who went to all of the animal rights events," she said.
"He was laid-back and came across real friendly. He'd show up and
lurk around and talk to people. Usually someone would recognize
him and go over and say, 'He works for Perceptions Press.' "[40]

Perceptions Press was the publishing arm of a two-company operation owned by Jan Reber, an unlicensed "private investigator" whose
other business, Perceptions International, provided "information gathering" and "security" services to transnational corporations, including "research on coercive trends and movements that affect
business"—in particular, animal rights activists and environmentalists.[41] Its clients included Leon Hirsch, the controversial president of
the US Surgical Company in Norwalk, Connecticut. US Surgical manufactures surgical staples, used in place of conventional sutures to
close wounds and surgical incisions. Financially, the company was
a smashing success, with $91.2 million in profits in 1991, of which
$23.3 million in salary and stock options went to Hirsch himself.[42]

Hirsch called himself an "only in America" success story, but
animal rights activists were upset with the methods the company
used to market its product. To demonstrate the advantages of staples
over sutures, US Surgical conducts "training demonstrations" for sur-
geons in which they cut open live dogs and staple their intestines.
After the demonstration, the dogs are killed. By US Surgical's own
estimate, it disposes of over 1,000 dogs a year.[43]

In 1981, a local newspaper wrote an article about the company's
use of dogs, prompting a series of protests outside US Surgical Headquarters by a Norwalk animal rights group, Friends of Animals (FOA).
Following one demonstration, FOA vice-president Sarah Seymour discovered that she was being followed by Bud Vestermark and Jan
Reber. They tailed her by car to her child's school and took photo-

Activists turned the tables on Seymour "Bud" Vestermark, Jr., by taking this picture of him as he spied on an animal rights rally. (photo courtesy of Friends of Animals)

graphs of her. Sarah Seymour went over to confront them, and Reber denied that he was following her. "I'm just here to pick up my own kid," he said. Seymour checked and learned that none of Reber's children were enrolled at the school. The incident upset her. It seemed like an attempt at intimidation. But it was nothing compared to later events.

Bombing the Boss

According to journalist Lisa McGurrin Driscoll, Mary Lou Sapone entered the animal rights movement in the summer of 1987 when she appeared at a conference in Washington, DC. "She just burst on the scene," said Julie Lewin, FOA's Connecticut coordinator. A friendly, talkative woman, Sapone immediately became involved in at least a half dozen animal rights groups. She seemed to be everywhere, traveling all around the country to participate in protests, meetings and conferences.[44]

Animal rights activists began to have suspicions about Sapone. Unlike most activists, she seemed to have unlimited time and money.

She seemed unusually inquisitive, making a point of getting to know all of the key people in the movement. "She always asked questions and carried a pad of paper, taking notes," said Kim Bartlett, editor of a magazine called *Animals Agenda,* who first met Sapone in June, 1987, at a demonstration in Massachusetts. Bartlett noticed that Sapone's statements "didn't add up. . . . First she said she was a psychologist, then a Lamaze instructor and then a social worker." Betsy Swart, chairwoman of a San Francisco-based animal rights group, became so suspicious of Sapone's questions that "I made up a date and told her there would be a demonstration." Within days, Swart said, she received a call from a government official asking about the "demonstration."[45]

Sapone frequently urged others to commit violent or illegal disruptions. "She showed a lack of judgment, always looking for action. This woman clearly seemed to be reckless, with no appreciation for the political and moral ramifications of violence," Lewin said.[46]

In April 1988, Sapone and Lewin attended a demonstration in New York City, where Sapone introduced Lewin to a woman named Fran Stephanie Trutt, a 33-year-old part-time math teacher who Sapone described as "someone who lobbies in New York." Lewin was not impressed with Trutt, who "seemed disheveled and not too tightly wrapped. She wore lumpy clothing, and her hair was askew." After talking to her briefly, Lewin decided that Trutt was "pretty crazy" and excused herself.

FOA president Priscilla Feral had met Trutt two years earlier at a US Surgical demonstration, and formed a similar opinion. "My assistant saw her stomping on azaleas. She seemed particularly angry," Feral recalled.[47]

Unlike the other animal rights activists, Mary Lou Sapone took an active interest in Trutt, befriending her and cultivating a close relationship. Over the course of the next six months, Sapone and Trutt spoke by phone at least two or three times a week.[48] Unbeknownst to Trutt, Sapone—a spy for Perceptions International—was secretly tape-recording the conversations and giving the tapes to US Surgical, along with written reports detailing her efforts to incite Trutt into carrying out a murder attempt against US Surgical president Leon Hirsch. In 1988, US Surgical paid Perceptions International over $500,000 for its services, of which $65,000 went to pay Sapone.[49] Normally, of course, company presidents do not pay to arrange their own murder, but Hirsch was neither crazy nor suicidal. He was trying to engineer an embarrassing scandal that would discredit the animal rights movement, and—if the resulting sensational court case had not unearthed tape transcripts and other confidential company documents—he probably would have succeeded.

Fran Trutt was a vulnerable, lonely, angry woman. She talked wildly of killing her ex-lover. The transcripts of Sapone's phone conversations with Trutt show Sapone's efforts to direct that anger toward Leon Hirsch. On May 23, for example, the two women reviewed possible murder scenarios. Trutt commented that the police would probably identify her as a suspect if she killed her ex-lover.

Sapone replied: "Well, maybe you could, so maybe you should do Leon first."

Trutt laughed, and Sapone added, "I mean, if you think that this, with this other guy that they should come to you—"

"Well, the other one, they're going to come to me first. There's no question about that," Trutt said.

"So maybe you should do Leon first," Sapone repeated.[50]

When Trutt showed signs of losing her resolve, Perceptions orchestrated a supposedly "accidental" meeting in September 1988 between Trutt and another agent, Marcus Mead. The meeting took place in a pizza shop, where Mead struck up a conversation with Trutt by asking her for advice on taking care of his puppies. Mead, whose sister was employed by US Surgical, was paid $500 a week to befriend Trutt and to help egg her on. To help him impress her, US Surgical loaned him the use of a Porsche and an Alfa-Romeo.[51]

Sapone and Mead gave Trutt money to buy bombs. In a tape-recorded conversation on November 10, Trutt thanked Sapone for giving her $100 which Trutt used for rent. Sapone replied, "if you want to use it for the bomb first or the rent first, I mean, I didn't care because, you know, you knew what you had to do."[52] The following day, Mead drove Trutt and two pipe bombs from New York to US Surgical headquarters in Connecticut, where she was arrested under a pre-arranged deal with the Norwalk Police Department.[53] Animal rights activists later wondered why the police had allowed Mead to drive an explosive device across interstate highways rather than simply arrest Trutt at her home where the bombs had been stored. The arrest seemed staged for maximum publicity value, with public safety a secondary concern.

News of the arrest spread quickly through the animal rights movement. Shocked and alarmed, Julie Lewin phoned Sapone trying to figure out who Trutt was. In the ensuing conversation, which was also secretly recorded, Sapone withheld information about her relationship with Trutt and pretended to search her memory.

"I think the name is familiar," Sapone said. "I'm trying to piece this together. . . . I remember the last name because it was kind of distinctive. It was like a strong—you know, I remember. I remember names sometimes. . . ."

A local reporter had informed Lewin that a tip had thwarted the bombing, prompting Lewin to speculate that the bombing might have been "*agent provocateur* kind of stuff, like in the '60s."

"What would that gain?" Sapone asked with false naïveté.

"It gains a blackening of our movement."

"Oh, I see."

"No one that I work with in the state would ever consider such an act," Lewin said. "We'd be the first to turn them in."

"Gosh," said Sapone the *provocateur,* "this is like a nightmare."[54]

For US Surgical, of course, the "nightmare" was a long-cherished dream. The *Animal Rights Reporter* lost no time in denouncing Trutt's action as a comparable to "the shooting down of a civilian Rhodesian airline by a local terrorist group" and "murderous attacks like the Achille Lauro incident."[55]

Even after Sapone's role in befriending and encouraging Trutt was disclosed, US Surgical continued to claim that the incident was an example of "terrorist" tendencies in the animal rights movement. "People think of animal rights as protecting the birds in the winter and the little puppies," said US Surgical Attorney Hugh F. Keefe. "I don't think they realize the militancy that has invaded some of these groups." Keefe used pretrial proceedings to seek exhaustive information about Friends of Animals, including lists of all contributors, Julie Lewin's personal diary and personal income tax returns, and all of her medical and psychiatric records—a request she interpreted as an effort to dig up dirt on the animal rights movement.[56]

"The people who are challenging this corporation are very small," said New Haven attorney John Williams, who represented both Trutt and Lewin. "US Surgical is going berserk and spending enormous amounts of money. It's become a personal vendetta for Leon Hirsch. The kinds of abuses that we associate with the FBI under J. Edgar Hoover are now in the realm of private corporations subsidizing a private security force."[57]

CHAPTER SIX

Divide and Conquer

We see then that there are many ways to one's object in War; that the complete subjugation of the enemy is not essential in every case.

CARL VON CLAUSEWITZ
On War

In 1980, a drunk driver killed the 13-year-old daughter of Candy L. Lightner. Devastated and angry, Lightner created an organization called Mothers Against Drunk Driving (MADD), to publicize the suffering caused by drug and alcohol abuse. Hollywood publicist Michael Levine described Lightner as a natural practitioner of what he calls "guerrilla PR." In his book by that title, Levine praised "this dynamic woman" who "used the sheer strength of her character to forge a movement." After Lightner and her surviving daughter held a press conference to describe the consequences of drunk driving, Levine said, "a photo of the tearful mother and daughter flashed around the world, and suddenly the agony of death from driving under the influence had a face and a name: Candy Lightner."

"We hadn't planned scenes of crying," Lightner said. "But instinctively we knew the media need something dramatic." After seeing the reaction to the photo, she learned to use visuals in dramatizing her cause. In a campaign to pass a California bill requiring a five-cent tax on alcohol, she sent her daughter to buy a six-pack with a fake ID. She then held a press conference—with her daughter sitting behind a small mountain of beer cans she'd just bought, illustrating how enormous the problem actually was.[1]

MADD quickly grew to three million members in the US alone, but Lightner's talents have been diverted to other purposes. In 1985 she left the organization over disagreements that included her desire to have MADD receive financial contributions from the liquor industry. She moved to Washington, DC, where she was hired by the American Beverage Institute, a liquor industry trade group, to help defeat MADD-supported laws that would toughen blood-alcohol tests.[2]

Dealing With Idealists

Since at least the days of Aristotle, practitioners of the art of rhetoric have understood that an endorsement from their opponent carries more persuasive power than anything they can say themselves. The public relations industry therefore carefully cultivates activists who can be coopted into working against the goals of their movement. This strategy has been outlined in detail by Ronald Duchin, senior vice-president of PR spy firm Mongoven, Biscoe and Duchin. A graduate of the US Army War College, Duchin worked as a special assistant to the Secretary of Defense and director of public affairs for the Veterans of Foreign Wars before joining Pagan International and MBD. In a 1991 speech to the National Cattlemen's Association, he described how MBD works to divide and conquer activist movements. Activists, he explained, fall into four distinct categories: "radicals," "opportunists," "idealists," and "realists." He outlined a three-step strategy: (1) isolate the radicals; (2) "cultivate" the idealists and "educate" them into becoming realists; then (3) coopt the realists into agreeing with industry.[3]

According to Duchin, radical activists "want to change the system; have underlying socio/political motives" and see multinational corporations as "inherently evil. . . . These organizations do not trust the . . . federal, state and local governments to protect them and to safeguard the environment. They believe, rather, that individuals and local groups should have direct power over industry. . . . I would categorize their principal aims right now as social justice and political empowerment."

Idealists are also "hard to deal with." They "want a perfect world and find it easy to brand any product or practice which can be shown to mar that perfection as evil. Because of their intrinsic altruism, however, and because they have nothing perceptible to be gained by holding their position, they are easily believed by both the media and the public, and sometimes even politicians." However, idealists "have a vulnerable point. If they can be shown that their position in opposition to an industry or its products causes harm to others and cannot be ethically justified, they are forced to change their position. . . . Thus, while a realist must be negotiated with, an idealist must be educated. Generally this education process requires great sensitivity and understanding on the part of the educator."

By contrast, opportunists and realists are easier to manipulate. Duchin defines opportunists as people who engage in activism seeking "visibility, power, followers and, perhaps, even employment. . . . The key to dealing with opportunists is to provide them with at least the perception of a partial victory." And realists are able to "live with trade-offs; willing to work within the system; not interested in radical change; pragmatic. The realists should always receive the highest priority in any strategy dealing with a public policy issue. . . . If your industry can successfully bring about these relationships, the credibility of the radicals will be lost and opportunists can be counted on to share in the final policy solution."[4]

Flacks to Greens: "Grow Up and Take the Cash"

The February 1994 issue of *O'Dwyer's PR Services Report* gives a candid description of the PR industry's strategy for encouraging sectors of the environmental movement to enter into "partnerships" with major polluters: "The lessons of the recent recession have taught PR people that no matter how idealistic a company sounds, it puts the bottom line ahead of cleaning up its mess,"[5] admits an editorial accompanying the report. As a cost-effective alternative, "such companies are finding that cold cash will buy them good will from the environmental movement. Cash-rich companies, PR people say, are funding hard-up environmental groups in the belief [that] the imprimatur of activists will go a long way in improving their reputation among environmentally aware consumers."[6]

On the other side of the "partnership," *O'Dwyer's* observes, "nonprofit groups are beginning to realize that private sector cash can increase an organization's clout and bankroll membership building programs." *O'Dwyer's* sees this increased willingness to take "private sector cash" as evidence of "maturing" in the environmental movement.[7]

O'Dwyer's interviewed Dale Didion of Hill & Knowlton in Washington, DC, the nation's third largest "environmental PR firm." Didion said companies are learning that they can "hire members of the environmental group's staff to help on certain projects. This is a tremendous benefit for a company that wants to have access to top green experts. Companies can avail themselves of talented researchers, scientists and analysts at very reasonable prices."[8]

Getting a relationship started between a company and an environmental group carries some risks as well. "It might be in both parties' interest at first to keep their relationship out of the news," says Didion. "Work out early how and when the relationship will be announced to the media—and what measure should be taken if word leaks out prematurely," he advises.

O'Dwyer's suggested some "cost-free and virtually risk free" ways to "test the waters" when entering into a relationship with an environmental group: "Help them raise money. Offer to sit on their board of directors. That can open up a good symbiotic relationship." Another effective tool is for the company to bankroll a conference on a topic of mutual interest, or fund an issue-specific publication for the nonprofit group. "The company gets substantial input into the content because the publication has its name on it," Didion said.[9]

Strange Bedfellows

To help industry determine how and which activists can be coopted, the Public Affairs Council, a trade association for public relations executives, sponsors a tax-exempt organization called the Foundation for Public Affairs. Funding comes from a who's-who list of America's corporate establishment including Ameritech, Ashland Oil, Boeing, Dow Chemical, Exxon, Health Insurance Association of America, Philip Morris, Mobil, Pharmaceutical Manufacturers Association, RJR Nabisco, and Shell Oil. Many PR/lobby firms also are members, including Bonner & Associates; Burson-Marsteller; E. Bruce Harrison; The Jefferson Group; and Mongoven, Biscoe & Duchin.[10]

The Foundation for Public Affairs monitors more than 75 specialized activist publications, and gathers information on "more than 1,300 activist organizations, research institutions, and other groups."[11] Until 1993, the Foundation published an impressive bi-annual directory titled *Public Interest Profiles* which offered "intelligence on 250 of the nation's key public interest groups" including "current concerns, budget, funding sources, board of directors, publications, conferences, and methods of operation."[12] In the 1992–93 version of this phonebook-sized tract, groups were profiled in chapters headed "Community/Grassroots," "Corporate Accountability/Responsibility," "Environmental," "Think Tanks," etc.[13]

Once a year, the Foundation for Public Affairs organizes a two-day Annual Conference on Activist Groups and Public Policymaking, where professional activists and staff members of prominent DC-based consumer and environmental organizations are invited to rub shoulders with influential corporate PR executives. The conference helps corporate flacks learn how to dissect the strategies, tactics and agendas of these activists, to better defeat or coopt their activism. The meeting is billed as a strictly off-the-record affair, "a one-of-a-kind opportunity to explore the agendas, strategies and influence of leading public interest groups." [14]

According to a promotional brochure, the purpose of the 1993 conference was to help PR executives find out the answers to questions such as: "What tactics are being employed by activists to achieve their goals? What methods can be used by business in cultivating ties with activist groups and what are the potential benefits . . . and/or drawbacks?" [15] Corporate attendance cost $545. Featured speakers included MBD's Ronald Duchin, along with Gene Karpinsky, head of the US Public Interest Research Group, and Gustav E. Jackson of the Citizens Clearinghouse for Hazardous Wastes. Stephen Brobeck, executive director of the Consumer Federation of America, also spoke for an hour "on what the dominant consumer issues and trends will be throughout the decade and what it all portends for corporate America." Conference attendees also heard from right-wing speakers including Patrick Noonan, the President of the Conservation Fund who sits on the Board of Ashland Oil; Ralph Reed, Executive Director of the Christian Coalition; and Fred Smith of the Competitive Enterprise Institute. [16]

The Best Friends Money Can Buy

The American Civil Liberties Union is one of the organizations that has been successfully recruited by the tobacco industry to promote the myth that smoking is a "civil right" comparable to freedom of speech and association. The ACLU denies charges by the Advocacy Institute that it is beholden to tobacco interests, but it cannot deny its own financial records, which show that the ACLU solicited and accepted about $500,000 in contributions from tobacco interests between 1987 and 1992, without disclosing the largesse to its ACLU membership. [17]

In Monsanto's campaign for approval of bovine growth hormone, it was able to buy the support of Carol Tucker Foreman, formerly executive director of the Consumer Federation of America. Foreman took a job in early 1993 as a personal lobbyist for Monsanto's rBGH team, for what is rumored to be an exceptionally large fee. With her help, Monsanto has successfully prevented Congress or the FDA from requiring labeling of milk from rBGH-injected cows, and in fact the company has used threats of lawsuits to intimidate dairy retailers who *want* to label their milk "rBGH-free."

Foreman, a former Assistant Secretary of Agriculture, is also the coordinator and lobbyist for the Safe Food Coalition, which calls itself "an alliance of consumer advocacy, senior citizen, whistleblower protection and labor organizations." Formed in 1987 by Foreman, its members include such public interest heavyweights as Michael Jacobson's Center for Science in the Public Interest (CSPI), Ralph Nader's Public Citizen, and Public Voice for Food and Health Policy.[18]

When interviewed, Foreman said she saw no conflict of interest between lobbying for rBGH and for the Safe Food Coalition. "The FDA has said rBGH is safe," she explained, adding "Why don't you call CSPI, they say rBGH is safe too?" When asked how much money she has received from Monsanto to lobby for rBGH, she angrily declined to answer, saying "What in the world business is that of yours?" Her DC consulting firm, Foreman & Heidepreim, refused to provide further information and referred journalists to Monsanto's PR department.[19]

Playing Both Sides

In the November 22, 1993, *Legal Times,* writer Sheila Kaplan describes the work of Porter/Novelli, a New York-based PR firm that specializes in what founder William Novelli refers to as "cross-pollination." By providing free work for health-related charities, Porter/Novelli is often able to persuade them to support the interests of its paying corporate clients. In spring of 1993, for example, produce growers and pesticide manufacturers represented by Porter/Novelli were alarmed to learn that the Public Broadcasting Service was about to air a documentary by Bill Moyers on the cancer risks that pesticides pose to children. To rebut the documentary, they turned to the government's National Cancer Institute (NCI) and the American Cancer Society (ACS). Porter/Novelli works for NCI and has provided free services to the ACS for over 20 years. It persuaded the national office of ACS to issue a memo downplaying the risk of cancer from pesticides. "The program makes unfounded suggestions . . . that pesticide residues in food may be at hazardous levels," said the memo, which the pesticide industry cited as "evidence" that the Moyers documentary overstated dangers to children from pesticides.[20]

"I have a longstanding concern that contractors work both sides of the street and that government agencies are unaware of these conflicting relationships," said Senator David Pryor (D-Ark.), the chairman of the subcommittee that oversees federal contracts. "This remains a glaring deficiency."[21]

Hill & Knowlton executive Nina Oligino used a similar "cross-pollination" strategy in 1994 to line up national environmental groups behind a coalition called "Partners for Sun Protection Awareness," a front group for Hill & Knowlton's client, drug transnational Schering-Plough. Best known for Coppertone™ sun lotion, Schering-Plough uses the coalition to "educate" the public about the dangers of skin cancer deaths, cataracts and damaged immune systems due to the atmosphere's thinning ozone layer and increased ultraviolet radiation. The campaign urges people to "liberally apply a sunscreen . . . to all exposed parts of the body before going outdoors."[22]

Hill & Knowlton successfully enlisted leaders of the Natural Resources Defense Council and the Sierra Club to add their names to the "Partners for Sun Protection" letterhead. Apparently these groups are little more than a dash of green window-dressing for the campaign. The "Partners" offered no proposals for preventing further thinning of the ozone layer. A representative of one of the environmental groups, who asked not to be named, said he was ignorant of the Schering-Plough funding and its hidden agenda to sell sun lotion.

The best prevention for sun-caused skin cancer is, of course, to cover up completely, but saying so would be market suicide for the world's largest maker of suntan lotion and purveyor of the sexy "Coppertone™ tan." One of the campaign's clever "video news releases" shows scores of sexy, scantily-clad sun worshippers still over-exposing themselves to UV rays, while slathering themselves with sun oil. The VNR does not mention Schering-Plough, the funder of the PR campaign.[23] Ironically, Hill & Knowlton has also worked for corporate clients who hired them to belittle the environmental risks of global climate change.[24]

Going the Extra Mile

Some companies, such as Ben & Jerry's ice cream and the Body Shop cosmetics, use progressive political rhetoric and claims of "social responsibility" as the centerpiece of their marketing campaigns. The Body Shop and Ben & Jerry's are among the founders of an association calling itself "Business for Social Responsibility," launched in 1992 by 54 companies with progressive reputations including the Stride Rite Corporation and Levi Strauss. By 1995 it had grown to over 800 companies, including many whose "social responsibility" is dubious at best. In order to increase its funding and corporate clout, BSR has actively recruited major corporations as members, including FedEx, Home Depot, Viacom, The Gap, AT&T, the Clorox Company, Kidder Peabody & Co., Reebok, Starbucks Coffee Co., Polaroid Corporation, Honeywell, Time-Warner, Taco Bell—and Monsanto.[25]

According to Craig Cox, former editor of *Business Ethics* magazine, Monsanto claims to have cut its toxic air emissions substantially, and is attempting to adopt other socially responsible business practices advocated by BSR.[26] However, these improvements in Monsanto's production *process* don't change the fact that the company's most profitable *products* include dangerous pesticides, artificial food additives, and risky bioengineered products. Monsanto's membership in BSR underscores a fundamental dilemma: How does the movement for socially responsible business define "social responsibility"? If Monsanto belongs in the club, why not "socially responsible" nuclear arms dealers? Can the tobacco industry join?

This dilemma forced the BSR board of directors to define its policy on eligibility for membership. After discussion, the board decided it would be counter-productive to impose specific standards of social responsibility on members. According to BSR President Bob Dunn, the board adopted an "all inclusive membership policy so long as companies demonstrate that they understand our mission, understand the principles of the organization and they wish to be a member because of their own interest in improving their policies and practices."[27]

The bottom line is that BSR's membership now includes some of the most environmentally destructive corporations on the planet, and more are sure to join. Some of the companies that have joined BSR are also financially supporting corporate front groups and business associations lobbying to weaken important environmental, consumer protection and civil rights laws, and funding right-wing advocacy groups set up to spread the message that environmental protection is incompatible with a healthy economy.

BSR's value as a vehicle for social change is further limited by the organization's decision not to take positions on specific legislation. This political neutrality stands in noticeable contrast to the right-wing activism of other corporate-sponsored associations such as the US Chamber of Commerce and the Business Roundtable, which are leading the charge to undermine even the mildest efforts to challenge the political power of big corporations.

BSR compensates for its limited commitment to social change with a seemingly unlimited devotion to glowing rhetoric. "For the last 10 years, it's been a very Pollyanna-ish type of movement," Cox admits.[28] Speaking to a 1994 meeting of the Public Relations Society of America, BSR founder Michael Levett said the organization's goal is to "benefit our companies, employees, environment and communities," and "demonstrate the growing link between corporate responsibility and corporate prosperity."[29] A similar upbeat spirit pervaded BSR's 1994 annual conference in Cambridge, Massachusetts. Titled *Beyond the Bottom Line: Putting Social Responsibility to Work for your Business and the World,* the conference featured cheerleading about the power of the private sector to build "markets and demand for socially responsible business and . . . broad public support for . . . environmental and energy-related efforts." It featured an appearance via satellite of First Lady Hillary Rodham Clinton. PR workshops included "Communicating Your Socially Responsible Message with Integrity" and "Negative Press: Best Practices, Worst Nightmares."

Many PR firms have joined BSR including Cone/Coughlin Communications, DDB Needham, the Delahaye Group, the Kamber Group, and Ketchum Communications.[30] BSR's goals, stated in its literature, include "connecting member companies with the press, and developing a higher level of visibility for our members' efforts." BSR thus enables its member companies to build an *image* of social responsibility, and to persuade consumers that buying their products will contribute to building a better world. But even leaders within the BSR movement like Ben & Jerry's ice cream have found it easier to improve their image than it is to reconcile social responsibility with profitability.

"In 1994, Ben & Jerry's did its first social audit," said Craig Cox. "Paul Hawken looked at the company's operations and internal practices versus marketing. The result was fairly sobering for folks at Ben & Jerry's. Major media proclaimed that Ben & Jerry's wasn't as pure as they had marketed themselves to be or as consumers had believed them to be. . . . Ben & Jerry's didn't purposefully greenwash, but there was a misleading public perception which they helped to create."[31]

The gap between words and deeds actually became a major scandal for the Body Shop, a cosmetics company which is so outspoken in its progressive rhetoric that owner Anita Roddick has been dubbed the "Mother Theresa of capitalism." In a cassette version of her autobiography titled *Body and Soul: Profits with Principles,* Roddick laid out her personal manifesto: "I hate the beauty business. It's an $80 billion a year industry that sells unattainable dreams. It lies, it cheats, it exploits women and makes them unhappy. . . . It wastes the time, energy and resources of consumers, workers and of the earth itself. All of that in order to sell what amounts to packaging for exorbitant prices. To me the whole notion of making beauty into a business is profoundly disturbing." By contrast, Roddick claimed, "We simply and honestly sell wholesome products that women want. We sell them at reasonable prices without exploiting anyone, without hurting animals, without hurting the earth. We do it without lying, cheating and without even advertising."[32]

In place of traditional paid advertising, Roddick mastered the public relations art of obtaining "free publicity" for her company by linking herself to a variety of progressive causes. Reporters flocked to cover the Body Shop's use of "natural" ingredients in its products, opposition to animal testing and support for organizations such as Amnesty International and Greenpeace. To highlight its concern for indigenous cultures in the Third World, the Body Shop publicized its "Trade Not Aid" program, which claimed to support indigenous groups by buying ingredients for its cosmetics from them.

"It was a great two-for-one sale: buy a Body Shop lotion and get social idealism for free,"[33] said journalist Jon Entine. In 1994, however, Entine began a series of investigative reports and discovered that only a miniscule fraction of the Body Shop's ingredients come from Trade Not Aid. Entine also discovered that the company:

- used many outdated, off-the-shelf product formulas filled with non-renewable petrochemicals;
- used animal-tested ingredients; and
- had a history of quality control problems, including selling products that were contaminated and contained formaldehyde.

To begin his research, Entine said, "The very first thing I did was contact the Body Shop's PR department in New York. They were not used to people asking real questions. They were quite shocked when I asked if there was some kind of outside auditing procedure that verified their claims; they looked at me like I was a man from Mars. They promised they'd send me many, many documents to verify their claims. Instead within the next two or three weeks I received libel threats from their lawyers in New York and London. Over the next three weeks while I was at ABC, every three or four days they came up with a new set of letters. They'd make these accusations but they never would attach a name to them. I had never been treated that way by any subject of a story before. They would react with this incredible anger. It was all part of their orchestrated theatrics. Anyone who cared about social responsibility and took the issues of honesty and integrity seriously was threatened. Anyone who questioned the Body Shop in a serious way was subjected to threats."[34]

To combat Entine's story, which appeared in *Business Ethics* magazine, the Body Shop turned to their PR guru, Frank Mankiewicz of Hill & Knowlton. A former president of National Public Radio, Mankiewicz assailed his former NPR colleagues for running a piece critical of the Body Shop. NPR acquiesced by removing the original NPR reporter and editor from the story.[35]

The fallout over the Body Shop also prompted Ben Cohen—the "Ben" of Ben & Jerry's—to resign from the advisory board of *Business Ethics* magazine in protest against the publication of Entine's exposé. "Ben's response was extremely disappointing and made me wonder where his heart is really at," said magazine editor Craig Cox. "A full week before our story was distributed to anyone, he sent us a letter demanding that we pull the story. In the letter he said that the story was a bundle of lies. He had never seen the story. Ben's response was a horrible overreaction that said to me that he had more allegiance to Anita Roddick than he had to this movement's state. . . . The thing about Ben was that when the article went to print he knew that Jon Entine was investigating Ben & Jerry's about their Trade Not Aid stuff. He knew that his company may be next on the front line. He knew that this story was going to raise fundamental questions about socially responsible business and that his company would be scrutinized more than ever before."[36]

In addition, Cox charged that Hill & Knowlton used another firm as an intermediary to obtain the mailing list of *Business Ethics* subscribers so the Body Shop could send them a ten-page letter attacking Entine's article. "Apparently a company named Hoffman and Associates called our list broker and said they wanted to rent the list to do a mailing of a nonprofit catalog," Cox said. "Apparently Hoffman and Associates gave the list to the Body Shop. The point that has to be made about various attempts to refute the story is that in more than 20 pages they wrote to our subscribers and editorial board, the Body Shop was not able to refute one statement of fact. . . . We are a five-member staff and we're having to respond to a PR machine, Hill & Knowlton, that has more resources than any other PR machine in the world. Hill & Knowlton is the best known and most powerful PR firm in the US and they are hitting us with everything they've got."[37]

According to Entine, the story of the Body Shop's rise and fall as an icon of social responsibility teaches an important lesson for citizens: "The Body Shop is a corporation with the same privileges and power in our society as all others. Like other corporations it makes products that are unsustainable, encourages consumption, uses nonrenewable materials, hires giant PR and law firms, and exaggerates its environmental policies. If we are to become a sustainable society, it is crucial that we have institutions, whether they be corporations or not, that are truly sustainable. The Body Shop has deceived the public by trying to make us think that they are a lot further down the road to sustainability than they really are. We should recognize and encourage corporations that are moving in the right direction; but no longer should the public lionize the Body Shop and others who claim to be something they are not."[38]

In fact, warns author Paul Hawken, overhyped claims of "social responsibility" create dangerous illusions that may prevent society from recognizing the magnitude of the dangers it faces and moving in the direction of true sustainability. "If every company on the planet were to adopt the best environmental practices of the 'leading' companies—say, Ben & Jerry's, Patagonia, or 3M—the world would still be moving toward sure degradation and collapse," Hawken writes in *The Ecology of Commerce: A Declaration of Sustainability.* "So if a tiny fraction of the world's most intelligent managers cannot model a sustainable world, then environmentalism as currently practiced by business today, laudable as it may be, is only a part of an overall solution. Rather than a management problem, we have a design problem, a flaw that runs through all business."[39]

CHAPTER SEVEN

Poisoning the Grassroots

The people, I say, are the only competent judges of their own welfare.
AMERICAN REVOLUTIONARY JOSIAH QUINCY, 1774

The American Revolution viewed "the people" as the sole legitimate source of all government power. Grassroots empowerment was both the means and the end of America's successful rebellion against King George's colonial empire. It reflected a fundamental shift in thinking. Instead of subjecting the common people to the "God-given authority" of the British monarchy, the Declaration of Independence announced a visionary new doctrine, stating boldly and clearly that the people have the right to "alter or to abolish" any government that does not obey *their* wishes.

At the time of the revolution, neighbors and townfolk participated in grassroots decision-making, sharing their opinions with each other directly and through a rich environment of communications forums that included public meetings, political debates, pamphlets like Tom Paine's *Common Sense*, posted "broadsides" and newspapers. Democracy was also strengthened by America's good fortune in avoiding the huge gap between rich and poor that existed in Europe. "The truth is," wrote Benjamin Franklin, "that though there are in the United States few people so miserable as the poor of Europe, there are also very few that in Europe would be called rich; it is rather a general happy mediocrity that prevails."[1]

Unfortunately, America has changed a lot since Ben Franklin's day. In April 1995, the *New York Times* reported that "the United States has become the most economically stratified of industrial nations. . . . The wealthiest 1 percent of American households—with net worth of a least $2.3 million each—owns nearly 40 percent of the nation's wealth." And "the top 20 percent of Americans . . . have more than 80 percent of the country's wealth, a figure higher than in other industrial nations." [2]

The old joke about the "golden rule" says that "whoever has the gold makes the rules," and with the United States entering the 21st century as the most business-dominated nation in the world, it is increasingly clear that social inequality leads naturally to a widening gap between the people and their government. The grassroots democracy that inspired our revolutionary forebears has given way to political elitism, corruption and influence peddling.

In President Clinton's 1995 State of the Union Address, he alluded to the citizenry's alienation from government: "Three times as many lobbyists are in the streets and corridors of Washington as were here 20 years ago. The American people look at their capital and they see a city where the well-connected and the well-protected can work the system, but the interest of ordinary citizens are often left out." Today even the loudest advocates of big business, such as Public Affairs Council President Ray Hoewing, publicly admit the obvious: "There is rising evidence of a system that favors the rich, the famous and the entrenched. . . . Does anyone seriously believe that it is pure coincidence that 27 US Senators are millionaires?" [3]

The business class dominates government through its ability to fund political campaigns, purchase high priced lobbyists and reward former officials with lucrative jobs. Meanwhile, the working-class majority of the American people has felt its economic and political power diminish or disappear. It has become necessary to work longer and harder to pay bills and earn a living. People have less free time for community involvement and grassroots citizen action. Many of the social institutions that should be the bulwark of grassroots democracy—stable neighborhoods, vigorous unions, independently-owned small farms and businesses—are rapidly disappearing. Fewer than half of eligible Americans even bother to vote, and those who do vote have little faith that good will come of it, telling pollsters they are often voting for the "lesser of two evils." Both major parties have become wholly dependent upon the same corporate dollars to pay a new professional class of PR consultants, marketers and social scientists who manage and promote causes and candidates in essentially the same manner that advertising campaigns sell cars, fashions, drugs and other wares.

Ironically, the dominance of PR in the political process has created a massive image problem for the politicians who have come to rely upon its services. In fact, politicians are held in such low esteem that they often build their election campaigns around the pretense that they are anything *but* "professional politicians." Campaign consultants tell their candidates that the best way to join the Washington establishment today is to tell voters that they hate Washington. This tactic is like a drug that has to be administered in stronger and stronger doses. Although it is effective at winning elections for individual politicians, it further feeds the disdain that citizens feel toward the system. Cynicism, alienation and disappointment have come to typify attitudes toward government, forcing members of the Washington establishment into increasingly hypocritical self-denials in order to retain their attachment to power.

This degraded political environment has created a rich bed of business opportunity for the public relations industry. As citizens remove themselves in disgust from the political process, the PR industry is moving in to take their place, turning the definition of "grassroots politics" upside down by using rapidly-evolving high-tech data and communications systems to custom-design "grassroots citizen movements" that serve the interests of their elite clients. Lloyd Bentsen, himself a long-time Washington and Wall Street insider, is credited with coining the term "astroturf lobbying" to describe the synthetic grassroots movements that now can be manufactured for a fee by companies like Hill & Knowlton, Direct Impact, Optima Direct, National Grassroots & Communications, Beckel Cowan, Burson-Marsteller, Davies Communications or Bonner & Associates. *Campaigns & Elections* magazine defines "astroturf" as a "grassroots program that involves the instant manufacturing of public support for a point of view in which either uninformed activists are recruited or means of deception are used to recruit them."[4] Journalist William Greider has coined his own term to describe corporate grassroots organizing. He calls it "democracy for hire."[5]

"Astroturf" organizing is corporate grassroots at its most deceitful. Even PR practitioners use the term to deride their competitors' work, promising that their own grassroots programs are more professional and legitimate. "Real Grass Roots—Not Astroturf", screams a full-page ad on the back cover of *Campaigns & Elections* magazine, touting the services of a firm called National Grassroots & Communications.[6] But "real" in PR terms has a very different definition than its common meaning in the "real world." PR professionals use the term "real grass roots" to refer to orchestrated mass campaigns that are so well-designed that they *look* real.

"Total Community Support"

In the old days, lobbyists relied on the "three Bs"—booze, blondes and bribes—to induce politicians to vote their way on the issues. These venerable persuaders have never been abandoned, but the advance of modern science has developed other methods which are more subtle and often more effective. The public relations industry now possesses something approaching a "unified field theory" of the methodology for motivating elected officials.

In the early 1970s, writes author Susan Trento, Hill & Knowlton's Washington office conducted a survey on Capitol Hill to determine the most effective approaches for lobbying. "They learned, in order of priority, that old friends, businessmen from the state or congressional district, and ordinary constituents make the biggest impact. Visits are better than letters. Handwritten or personalized letters are better than form letters or preprinted postcards. Letters are better than telephone calls."[7]

Guided by this analysis, Hill & Knowlton executive Robert Keith Gray began systematically hiring friends and family of prominent Washington politicos. This technique, which is now widely used by industry, was dubbed "grasstops communications" by PR executive Matt Reese, one of the technique's pioneering practitioners in the early 1980s. Until his retirement in 1987, Reese ran Reese Communications Companies, serving clients such as AT&T, Philip Morris, McDonnell Douglas and United Airlines.[8] Reese touted "grasstops communications" as "the ultimate in corporate legislative leverage . . . a bold, unique method of cutting through the special interest tangle to make an industry's message heard . . . and make the legislator sit up and listen."[9]

To target an individual legislator, Reese Communications said it begins by hiring a "District Liaison" from the ranks of the legislator's "influential friends and leading business associates." In addition to having "a close personal relationship with the legislator and his/her staff . . . this person should also be actively involved in the community and have some media contact." Once hired, the District Liaison works to personally lobby the legislator, and helps organize "a powerful business roundtable whose members are identified and recruited by the District Liaison. This roundtable consists of key business and community leaders . . . and friends and supporters of the legislator. . . . In other words, we create a 'kitchen cabinet.' . . . These are not just any leaders—but specifically those individuals who are well-connected to the legislative target, are receptive to the clients' goals and who may have similar legislative concerns in their own business or industry." Like the District Liaison, the roundtable members are recruited from the "legislator's business associates, major political contributors and social contacts." Through "repetitive, persuasive contact by friends, acquaintances and influential members of the legislator's home district," the District Liaison and members of the roundtable create an artificial bubble of peer influence surrounding the targeted politician, so that "legislators will get the feel of *total community support* for an issue."[10]

Organizing From the Bottom Up

Politicians rely like anyone else on family and friends for advice and support, and they rely on people with money to fund their campaigns. Ultimately, however, they also need votes from the community at large to win election and re-election. Lobbyists therefore need to convince politicians that "the masses" are desperately concerned about the issue they want pressed. By the 1980s, PR firms like Hill & Knowlton were developing techniques not only for targeting legislators but also for serving up their constituents. Since then the business of organizing grassroots support for pro-business positions has become a half-billion-dollar-a-year PR subspecialty—"one of the hottest trends in politics today," according to former state legislator Ron Faucheux, now the editor of *Campaigns & Elections* magazine. "In the modern world, few major issues are merely *lobbied* anymore," Faucheux writes. "Most of them are now *managed*, using a triad of public relations, grassroots mobilization and lobbyists."[11]

Jack Bonner, one of the pioneers in the field of corporate grassroots organizing, is profiled in William Greider's important 1992 book, *Who Will Tell the People*. Greider's book issued a blunt, eloquent warning: "American democracy is in much deeper trouble than most people wish to acknowledge. Behind the reassuring facade, the regular election contests and so forth, the substantive meaning of self-government has been hollowed out. What exists behind the formal shell is a systemic breakdown of the shared civic values we call democracy. . . . The representative system has undergone a grotesque distortion of its original purpose."[12]

Greider described Jack Bonner's "grassroots organizing" shop, located on one of Washington's main boulevards, as a "boiler room" operation with "300 phone lines and a sophisticated computer system, resembling the phone banks employed in election campaigns. Articulate young people sit in little booths every day, dialing around

America on a variety of public issues, searching for 'white hat' citizens who can be persuaded to endorse the political objectives of Mobil Oil, Dow Chemical, Citicorp, Ohio Bell, Miller Brewing, US Tobacco, the Chemical Manufacturers Association, the Pharmaceutical Manufacturers Association and dozens of other clients. This kind of political recruiting is expensive but not difficult. . . . Imagine Bonner's technique multiplied and elaborated in different ways across hundreds of public issues and you may begin to envision the girth of this industry. . . . This is democracy and it costs a fortune."[13]

Jack Bonner, of course, takes issue with Greider's negative opinion of his trade. "I see it as the triumph of democracy," Bonner told a writer for the the *Washington Post.* "In a democracy, the more groups taking their message to the people outside the Beltway, and the more people taking their message to Congress, the better off the system is."[14]

What puts the lie to Bonner's claim is that his clients are not "people," but corporations and business trade associations buying the *appearance* of public support and citizen advocacy. Democracy is based on the principle of "one person, one vote." Bonner relies instead on the principle of "one *dollar,* one vote," mobilizing resources that would break the budget of even the best-funded environmental or consumer organization. His services "do not come cheap," noted the *New York Times* in 1993. "A campaign aimed at a handful of lawmakers on a subcommittee could cost in the tens of thousands of dollars, but one trade association in an uphill fight on the Senate floor paid $3 million for a single month's work."[15] As Greider points out, "Only those with a strong, immediate financial stake in the political outcomes can afford to invest this kind of money in manipulating the governing decisions. Most Americans have neither the personal ability nor wherewithal to compete on this field."[16]

Every Move You Make

The business of grassroots campaigning begins with opinion polling, one of the public relations industry's staple technologies. The science of reliable polling was first developed in the 1930s for businesses alarmed by the implications of Franklin D. Roosevelt's landslide election victory, which reflected widespread Depression-era disenchantment with capitalism. Beginning in 1937, the Psychological Corporation, a business established by 20 "leading psychologists," began systematic and continuous monitoring of public opinion on questions of political importance to business. At first, polls were used to gauge the mood of "the public at large," but progressive refinements have enabled pollsters to zero in on the opinions of narrower and narrower segments of the population.

In the 1950s, notes Canadian author Joyce Nelson, business adapted the techniques of military "wargaming," which uses computer technology to run complex simulations of battle, giving numerical weights to factors like population densities, environmental conditions, and weapon deployments to create detailed projections of probable outcomes. Using similar computer models, companies were able to enter their own sets of numbers, representing variables such as demographic factors, economic conditions and polling data to generate marketing scenarios.[17]

At the same time that opinion polling was providing an ever-more-detailed map of the public's collective psyche, computer databases were also evolving in sophistication and ability to track the thoughts and preferences of individuals. The junk mail that arrives at every home every day is generated by "direct marketing," a science that enables organizations to target their pitches directly to the individuals whose past history shows that they are most likely to respond, using computerized lists that track people according to characteristics such as membership in organizations ranging from the ACLU to the Christian Coalition; income; recent change in address; magazine subscriptions; hobbies; attitudes toward crime; ethnic background; buying habits; and religion, to name just a few. Through computerized "merge/purge" techniques, companies can produce hybrid lists—for example, of white Democrat male gun owners who have recently moved, or of upper-income NOW members who subscribe to the *National Review*. By combining this capability with the "psychographic" maps generated by opinion polling, corporations can draw a remarkably detailed portrait of you, using the information they *do* have to make calculated guesses about your likely attitude on gun control, taxes, nuclear power or any other issue. According to PR executive Robert L. Dilenschneider, Hill & Knowlton subsidiary Reese Communications used this technique a few years ago to help AT&T identify "1.2 million people who actually wrote their senators to raise their phone bills. It was all a question of correlating characteristics, values, and geography so that a targeted direct-action campaign could be waged."[18]

"This isn't rocket science; in fact, it's 'Direct Marketing 101,' " says Mike Malik, vice-president of Optima Direct, which offers "issue communications" and "grassroots mobilizations" to corporate clients. "We do junk mail and junk phone calls. Everybody hates that stuff but it works. . . . Our two major clients are Philip Morris and the National Rifle Association. . . . You can learn from those two organizations and what they do—they're very efficient, very effective at grassroots." [19]

Like most of today's political wizards, Malik is young but experienced, confident and well compensated. Raised in Iowa, he graduated from Columbia University with a political science degree in 1985, then returned for his masters in business administration in 1991. Malik spent over seven years with Philip Morris developing a grassroots tobacco lobby that he proudly calls "one of the best citizen action grassroots programs in the nation today." In December 1994, he explained how it works at a corporate seminar in Chicago titled "Shaping Public Opinion: If You Don't Do It, Somebody Else Will."

"Mail is what you do when you have more time," Malik said. "The mass of Americans don't care. So you want to find the people who do care, and then you want to find the people who will take action on your side of the issue. You've got to communicate to them in their manner. It's really easy to get lists of people who might be effected by your issue. . . . Build a data base today that will track mail response. . . . Follow it up with a phone call, find out where they stand, mark it down in a database so you can target who you want to call again right before a vote."

When an issue is actually coming up for a vote, Malik turns to his phone banks: "Phones are for speed. Another advantage of phones is that it's really flexible. You test mail, get results in three weeks, and make adjustments. With phones you're on the phones today, you analyze your results, you change your script and try a new thing tomorrow. In a three-day program you can make four or five different changes, find out what's really working, what messages really motivate people, and improve your response rates."

Telephones can also be used very effectively to deluge a targeted legislator with constituent phone calls, using "patch-through," a contact technique in which a phone bank for a lobbying organization gets one of its supporters on the line and directly connects him or her to the targeted public official to deliver a personal message. Optima Direct has communications switches specially designed for this purpose. Malik explains: "I'm talking to you, and I say, 'Hey, are you with me on the issue?' and we have a little conversation. You say, 'Yeah, I'll talk to my legislator.' I say, 'Great, I'll connect you now.' You need a shop that has a switch that you can push a button and they are connected, and they are off, and your live operator is on the outbound talking to the next person. That's advanced switches, people."

"There are bad patch-through jobs out there," Malik warned, sounding like the used car salesman he so much resembles. Optima Direct, he says, does quality work—patch-through jobs so sophisticated they look like spontaneous manifestations of popular sentiment. "Space the calls out throughout the day—it's got to look real," he advises. "Talk to your lobbyists and find out what the call flow patterns are. . . . Make it look as real as possible." [20]

Onward Christian Soldiers

High-tech, well-funded "grassroots organizing" is the basis for the remarkable growth of the Christian Coalition, led by boyish-looking executive director Ralph Reed. The Christian Coalition is largely responsible for the swelling tide of far-right politics in recent US elections, representing an ungodly alliance of right-wing Christians and corporate America using a high-tech version of the direct action organizing tactics pioneered in the 1960s by the New Left. Former felon Oliver North, who narrowly missed his bid to become a US senator from Virginia, was one of the rare candidates supported by the right-wing Christian Coalition who failed to win office in 1994, despite massive financing, energetic, mobilized Christian troops, and an angry message that spoke to the bitter mood of American voters.

Reed has become the single most important pro-business activist on the political Right, making him a favorite speaker at conferences sponsored by the Public Affairs Council, the PR industry's leading political association. In February 1994, he joined PR consultants Michael Dunn, Neal Cohen and other speakers at an expensive and exclusive conference held in Sarasota, Florida. "You're beginning to see the emergence of genuine grassroots citizen-based movements that I think are going to be the future of American politics in the '90s and into the next century," Reed told the assembled public relations executives from America's biggest companies. He pointed out that both political parties are "in irreversible, precipitous decline." [21]

The Christian Coalition is filling that void, not with a party, but with what Reed calls "a civic league." By the millennium, the Christian Coalition plans to establish 3,300 county chapters and 175,000 precinct organizations, one for each county and precinct in the United States. Founded in 1990, it already has more than 1.5 million members and 1,200 chapters that are supported by an annual budget of $20 million. "The size of our annual budget and the size of our mailing list will [soon] exceed that of the Republican Party," Reed predicted. The Coalition plans to build that base by reaching out to two demographic groups: pro-life Catholics and the 24 percent of the electorate who define themselves as born-again evangelicals.

The Coalition's success is based partly on technological wizardry. The group's Chesapeake, VA, headquarters are equipped with a phone system capable of generating 100,000 calls in a single weekend. Aided by a sophisticated computer system, the Coalition is obtaining the public voting records from every precinct in the United States—records that often include a history of which elections a voter has participated in and, if they voted in a primary, whether they picked a Democratic or Republican ballot.

The Coalition provides each of its 1,200 chapters with the computerized voter rolls for their county. Using those lists the chapters build what Reed calls "a voter ID file." Volunteers and hired workers (who are paid $5 per hour and must meet a quota) call each voter in the county and ask three questions. First, voters are asked whether or not they are in favor of raising taxes, a question that identifies economic conservatives. Next they are asked about abortion—this identifies who is pro-life or pro-choice. Third, voters are asked what is the most important issue facing their community, and that response is coded as belonging to one of 43 identified hot-button issues, such as crime, homosexuality and humanism.

Reed explained that the Coalition's success is based on the group's realization that its potential supporters are not a monolithic voting bloc. For example, many evangelicals will not respond to an anti-abortion argument, but can be reached with an anti-tax message. Armed with these ideological IDs on each voter, Christian Coalition-backed candidates can generate elaborate direct-mail campaign appeals. "There is no replacement for knowing what somebody cares about," said Reed.

As an example, Reed told the assembled PR executives how the Christian Coalition had success in targeting Sonny Stallings, an up-and-coming Democratic state legislator from Virginia Beach. "In 1991 there was a state senator [Stallings] that we did not care for, the business community did not care for and the National Rifle Association did not care for. . . . [He] was positioning himself to run for attorney general in Virginia two years hence," said Reed. "None of us together could afford to take the chance that he might be elected because in Virginia attorney general is a nice stepping stone to governor. So we figured it would be a lot cheaper to move him back to his law practice in a state senate race than it would be to do it in a statewide race."

So Reed and company, working stealthily, nipped Stallings' political ambitions in the bud and helped a Christian Republican, Ken Stolle, capture his seat. First, the Coalition surveyed the electorate and discovered that the No. 1 issue concerning district voters was the city's inadequate water supply. Second, the Coalition helped Stolle, who "represented the more conservative pro-family and pro-business viewpoint," send out personalized letters to potential voters.

The letters arrived the Saturday before the election. To those who had voiced concern about water, Stolle declared himself to be the "water candidate." To those voters who said crime was the most important issue, Stolle was packaged as the "crime candidate," and so on. Consequently the Coalition, by picking and then exploiting the right issues, was able to elect Stolle, a right-thinking Republican, to a seat that Democrats had held since Reconstruction.

Reed also offers his Coalition's services to help corporations mobilize citizens on issues that go beyond the Christian Coalition's litany of evils: abortion, condoms and secularism. He acknowledged that many of the PR executives gathered in Sarasota didn't share his views on these subjects. They could agree to disagree, but there were other areas of common ground, such as environmental issues, especially "if a corporation is involved in getting a lot of harassment" from activists. The Christian Coalition also did its part to defeat Clinton's 1994 health care reform proposal. Reed told of plans to "drop into 60,000 evangelical churches 32 million postcards that have a picture of a 4-year-old child getting a shot." The caption under the picture read, "Don't let a government bureaucrat in this picture." [22]

Democratic Centralism

Like the Christian Coalition, corporate grassroots strategies are designed to mobilize the masses in political campaigns while keeping effective control of actual political debates concentrated in the hands of a select few. Speaking at the same conference as Reed, Neal Cohen, the director of political support services at APCO Associates in Washington, explained the relationship between "broad-based membership" and tightly centralized decision-making: "Broad-based membership is: What does the public see? What do the legislators see? Decision-making is: a core group of three or so people who have similar interests and who are going to get the job done and not veer off." [23]

Another speaker, Michael Dunn of the Washington-based PR firm Michael E. Dunn and Associates, agreed: "The purpose of the grassroots program is *not* to get more Americans involved in the political system," Dunn explained. "The purpose of a grassroots program is one purpose period, and that is to influence legislative policy. . . . The reality is you are going to be involved in this political process whether you want to or not. The only real question is whether or not you are going to win. And if you do not have a grass-roots program your odds of winning have seriously diminished."[24]

Fortunately, Dunn said, corporations can use the same technology as the Christian Coalition. First, companies must systematically build a political propaganda effort targeted at their employees, retirees, vendors and customers. The aim of this indoctrination is to make the majority of employees at each corporate outpost "sensitive to the impact government has on what they are trying to do and to realize they've got to play a role in that whole program." To complement this broad-based indoctrination program, he urged companies to set up a "key contact program" that recruits employees from each corporate outpost to develop "a personal relationship with the elected official to whom they are assigned. In order to have a quality relationship that key contact has to basically be willing to integrate into that lawmaker's political organization, and become part of their political campaign apparatus, be a part of the social circle of which that lawmaker is a part," said Dunn, describing an in-house "grasstops" strategy. Employees are being told, in short, that to keep their jobs and rise within the company, they should become political operatives for the company, befriending candidates and becoming the grassroots eyes and ears for the corporation in local politics. Dunn even advocated putting this "key contact responsibility into a job description."

Dunn didn't discuss, of course, how the company should deal with employees who fail to get with the "program." But such a possibility touches on issues of political liberties and the integrity of democratic institutions. Dunn's system of "grassroots mobilization" is in fact a top-down command system, under which employees are expected to vote and agitate not for what they as free citizens consider politically good or desirable but for the political interests of the company that employs them. Dunn sees these "grassroots agents" as corporate soldiers, whose loyalty is essential for victory in today's competitive environment. "This is a battle, folks. There is a German general who once said politics is war without bullets. And if you think you are not in a war right now, you have not been in the trenches yet. This is a war," he thundered. "Ultimately, every organization in America has to move to a broad-based program. Until we get all of our people involved in understanding, we are going to continually lose the political marketplace." [25]

Stick It Up Your Back Yard

Grassroots organizing is industry's weapon of choice against "NIMBY" or "Not In My Back Yard" movements—local community groups that organize to stop their neighborhood from hosting a toxic waste dump, porno bookstore or other unwanted invader. NIMBYs are the "white blood cells" of the democratic body politic—small, quickly mobilized, and effective at killing off foreign intrusions. Like white blood cells, they sometimes attack harmless or even beneficial newcomers, but they are authentic and deeply-felt expressions of democracy, reflecting the right of citizens to shape their own environment and destiny.

John Davies helps neutralize these groups on behalf of corporate clients including Mobil Oil, Hyatt Hotels, Exxon, American Express and Pacific Gas & Electric. He describes himself as "one of America's premier grassroots consultants," and runs a full-color advertisement designed to strike terror into the heart of even the bravest CEO. It's a photo of the enemy—literally a "little old white-haired lady," holding a hand-lettered sign that reads, "Not In My Backyard!" A caption imprinted over the photo says, "Don't leave your future in her hands. Traditional lobbying is no longer enough. . . . To outnumber your opponents, call Davies Communications." [26]

Davies' promotional material claims that "he can make a strategically planned program look like a spontaneous explosion of community support. Davies has turned grassroots communications into an art form." Speaking at a PR conference in December 1994, Davies said his clients "usually come to us when they really need a friend. A local community is going to shut down your business and you call up a public affairs firm and say, 'Oh shit.' Mark Twain said it best: 'When you need a friend, it's too late to make one.' " [27]

Davies manufactures friends for needy corporate clients by using mailing lists and computer databases to identify potential supporters. He explained how his telemarketers turn passive supporters into what appear to be advocates concerned enough to pen a personal letter to a politician, newspaper or city commissioner: "We want to assist them with letter writing. We get them on the phone, and while

"The enemy" as seen in a copyrighted commercial message by the PR firm Davies Communications. This ad appeared in the December/January 1995 issue of *Campaigns & Elections* magazine, which was dedicated to the topic of corporate grassroots lobbying.

we're on the phone we say, 'Will you write a letter?' 'Sure.' 'Do you have time to write it?' 'Not really.' 'Could *we* write the letter for you? I could put you on the phone right now with someone who could help you write a letter. Just hold, we have a writer standing by.'" The call is then passed on to another Davies employee who creates what appears to be a personal letter to be sent to the appropriate public official. "If they're close by we hand-deliver it. We hand-write it out on 'little kitty cat stationery' if it's a little old lady. If it's a business we take it over to be photocopied on someone's letterhead. [We] use different stamps, different envelopes. . . . Getting a pile of personalized letters that have a different look to them is what you want to strive for."[28]

Pamela Whitney, the CEO of National Grassroots & Communications, also specializes in fighting local community groups. "My company basically works for major corporations and we do new market entries. . . . Wal-Mart is one of our clients. We take on the NIMBYs and environmentalists." National Grassroots also assists "companies who want to do a better job of communicating to their employees because they want to remain union-free. They aren't quite sure how to do it, so we go in and set that up."[29]

Whitney began her political career as a "gopher" in Democratic Senator Ed Muskie's press office in 1969, then graduated to traveling advance work for the Barnum & Bailey Circus, where she "learned the value of a visual. There's nothing better than a guy walking behind an elephant to make the evening TV news. It was great training for me." In 1980 Whitney joined the nation's second largest PR firm, "working for corporate America to defeat legislation that was pro-union. At the same time I was married to a member of Congress [Pennsylvania's Peter Kostmayer] who was in the pocket of unions." Notwithstanding the contradiction, Whitney campaigned aggressively for her husband, "shaking 27,000 hands in 41 days in 1982 campaigning on the front lines. . . . Between that and my experience with Mothers Against Drunk Driving I really learned the value of grassroots support."

National Grassroots specializes in "passing and defeating legislation at both the federal and state level," setting up its own local organizations, using a network of professional grassroots organizers. "We believe very strongly in having what we term 'ambassadors' on the ground. One of the things we *don't* like to do is hire a local PR firm. . . . They are not part of the community. We hire local ambassadors who know the community inside and out to be our advocates, and then we work with them. They report to us. They are on our pay-roll, but it's for a very small amount of money."

Who are these on-the-cheap organizers-for-hire? "We have found that our best community ambassadors are women who have possi-bly been head of their local PTA; they are very active in their local community—or women who are retired and who have a lot of time on their hands. We find them to be the very best activists." To super-vise these grassroots grannies, Whitney hires professionals who "have had field organizing experience" on electoral campaigns, operatives who "can drop in the middle of nowhere and in two weeks they have an organization set up and ready to go."

When outside organizers are sent in, they dress carefully to avoid looking like the high-priced, out-of-town hired guns that they really are. "It's important not to look like a Washington lobbyist," Whitney explained. "When I go to a zoning board meeting I wear absolutely no make-up, I comb my hair straight back in a ponytail, and I wear my kids' old clothes. You don't want to look like you're someone from Washington, or someone from a corporation. . . . You want very much to fit in with the environment." Wearing a baseball cap "is how you fit in, that's how you're one of them instead of some-body from the outside coming in. . . . People hate outsiders; it's just human nature."[30]

Not In *Our* Bottom Line

The growing proliferation of phony grassroots groups prompted a May 1994 article titled "Public Interest Pretenders" in *Consumer Reports* magazine. "That group with the do-good name may not be what it seems," warned the magazine. "There was a time when one usually could tell what an advocacy group stood for—and who stood behind it—simply by its name. Today, 'councils,' 'coalitions,' 'alliances,' and groups with 'citizens' and 'consumers' in their names could as likely be fronts for corporations and trade associations as representatives of 'citizens' or 'consumers.' These public interest pre-tenders work in so many ways—through advertisements, press releases, public testimony, bogus surveys, questionable public-opin-ion polls, and general disinformation—that it's hard to figure out who's who or what the group's real agenda might be."[31]

As an example, *Consumer Reports* pointed to the Workplace Health & Safety Council, which is actually "a lobbying group com-posed of employers, and it has opposed a number of regulations aimed at strengthening worker safeguards. Similarly, someone looking at the logo of the National Wetlands Coalition, which features a duck flying over a marsh, would have no clue that the coalition is made up mainly of oil drillers, developers, and natural gas companies. . . . Today, inventing phony 'citizens' groups is an industry in its own right. . . . Public relations specialists have discovered countless ways to create at least the illusion of citizen involvement."

The auto and oil industries are also active in grassroots organizing. *Consumer Reports* noted that the American Petroleum Institute retained the Beckel Cowan PR firm in 1989 to organize "Americans Against Unfair Gas Taxes, a national organization with over 15,000 members" that helped kill a proposed hike in the federal gas tax. In Nevada, the auto industry created a front group called Nevadans for Fair Fuel Economy Standards to "impress Nevada Senator Richard Bryan." A PR firm called the FMR Group worked "to find Nevadans who owned . . . gas guzzlers, and spread the word" that a law supported by Bryan to foster greater gas efficiency "would make such vehicles unaffordable. FMR recruited 20 Nevada residents, put their names on the group's letterhead, and sent letters to organizations and individuals, asking them to write Senator Bryan. . . . The letters to constituents didn't mention the auto industry's sponsorship."[32]

Insurance companies are also mobilizing, according to Barbara Bey, the managing director of public affairs at the American Council of Life Insurance in Washington, a trade association of more than 600 companies. Bey was also the Public Affairs Council's 1995 chairperson. Bey told *Impact,* the Council's monthly newsletter, how the American Council of Life Insurance is preparing for action. "Technology is what allows us to do it and do it efficiently, and do it well," Bey said. "We're building an interactive database for grassroots use in explaining concerns to members, legislators and other stakeholders before these concerns escalate into issues. We are also developing a key contact program to expand and take the grassroots program to 'the next step.' "[33]

There is just no substitute for grassroots campaigns, according to Eric Rennie, the director of public policy communication at the ITT-Hartford Insurance Group. Rennie told *Impact:* "In a top-down organization such as ours, when the local general manager wants employees to sit down and write letters to their legislators, it's often done right there at work. The employees are given the paper, the pens, the stamps and the envelopes. Afterwards, copies are made so we know what kind of response we have achieved. Because we don't feel comfortable doing that with our customers, we don't know what proportion of them actually responded or along what lines." And that is where grassroots mobilization comes in. "These days," Rennie continued, "corporate grassroots campaigns require that we knock on more and more doors, the doors of our customers, distributors, suppliers, related industries and other members of our 'extended family.' "[34]

Robert C. Kirkwood, the director of government affairs at Hewlett-Packard, is another true believer. He told *Impact:* "We had an epiphany . . . in the NAFTA effort. For the first time, we went to a widespread grassroots program that involved employees throughout the country. My sense is that we will use that as a part of our regular arsenal. . . . The environmental movement will be upset, labor will be troubled. Everyone hasn't tooled up yet, but they will."[35]

Amputating Health Reform

During the 1992 presidential campaign, opinion polls showed that voters were especially concerned by skyrocketing costs for health care. Candidate Bill Clinton talked frequently about his interest in a "managed competition" approach to health reform. In fact, observes James Fallows in the January 1995 issue of *The Atlantic,* demand for health reform was so strong that "through most of 1993 the Republicans believed that a health reform bill was inevitable, and they wanted to be on the winning side. [US Senator] Bob Dole said he was eager to work with the Administration and appeared at events side by side with Hillary Clinton to endorse universal coverage. Twenty-three Republicans said that universal coverage was a given in a new bill."[36]

Critics have pointed to numerous flaws in the Clinton Administration's health care proposals. In a democratic system, however, flawed initial proposals are common, perhaps even inevitable. A healthy democratic process brings together people from differing perspectives to debate and revise plans until a consensus emerges. In the case of the Clinton health plan, however, astroturf tactics—funded primarily by the insurance and drug industries—managed to quash the debate in its entirety, crushing not only the Clinton plan but all proposed alternatives for reforming the US health care system. What had been the centerpiece of the Clinton administration's domestic policy was relegated to the dustbin of political history. By 1995 the issue was not even on the political map.

The first salvo in the campaign was fired in 1993, when the Clinton administration attacked high prices for prescription drugs and hinted at the possibility of government-imposed price controls. In response, the pharmaceutical industry hired the Beckel Cowan PR firm, whose principals had managed the Mondale for President campaign. Beckel Cowan created an astroturf organization called "Rx Partners" and began deploying state and local organizers to, in the words of a company brochure, "generate and secure high-quality personal letters from influential constituents to 35 targeted Members of Congress. Simultaneously, Beckel Cowan managed a targeted mail and phone campaign which produced personal letters, telegrams, and patch-through calls to the targeted Members' local and Washington, DC, offices." The firm claimed that the campaign generated "in excess of 50,000 congressional contacts" and "built an extensive network of supporters in 35 congressional districts and states." [37]

Robert Hoopes, who also started his career working for liberal Democrats, was another key player in the PR campaign against health care reform. In 1986, Hoopes was a college freshman when he picked up a *Time* magazine, saw Michael Deaver on the cover, and decided, "I want to be a lobbyist, because this looks like a great job. You sit in the back of a limousine, you're on the phone, you've got a view of the Capital, and get paid big bucks." In pursuit of this dream, Hoopes went to work for liberal Democrats including Senators Joe Biden and Christopher Dodd. In 1992 he worked for the Clinton/Gore campaign. In October 1993, he was named the first 'grassroots coordinator/political education specialist' for the the 300,000-member Independent Insurance Agents of America (IIAA). According to Hoopes, the IIAA has made grassroots lobbying "the cornerstone of our public affairs agenda since 1987," making it a frequently-cited model for lobbyists in other industries. [38]

"Health care was a very slow moving train," Hoopes said. "We saw it coming in Clinton's State of the Union address. We had time to gin up the grassroots, mail our letters, educate our membership, have town hall meetings; I could travel all over the country and get my members excited about it. When it came time for a vote we were ready." According to *Campaign & Elections* magazine, the IIAA activated "nearly 140,000" insurance agents during the health care debate, becoming what Hoopes describes as a new breed of Washington lobbyists: "The new lobbyists, good lobbyists, wear unpressed pants, tacky name tags, and are in the Capitol to represent themselves . . . 300,000 independent insurance agents across the country. Our [Washington] lobbyists have behind them an army of independent insurance agents from each state, and members of Congress understand what a lobbyist can do with the touch of a button to mobilize those people for or against them. This change is a direct result of technology." [39]

The Coalition for Health Insurance Choices—an insurance industry front group—led the effort to kill health reform. The Coalition admitted that it received major funding from the National Federation of Independent Businesses (NFIB) and the Health Insurance Association of America (HIAA), a trade group of insurance companies. According to *Consumer Reports,* "The HIAA doesn't just support the coalition; it created it from scratch." [40]

The Coalition's mastermind was Blair G. Childs, who has been organizing grassroots support for the insurance industry for a decade. From 1986-89 he orchestrated a media, grassroots and coalition-building campaign for the industry's American Tort Reform Association. Then he moved to Aetna Life and Casualty where he instituted one of the most sophisticated corporate grassroots systems in the nation. He wasn't the only PR genius behind the anti-health care campaign, but his coalition can honestly claim the kill. "Through a combination of skillfully targeted media and grassroots lobbying, these groups were able to change more minds than the President could, despite the White House 'bully pulpit.' . . . Never before have private interests spent so much money so publicly to defeat an initiative launched by a President," states Thomas Scarlett in an article titled "Killing Health Care Reform" in *Campaigns & Elections* magazine. [41]

In 1993, Childs recalled, "The insurance industry was real nervous. Everybody was talking about health care reform. . . . We felt like we were looking down the barrel of a gun." Forming coalitions, he explained, is a way to "provide cover for your interest. We needed cover because we were going to be painted as the bad guy. You [also] get strength in numbers. Some have lobby strength, some have grassroots strength, and some have good spokespersons. . . . Start with the natural, strongest allies, sit around a table and build up . . . to give your coalition a positive image." For the health care debate, his coalition drew in "everyone from the homeless Vietnam veterans . . . to some very conservative groups. It was an amazing array, and they were all doing something." [42]

Instead of forming a single coalition, health reform opponents used opinion polling to develop a point-by-point list of vulnerabilities in the Clinton administration proposal and organized over 20 separate coalitions to hammer away at each point. "In naming your coalition . . . use words that you've identified in your research," Childs said. "There are certain words that . . . have a general positive reaction. That's where focus group and survey work can be very beneficial. 'Fairness,' 'balance,' 'choice,' 'coalition,' and 'alliance' are all words that resonate very positively." The Coalition for Health Insurance Choices (CHIC), for example, focused on opposing the Clinton plan's proposed "mandatory health alliances."[43]

To drive home the message, CHIC sponsored a now-legendary TV spot called "Harry and Louise," which featured a middle-class married couple lamenting the complexity of Clinton's plan and the menace of a new "billion-dollar bureaucracy." The ad was produced by Goddard*Claussen/First Tuesday, a PR and election campaign management firm that has worked for liberal Democrats, including the presidential campaigns of Gary Hart, Bruce Babbitt and Jesse Jackson. According to Robin Toner, writing in the September 30, 1994, *New York Times,* "'Harry and Louise' symbolized everything that went wrong with the great health care struggle of 1994: A powerful advertising campaign, financed by the insurance industry, that played on people's fears and helped derail the process." [44]

CHIC and the other coalitions also used direct mail and phoning, coordinated with daily doses of misinformation from radio blowtorch Rush Limbaugh, to spread fears that government health care would bankrupt the country, reduce the quality of care, and lead to jail terms for people who wanted to stick with their family doctor.

Every day 20 million Americans tune in and turn on to the Limbaugh talk radio show, which is aired on 650 stations across the United States. However, few people realize the degree of technologically sophisticated orchestration behind Limbaugh's power. Childs explained how his coalition used paid ads on the Limbaugh show to generate thousands of citizen phone calls urging legislators to kill health reform. First, Rush would whip up his "dittohead" fans with a calculated rant against the Clinton health plan. Then during a commercial break listeners would hear an anti-health care ad and an 800 number to call for more information. Calling the number would connect them to a telemarketer, who would talk to them briefly and then "patch them through" directly to their congressperson's office. The congressional staffers fielding the calls typically had no idea that the constituents had been primed, loaded, aimed and fired at them by radio ads on the Limbaugh show, paid by the insurance industry, with the goal of orchestrating the appearance of overwhelming grassroots opposition to health reform.

"That's a very effective thing on a national campaign and even in a local area if the issue is right," Childs said. He said this tactic is now widely used, although few will discuss the technique.[45]

Childs also stepped in to provide corporate resources where members of the coalition were unable to do it themselves: "With one group we wrote a large portion of their direct mail package which went out to 4.5 million people and generated hundreds of thousands of contacts. We worked with a number of [business trade] associations to finance fly-ins to Washington, DC, where people lobbied their Representatives. . . . In some case we funded them entirely, in some cases funded part of them, in others we didn't have to fund, we just provided the background and message. In other cases we actually wrote the stuff. . . . With our coalition allies in some cases we were totally invisible. . . . We actually ended up funding some advertising that our coalition partners ran under their names, mostly inside the Beltway to effect lawmakers' thinking."[46]

By 1994, the barrage had substantially altered the political environment, and the Republicans became convinced that Clinton's plan—*any* plan—could be defeated. Their strategist, William Kristol, wrote a memo recommending a vote against any Administration health plan, "sight unseen." Republicans who previously had signed on to various components of the Clinton plan backed away. GOP Senator Robert Packwood, who had supported employer mandates for twenty years, announced that he opposed them in 1994, leading the *National Journal* to comment that Packwood "has assumed a prominent role in the campaign against a Democratic alternative that looks almost exactly like his own earlier policy prescriptions." In desperation George Mitchell, the Democratic Party's Senate majority leader, announced a scaled-back plan that was almost pure symbolism, with no employer mandates, and very little content except a long-term goal of universal coverage. Republicans dismissed it with fierce scorn.

In 1994, notes author James Fallows, the *Wall Street Journal* tested the reaction of a panel of citizens to various health plans, including the Clinton plan. First they tried describing each plan by its contents alone, and found that the panel preferred the Clinton plan to the main alternatives. "But when they explained that the preferred group of provisions was in fact 'the Clinton plan,' writes Fallows, "most members of the panel changed their minds and opposed it. They knew, after all, that Clinton's plan could never work."[47]

CHAPTER EIGHT

THE SLUDGE HITS THE FAN

The major public acceptance barrier which surfaced in all the case studies is the widely held perception of sewage sludge as malodorous, disease causing or otherwise repulsive. . . . There is an irrational component to public attitudes about sludge which means that public education will not be entirely successful.

US ENVIRONMENTAL PROTECTION AGENCY
1981 public relations document

The German politician Otto von Bismarck once said that "those who love sausage and the law should never watch either being made." Something similar might be said about the process we've gone through in writing this book. Take, for example, our title. We knew we wanted to write an exposé of the PR industry, but our publisher felt that using "public relations" in the title would "put people right to sleep." His advertising timeline required that we furnish a title before the manuscript was actually finished. We went through weeks of constant brainstorming in search of a title that would *say* public relations without actually using those words. We searched dictionaries for interesting phrases, and badgered friends to ask how they felt about titles such as *The Hidden Manipulators*, *Flack Attack*, *Sound Bites Back*, or *The Selling of the Public Mind*. We seriously considered lifting the title from Arnold Schwarzenegger's 1994 film, *True Lies*, or from J. Edgar Hoover's classic 1950s anticommunist diatribe, *Masters of Deceit*.

Our final title was borrowed from the "Tom Tomorrow" cartoon reprinted in chapter one. We tried it on a friend who thought *Toxic Sludge Is Good For You* sounded "too weird" to be taken seriously, but our publisher felt it would stick in people's heads and make the book easier to market. In the end, therefore, our decision boiled down to commercial calculations. We weren't planning to write about "toxic sludge" per se. We were trying to reach so-called "Generation X" readers with a "Generation X" title—a cynical, exaggerated parody of deceptive public relations.

Then Nancy Blatt called, and we discovered that our "parody" is no exaggeration.

Nancy Blatt is an aggressively perky woman who serves as Director of Public Information for the "Water Environment Federation" (WEF). She phoned to say that she had seen an advance notice mentioning our book, and she was concerned that the title might interfere with the Federation's plans to transform the image of sewage sludge. "It's not toxic," she said, "and we're launching a campaign to get people to stop calling it sludge. We call it 'biosolids.' It can be used beneficially to fertilize farm fields, and we see nothing wrong with that. We've got a lot of work ahead to educate the public on the value of biosolids." Blatt didn't think the title of our book would be helpful to her cause. "Why don't you change it to *Smoking Is Good For You?"* she suggested. "That's a great title. People will pick it up. I think it has more impact. You can focus in on all the Philip Morris money. I think it's a grabber."

We thanked her for the suggestion, but explained that we don't want our book to be confused with Christopher Buckley's hilarious satire of the PR industry, titled *Thank You For Smoking.*

Blatt took pains to insist that "I am not a flack for an interest that I don't believe in personally." She said she shared our dim view of PR representatives working to promote tobacco and other harmful products. She said the Water Environment Federation works to promote recycling by applying the nutrients in sewage waste as fertilizer to farm fields, a "natural process" that returns organic matter to the soil and keeps it from polluting water supplies.

"We were concerned that you might have heard some negative things about the campaign planned by our PR firm, Powell Tate," Blatt said.

That caught our attention. Powell Tate is a blue-chip Washington-based PR/lobby firm that specializes in public relations around controversial high-tech, safety and health issues, with clients from the tobacco, pharmaceutical, electronics and airlines industries. Jody Powell was President Jimmy Carter's press secretary and confidant. Sheila Tate similarly served Vice-President George Bush and First Lady Nancy Reagan. Tate is also the chairperson of the Corporation for Public Broadcasting.

Realizing we might be on to something, we asked Nancy Blatt to send more information about the Water Environment Federation. She dutifully mailed a glossy brochure and some other promotional materials, along with a letter reiterating her concern that our book might "do a disservice to the public and the environment."[1] Her cooperation quickly turned to stonewalling, however, when we requested strategy documents, memos, opinion surveys and other materials from Powell Tate. Legally we are entitled to these documents, since the Water Environment Federation is partially funded at taxpayer expense. WEF's refusal to voluntarily produce them forced us to file a Freedom of Information Act request with the federal government. As this book goes to press, the EPA is still stalling on our information request.

Our investigation into the PR campaign for "beneficial use" of sewage sludge revealed a murky tangle of corporate and government bureaucracies, conflicts of interest, and a coverup of massive hazards to the environment and human health. The trail began with the Water Environment Federation—formerly known as the "Federation of Sewage Works Associations"—and led finally to Hugh Kaufman, the legendary whistleblower at the hazardous site control division of the Environmental Protection Agency.

In the 1980s, Kaufman refused to remain silent about the collaboration between EPA officials and leaders of the industries they were supposed to regulate. His courageous testimony exposed the agency's failure to deal with mounting chemical wastes and brought down Anne Burford, President Reagan's EPA administrator. "His active protest resulted in a secret campaign to track his whereabouts and find evidence to fire him," report Myron Peretz Glazer and Penina Migdal Glazer in their 1989 book, *The Whistle Blowers*. "The EPA's inspector general became implicated in this scheme. Silencing Kaufman became official policy even if it meant invading his privacy in the futile hope of uncovering some personal indiscretion. . . . Kaufman gained national prominence and became a symbol of an employee who refused to be cowed by an oppressive bureaucracy."[2]

Today, Kaufman is attempting to raise a similar alarm about the so-called "beneficial use" of sewage sludge, a boondoggle he refers to as "sludge-gate . . . the mother lode of toxic waste."[3]

A Brief History of Slime

Prior to the twentieth century, indoor plumbing was an almost unheard-of luxury. Common people used outhouses, while the wealthy used a primitive indoor system—bedpans, which were carried away by servants. In either case, the waste ultimately returned to the soil near its point of origin. In traditional, agricultural societies, human waste was prized as a prime ingredient in what the Chinese called "night soil"—artfully composted, high-grade fertilizer.

Things changed with the industrial revolution, which brought people together in congested cities, far away from farmlands, where composting and recycling were no longer practical. Open gutters were dug to carry sewage from city streets into nearby bodies of water. When populations were small and water supplies seemed unlimited, the wisdom of using fresh water as a vehicle and receptacle for human waste was not questioned. By the 1920s and 1930s, large cities were piping large quantities of untreated sewage into rivers and oceans, creating serious pollution problems. Septic systems in thousands of small and medium-sized communities were failing due to overloading. Thousands of industries were also producing chemical wastes and needed to dispose of them.

The environmentally sound approach would have been to develop separate treatment systems for human and industrial waste. Biological wastes should have been recycled through a system that returned their nutrients to the soil, and businesses should have been required to separately treat their chemical wastes on-site so that they could be contained and re-used within the industries from which they came. At the time, however, it seemed easier and cheaper to simply dump everything into a single common sewer system. For businesses, the system provided tax-based aid to help them dispose of their toxic byproducts. For people, indoor plumbing that magically "carried everything away" was a luxury that marked their escape from frontier hardship and their entrance into modernity. The system helped limit the spread of communicable diseases, and for many it symbolized the difference between primitive crudity and the civilized benefits of technological society.

The problem with this system, however, is that it collects, mixes, and concentrates a wide range of noxious and toxic materials which are then very difficult, if not impossible, to separate and detoxify. According to Abby Rockefeller, a philanthropist and advocate of waste treatment reform, "conventional wastewater treatment systems . . . are not designed to produce usable end-products. Because this is so, it must be said that failure to solve the overall problem of pollution caused by the waste materials received by these systems *is a function of their design.*"[4]

"Today," observe environmental writers Pat Costner and Joe Thornton, "waterless treatment systems—on-site composting and drying toilets that process human wastes directly into a safe, useful soil additive—are available. These dry systems are more economical than water-flushed toilets and their attendant collection and treatment systems. However, water-flushed toilets are so entrenched in the cultural infrastructure that the transition to alternative waste systems has been blocked. Instead, billions of dollars are spent on perfecting the mistake of waterborne waste systems: wastes are first diluted in water and then, at great expense, partially removed. The products of this treatment are sludge—which requires even further treatment before disposal—and treated effluent, which carries the remaining pollutants into receiving waters."[5]

To cope with the mounting problem of water pollution, the United States launched what has become the largest construction grants program in US history, linking millions of homes and tens of thousands of businesses into central treatment facilities. As the 1970s dawned, front-page headlines across America told stories of polluted drinking water and quarantined beachfronts. Pressure from environmentalists spurred Congress to pass the Clean Water Act of 1972, which according to US Senator Max Baucus, "put us on the course to fishable and swimmable rivers at a time when one river was known as a fire hazard and others hadn't seen fish in a generation."[6] The Clean Water Act required communities to make sure that by 1977 their sewage plants could remove at least 85 percent of the pollutants passing through them, and allocated funding to pay for the additional treatment and filtering technologies needed to achieve this goal. By 1976, the federal government was spending $50 billion per year to help cities achieve water purity goals.[7]

In the 1980s, however, politicians responded to pressure for reduced federal spending by cutting funds for water treatment, and by the 1990s the money had been virtually eliminated.[8] In the meantime, the push for clean water had created another problem—tons of pollution-laden sewage sludge generated as a byproduct of the treatment process.

According to Abby Rockefeller, the hundreds of billions of dollars spent purifying water through central sewage processing plants has largely been wasted. "Leaving aside the immense costs of this option, both in energy and in money, there is the critical though inadequately recognized problem of the sludge," Rockefeller states. "The more advanced the treatment of the sewage (the more successful the separation), the more sludge will be produced, and the worse—the more unusable and dangerous—it will be. That is, the 'better' the treatment, the greater the range of incompatible materials that will have been concentrated in this highly entropic gray jelly."[9]

Secret Ingredients

The *HarperCollins Dictionary of Environmental Science* defines sludge as a "viscous, semisolid mixture of bacteria- and virus-laden organic matter, toxic metals, synthetic organic chemicals, and settled solids removed from domestic and industrial waste water at a sewage treatment plant."[10] Over 60,000 toxic substances and chemical compounds can be found in sewage sludge, and scientists are developing 700 to 1,000 new chemicals per year. Stephen Lester of the Citizens Clearinghouse for Hazardous Wastes has compiled information from researchers at Cornell University and the American Society of Civil Engineers showing that sludge typically contains the following toxins:

- *Polychlorinated Biphenyls (PCBs);*
- *Chlorinated pesticides*—DDT, dieldrin, aldrin, endrin, chlordane, heptachlor, lindane, mirex, kepone, 2,4,5-T, 2,4-D;
- *Chlorinated compounds* such as dioxins;
- *Polynuclear aromatic hydrocarbons;*
- *Heavy metals*—arsenic, cadmium, chromium, lead, mercury;
- *Bacteria, viruses, protozoa, parasitic worms, fungi;* and
- *Miscellaneous*—asbestos, petroleum products, industrial solvents.[11]

In addition, a 1994 investigation by the US General Accounting Office found that "the full extent of the radioactive contamination of sewage sludge, ash and related by-products nationwide is unknown." Most of the radioactive material is flushed down the drain by hospitals, businesses and decontamination laundries, a practice which has contaminated at least nine sewage plants in the past decade.[12]

In 1977, EPA Administrator Douglas Costle estimated that by 1990 treatment plants would be generating 10 million tons of sludge per year, a thought that "gives us all a massive environmental headache."[13] Today there are about 15,000 publicly-owned wastewater treatment works in the United States, discharging approximately 26 billion gallons per day of treated wastewater into lakes, streams and waterways. Before treatment, this wastewater contains over a million pounds of hazardous components. Sewage plants use heat, chemicals and bacterial treatments to detoxify 42 percent of these components through biodegradation. Another 25 percent escapes into the atmosphere, and 19 percent is discharged into lakes and streams. The remaining 14 percent—approximately 28 million pounds per year—winds up in sewage sludge.[14]

Once created, this sludge must be disposed of in some fashion. The available methods include: incineration (which releases pollution into the air), dumping into landfills (which is expensive, and often lets contaminants leach into groundwater), and ocean dumping (where it has created vast underwater dead seas). A fourth approach—gasification, using sludge to generate methanol or energy—is favored by EPA's Hugh Kaufman as the "most environmentally sound approach, but also the most expensive."[15] A fifth approach—using sludge as plant fertilizer—was considered hazardous to health and the environment until the 1970s, but it has the advantage of being inexpensive. As budget concerns mounted in the late 1970s, the EPA began to pressure sewage plants to adopt the cheapest method available—spreading sludge on farm fields.[16]

A Rose By Any Other Name

To educate the public at large about the benefits of sludge, the EPA turned to Nancy Blatt's employer, known today as the "Water Environment Federation." Although its name evokes images of cascading mountain streams, the WEF is actually the sewage industry's main trade, lobby and public relations organization, with over 41,000 members and a multi-million-dollar budget that supports a 100-member staff. Founded in 1928 as the "Federation of Sewage Works Associations," the organization in 1950 recognized the growing significance of industrial waste in sludge by changing its name to the "Federation of Sewage and Industrial Wastes Associations." In 1960, it changed its name again to the cleaner-sounding "Water Pollution Control Federation."[17]

In 1977, Federation director Robert Canham criticized the EPA's enthusiasm for land application of sludge, which he feared could introduce viruses into the food chain. "The results can be disastrous," he warned.[18] By the 1990s, however, Federation members were running out of other places to put the stuff. The Federation became an eager supporter of land farming, and even organized a contest among its members to coin a nicer-sounding name for sludge.

The proposal to create a "Name Change Task Force" originated with Peter Machno, manager of Seattle's sludge program, after protesters mobilized against his plan to spread sludge on local tree farms.

"If I knocked on your door and said I've got this beneficial product called sludge, what are you going to say?" he asked. At Machno's suggestion, the Federation newsletter published a request for alternative names. Members sent in over 250 suggestions, including "all growth," "purenutri," "biolife," "bioslurp," "black gold," "geoslime," "sca-doo," "the end product," "humanure," "hu-doo," "organic residuals," "bioresidue," "urban biomass," "powergro," "organite," "recyclite," "nutri-cake" and "ROSE," short for "recycling of solids environmentally."[19] In June of 1991, the Name Change Task Force finally settled on "biosolids," which it defined as the "nutrient-rich, organic byproduct of the nation's wastewater treatment process."[20]

The new name attracted sarcastic comment from the *Doublespeak Quarterly Review,* edited by Rutgers University professor William Lutz. "Does it still stink?" Lutz asked. He predicted that the new name "probably won't move into general usage. It's obviously coming from an engineering mentality. It does have one great virtue, though. You think of 'biosolids' and your mind goes blank."[21]

According to Machno, the name change was not intended to "cover something up or hide something from the public. . . . We're trying to come up with a term . . . that can communicate to the public the value of this product that we spend an awful lot of money on turning into a product that we use in a beneficial way."[22]

James Bynum, director of an organization called "Help for Sewage Victims," saw a more sinister motive behind the name change. In 1992 the EPA modified its "Part 503" technical standards which regulate sludge application on farmlands. The new regulations used the term "biosolids" for the first time, and sludge which was previously designated as hazardous waste was reclassified as "Class A" fertilizer. "The beneficial sludge use policy simply changed the name from sludge to fertilizer, and the regulation changed the character of sludge from polluted to clean so it could be recycled with a minimum of public resistance," Bynum wrote. "Sludge that was too contaminated to be placed in a strictly controlled sanitary landfill was promoted as a safe fertilizer and dumped on farmland without anyone having any responsibility. . . . There is a real concern for everyone, when a bureaucrat can write a regulation which circumvents the liability provisions of the major Congressional mandated environmental laws, by simply changing the name of a regulated material."[23]

A few months after the debut of "biosolids," the Water Pollution Control Federation dropped the words "pollution control" from its own name and replaced them with "environment." At the group's

64th annual conference, WEF President Roger Dolan explained the reasoning behind the latest name change: "We don't control pollution anymore; we eliminate it. To the outside world, our people came to be seen as pollution people. In today's world, the word 'control' just isn't good enough." In fact, this claim was largely rhetorical. "Virtual elimination has not been achieved for one single persistent toxic," said E. Davie Fulton, a Canadian official involved in sagging efforts to clean up the Great Lakes.[24]

So You See, It *Is* Good For You

In 1992, the Water Environment Federation, describing itself as a "not-for-profit technical and educational organization" whose "mission is to preserve and enhance the global water environment,"[25] received a $300,000 grant from the EPA to "educate the public" about the "beneficial uses" of sludge. "The campaign will tie in with the Federation's ongoing efforts to promote use of the term 'biosolids,' " reported the Federation's December 1992 newsletter.

"Beneficial use" is the industry euphemism for the practice of spreading sludge on farm fields. Even before the current push, sludge has been applied to soil for decades. Milwaukee's sewage sludge has been dried and sold nationally for 70 years as "Milorganite," a lawn and garden fertilizer. Other cities have offered sludge products such as "Nu-Earth" from Chicago, "Nitrohumus" from Los Angeles, and "Hou-actinite" from Houston.[26] In the early 1980s, Milorganite contained high levels of cadmium, a toxic heavy metal, and the fertilizer bag carried a warning: "Do not use on vegetable gardens, other edible crops or fruit trees. Eating food grown on soil containing Milorganite may cause damage to health."[27] Under current federal rules, however, most sludge products carry no such warning. Consumers are largely unaware that tens of thousands of acres, from Midwest dairy land to Florida citrus groves and California fruit orchards, are routinely "fertilized" with byproducts of industrial and human sewage. In theory, this approach harkens back to the time-honored natural system of composting. Of course, the organic farmers of previous centuries didn't have to worry that *their* "night soil" contained a synergistic soup of dioxins, asbestos, DDT and lead that could contaminate themselves, their groundwater, and their food.

"I am appalled at what I would term the 'total disregard for human health' and the fact that the Environmental Protection Agency is actively promoting and is, in fact, lulling communities throughout the United States into initiating programs for the composting of sewage sludge," said Melvin Kramer, an infectious disease epidemiologist who has been researching the issue since the late 1970s. He says the EPA's plan for sludge disposal poses "a significant health hazard to the population in general, but especially to the elderly, children, and the infirm, both in terms of nuisances as exemplified by excessive putrid odors and minor allergic reactions . . . to life-threatening diseases."[28]

Some environmental activists with Greenpeace and the Citizens Clearinghouse on Hazardous Waste have warned about the dangers of sludge, but most groups have bought into the argument that sludge farming is the least offensive way to deal with the problem of waste disposal. Some groups even *support* sludge farming. During the 1970s, these environmentalists worked for passage of the Clean Water Act. Now they find themselves in the awkward position of defending its consequence—huge mountains of poisonous sludge that need to be put *somewhere.* Sarah Clark, formerly of the Environmental Defense Fund, claims that sludge farming "is the best means of returning to the soil nutrients and organic matter that were originally removed. It is recycling a resource just as recycling newspapers or bottles is. If the right safeguards are taken, it can be environmentally protective and even beneficial."[29]

Unfortunately, "the right safeguards" are *not* being taken. Joseph Zinobile, a risk management consultant with the Pennsylvania-based Waste Risk Education Fund agrees that "human waste residue *can be* applied to land in a safe manner." The problem, he says, is that "*it is often not done safely at this time.* The primary reason that it is not always done safely at this time is a nearly complete subjugation of safety concerns by the US EPA in favor of their concern over solving their 'disposal dilemma.' "[30]

Dr. Stanford Tackett, a chemist and expert on lead contamination, became alarmed about sludge on the basis of its lead content alone. "The use of sewage sludge as a fertilizer poses a more significant lead threat to the land than did the use of leaded gasoline," he says. "All sewage sludges contain elevated concentrations of lead due to the nature of the treatment process. . . . Lead is a highly toxic and cumulative poison. Lead poisoning can cause severe mental retardation or death. It is now known that lead interferes with the blood-forming process, vitamin D metabolism, kidney function, and the neurological process. From the standpoint of lead alone, sludge is 'safe' only if you are willing to accept a lowered IQ for the young children living in the sludge area. And what about the other toxins?"[31]

Tackett is appalled "that the government would take the citizens' money and use it in such an odious way. The land spreading program for sewage sludge is a scam of enormous proportions, driven mainly by money," he charges. "The high sounding justifications such as 'sludge is a beneficial resource' and 'sludge is just as safe as manure' are clever excuses designed to fool the public. . . . In truth, only one to three percent of the sludge is useful to plants. The other 97 to 99 percent is contaminated waste that should not be spread where people live. . . . Land spreading of sewage sludge is not a true 'disposal' method, but rather serves only to transfer the pollutants in the sludge from the treatment plant to the soil, air and ground water of the disposal site."[32]

One Hand Washes the Other

Tackett also condemns the "selective science" and "manipulation of research money" used to rationalize sludge farming. "Millions of dollars have been made available through EPA and other federal, state and local agencies, for 'beneficial use' research. Toxicologists, public health scientists and medical researchers have not had a similar money pot available to study the potential dangers and adverse health effects of sewage sludge. It is no wonder then that the scientists selected by the EPA to serve on sludge advisory committees are the 'beneficial use' researchers, and the only research reports they deem acceptable for the purpose of adopting new sludge spreading regulations are from the 'beneficial use' studies. . . . The claims now made for 'sludge safety' sound eerily like the earlier claims that 'DDT is perfectly safe' and 'asbestos is a miracle fiber that poses no danger at all."[33]

In fact, the researchers, advocates, regulators and practitioners of sludge farming are a closely interwoven group. Dr. Alan Rubin, for example, served as chief of the Environmental Protection Agency's sludge management branch where he oversaw the development of new regulations for land farming of sludge fertilizer. In 1994 the EPA loaned Rubin to the Water Environment Federation, while continuing to pay half of his salary. Now Rubin the regulator is a full time cheerleader for "biosolids." Together he and Nancy Blatt are a team, barnstorming the nation, meeting the press, schmoozing with politicians, and debating critics.[34]

Dr. Terry Logan, a professor of soil chemistry at Ohio State University, is another sludge advocate who has conflicting roles and interests. He co-chairs the US EPA Peer Review Committee, a group described by the EPA as "the best scientific talent and data assembled" to help develop recent federal regulations that eased restrictions on sludge farming. Logan also receives $2,400 per month as a paid consultant and board member of the N-Viro International Corporation, which has developed a patented process for converting sludge into fertilizer by mixing it with dust from concrete kilns and heat-drying it to kill germs. N-Viro, a client of Hill & Knowlton PR, handles sludge treatment and disposal for sewer plants in New Jersey, Minnesota, Ohio and Harsham, England. At the recommendation of Logan's committee, the EPA promulgated a modification of its "Part 503" regulations that increased the allowable heavy metals in sludge fertilizer. At the same time that Logan was involved in developing the new, relaxed regulations, he held stock options in N-Viro whose value could have dropped substantially if he had recommended stricter requirements.[35]

Despite its many customers, N-Viro is in shaky financial condition. Since 1993, the value of its stock has plummeted from $9.50 to $1.50 a share.[36] One of its major problems has been the slow rate of acceptance of land farming of sludge. The company is banking on sludge regulator/promoter Alan Rubin to help overcome political and PR obstacles so the company and industry can flourish. In 1994, Dr. Logan was named "man of the year" by the EPA, and N-Viro, along with the Compost Council and the Rodale Institute, received a $300,000 grant from the US Congress to help promote its product.[37]

Criticism of EPA's sludge policy has emerged from within the EPA itself. William Sanjour has spent 16 years supervising hazardous waste management programs. In 1990 he testified before the Georgia State Senate on the "close working relationships formed with government officials who are lured by the huge profits made by the waste management industry. . . . There are many examples. . . . The power of this industry to influence government actions is further enhanced by the ease with which government regulatory officials are hired by the industry. Over thirty state and federal officials have gone over to the waste management industry in the southeast region alone including a former EPA Regional Administrator in Atlanta. This practice extends even to the highest levels of government. William Ruckelshaus, a former Administrator of EPA and a close advisor to President Bush, is CEO of the second largest waste management company in America. He is credited with getting William Reilly, the present Administrator, his job. . . . With this kind of influence and power, trying to have a meaningful hazardous waste reduction program . . . is, frankly, like trying to have a meaningful egg laying program after you've let the fox into the chicken coop."[38]

Our Sludge Doesn't Stink

The EPA's PR strategy for sludge was first outlined in a 40-page report published in 1981 with a classic bureaucratic title: "Institutional Constraints and Public Acceptance Barriers to Utilization of Municipal Wastewater and Sludge for Land Reclamation and Biomass Production" (imagine the acronym: ICPABUMWSLRBP). It warns that there is an "irrational component" to the public's attitude toward sludge, including the widely-held notion that sludge smells bad: "It is difficult to say to what extent odors emanating from sludge may be imagined. However, it is the most common ground voiced by opponents in taking action against land application projects." In addition, "the growing awareness about hazardous wastes and the inadequacy of their past disposal practices will inevitably increase public skepticism."[39]

While national environmental groups are usually no threat to sludge farming, ICPABUMWSLRBP warns that projects may be blocked by small local groups. Citizens who "feel their interests threatened" may "often mount a significant campaign against a project." To counter this opposition, ICPABUMWSLRBP advises project advocates to choose a strategy of either "aggressive" or "passive" public relations. "Aggressive public relations" uses "glossy brochures describing the project; open public meetings; presentations to specific interest groups; presentation of films about similar projects; local media coverage; technical education campaigns for the public and in schools; establishment of a hotline for quick response questions; and presentation of material stressing community benefits from the project." This approach, however, entails some risk: "A highly visible public relations campaign . . . would in itself alarm and harden opinion against the project." In some communities, therefore, ICPABUMWSLRBP recommends using "a passive public relations campaign" to introduce sludge farming. A "passive" campaign makes "little effort to reach out to particular segments or constituents of the public. Rather, information about the project [is] made available for individuals and groups which made the effort to obtain it." This secretive approach works best in small, rural communities "where the application site is relatively isolated."[40]

Kelly Sarber, a PR specialist in sludge crisis management, offered her advice to other sludge marketers in a 1994 article titled

"Campaign Tactics: How to Strategize for Successful Project Development." The article warns that "public opposition has taken its toll" on the sludge industry, which is experiencing "new, unprecedented levels of interest, discomfort and complaints from the public." To counter these stirrings of community self-determination, Sarber uses tactics that she attributes to sludge opponents, such as "creating photo opportunities, using a small number of vocal people to make it appear like a majority, and undermining messages through counter messages. . . . Countering the opposition without letting them determine the approval process is the most important goal of a good campaign manager. . . . This is called 'controlling the debate.' "⁴¹

To control the local media's coverage of the sludge issue, Sarber recommends "a pre-emptive strike" to "get positive messages out about the project before the counter-messages start." She advises sludge companies to identify and develop "several advocates or opinion leaders" who can persuade other community members that they "have taken the time to learn about the project and are comfortable with it from an environmental standpoint." They should be careful, however, to avoid seeking early public support from local politicians, because "a local community can be very unforgiving of a political leader believed to have come to some type of conclusion about what is best for the rest of the community before anyone else has heard about the project. . . . A better positioning of the politician is to provide education . . . while promoting the importance of the community having 'an open mind' about the project."⁴²

Sarber is especially proud of her PR work in 1991–1992 for Enviro-Gro Technologies, a sludge hauler now operating under the name Wheelebrator. Sarber quietly approached business leaders and politicians in the rural town of Holly, Colorado (population 1,400), which Enviro-Gro had targeted as a dumping-site for New York City sludge. When the proper groundwork had been laid, the pro-sludge campaign struck like a blitzkrieg, quickly deploying "third-party" scientific advocates to assure local citizens of the safety of sludge. Sarber bragged about stealing the media spotlight at a public meeting organized by opponents of sludge farming: "[Pro-sludge] advocates were placed directly on stage and demanded participation in the forum, which was granted. In addition, local advocates promoted the project through general grandstanding activities in the audience. . . . By targeting the press during the event, the spin of the story changed from an opposition meeting to one which showed that several farmers wanted to find out how they could get more biosolids. Rather than allowing the opposition to have a press 'success' in blasting the project, the media stories show support, with only a few dissenters. When Governor Romer of Colorado came out to throw a shovel full of New York City biosolids on a field, it was apparent that the initial siting of the project had been successful." [43]

Flush With Victory

Kelly Sarber has fought on the front lines of several other sludge campaigns involving sludge disposal for New York City. In addition to Enviro-Gro, her employers have included the New York Organic Fertilizer Company and Merco Joint Venture, the major players in the Big Apple's billion-dollar sludge disposal game. The city has signed contracts totalling $634 million with Merco and New York Organic, in exchange for which the two companies have committed to haul away over a thousand tons per day of city sewage sludge. [44]

New York has an especially messy history of waste disposal problems. In addition to sewage, the city used to dump its garbage into the ocean, and is famous for the 1987 "garbage barge" that was forced to sail for nearly 3,000 miles in search of a place to dump its cargo. New York's practice of dumping sludge into the ocean first came under fire from the EPA in 1981, prompting the city to file a lawsuit arguing that ocean dumping was environmentally preferable to land-based alternatives. In 1985, however, the EPA found that New York's ocean dumping site, located 12 miles offshore, had suffered heavy degradation, including bacterial contamination of shellfish, elevated levels of toxic metals, and accumulations of metals and toxic chemicals in fish. Federal legislation in 1987 forced New York to close the 12-mile site and begin dumping at a new site 106 miles from shore. Shortly afterwards, fishermen near the 106-mile site began to complain of decreased catches and diseased fish. In 1988, Congress passed the Ocean Dumping Reform Act, requiring a complete end to ocean dumping by June 1991 and imposing fines of up to $500,000 per day if New York failed to comply. [45]

As the city scrambled to meet the deadline, Merco and New York Organic used both "aggressive" and "passive" PR to persuade small towns in other states to take their sludge. Their efforts met with mixed success. Alabama residents shut off all attempts to export New York sludge to their pastures, and Merco's efforts in Oklahoma failed in four towns. In Thomas, Oklahoma (population 1,244), news of Merco's interest triggered what Thomas Mayor Bill Haney described as a "civil war." Within two weeks after the plan went public, state officials had received over 200 angry letters from Thomas residents.[46] The public outcry prompted the Oklahoma legislature to vote unanimously for a moratorium, signed into law by the governor on April 17, 1992, prohibiting land application of sludge that contains "significantly higher" concentrations of heavy metal than sludge produced in the state.[47]

"It's a scary thing at first to take New York's waste and spread it on the land that supports you," Sarber admitted. "In fact to some people it's the most scary thing they can think of. But after a little education most people eventually come around."[48]

In her work as an "environmental media consultant," Sarber faced questions that went beyond issues of nitrogen content and pH balance. She was called upon repeatedly to deny allegations that her employers were engaged in environmental violations, influence peddling and organized crime.

Merco came under criticism, for example, when it was discovered that one of its partners, Standard Marine Services, belonged to the Frank family barge empire, a group of companies labeled by the state as New York Harbor's worst polluter. Standard Marine owed over $1 million in taxes and judgments and was forced to drop out of Merco after it was unable to get financial bonding.[49]

In 1992, *Newsday* reported that New York deputy mayor Norman Steisel, whose duties included oversight of the city's sludge program, was a partner in New York Organic Fertilizer Co., and noted that the brother of New York Senator Alfonse D'Amato was a partner in the law firm that negotiated New York Organic's contract with the city. A probe was launched to investigate possible influence-peddling, and company spokesperson Sarber promised that "we will cooperate fully."[50]

A few months later, Alphonse D'Arco, a former boss for the Luchese crime family, testified during a June 1992 murder trial that two Merco partners—the John P. Picone and Peter Scalamandre & Sons construction firms—had paid $90,000 a year in payoffs to the Luchese family.[51] In separate but corroborating testimony, D'Arco and Gambino family turncoat Salvatore ("The Bull") Gravano also described Picone's involvement in a sweetheart deal involving bid-rigging and manipulation of New York labor unions to benefit the Gambino, Genovese, Luchese, Colombo and Bonanno crime families.[52] Picone and Scalamandre were unavailable for comment, but Sarber was brought out to state that her employers "have had no business or personal relationships with any of these people."[53]

In 1994, *Newsday* reported that Merco was using the Cross Harbor Railroad to ship its sludge, even though Salvatore Franco, a major Cross Harbor investor, had been banned for life from the waste industry in New Jersey. In response to a reporter's inquiry, spokesperson Kelly Sarber said Merco had no idea that Franco was involved with Cross Harbor.[54]

Walk Softly and Carry a Big Slick

On December 10, 1991, *Newsday* reported that "stealth is New York City's new weapon in its war on sludge. The city has decided to make a secret of where it plans to ship tons of the sewage gunk beginning next month. It hopes to secure permits for sludge disposal in some towns before the local gadflys can get all riled up about it. Thus, the names of towns where New York Organic Fertilizer . . . has applied for sludge permits are strictly hush-hush. Only town officials have been told. . . . The city . . . wants to avoid a political circus such as the one in Oklahoma, where three towns rejected another New York plan for sludge because they feared it could carry everything from AIDS to organized crime with it."[55]

Bowie, Arizona (population 400), was one of the communities targeted with "passive public relations" in 1992, when Bowie resident Ronald K. Bryce received state approval to apply 83 million pounds per year of New York sludge on his cotton fields. The rest of the community found out about the plan when someone overheard a conversation in a restaurant in the summer of 1993, shortly before the first deliveries of sludge were scheduled to begin. Bryce had received his permits without public hearings or even public notice. *Arizona Daily Star* reporter Keith Bagwell sought an explanation from Melanie Barton, a solid waste official with the Arizona Department of Environmental Quality. "Our approval was based on guidelines, which are like rules but without the public comment," Barton said. She added that sewage sludge had been applied to crops in Arizona at least since 1978. "But we still don't have rules," Barton said. "Only guidelines. We have no ability to enforce them legally."

Exposure of the sludge plan created a public furor, and the state hastily scheduled "informational" public meetings, but their explanations failed to allay fears. "Who knows what will happen in 20 years—we don't want another Love Canal," said Rhonda Woodcox, vice-president of the Bowie Chamber of Commerce.[56]

Further inquiry by Bagwell discovered that over 100 million pounds of sludge from Arizona's own Pima County sewers had also been spread on area farms since 1983. EPA regulations had enforced limits for only one metal and one chemical in the sludge, even though Pima County sewage treatment superintendent Donald Armstrong admitted that the county sewer system received wastes from about 1,500 industries, roughly half of which use toxic chemicals. Test data showed that the Pima County sludge contained over 80 "priority pollutants," including dioxin, phenol and toluene, along with high levels of cadmium, lead and other toxic heavy metals.

Actually, the Arizona sludge was relatively *clean* compared to the stuff being shipped in from New York. "Sludge from San Diego, Los Angeles or New York you have to look at carefully—it's different in highly industrialized areas," said Ian Pepper, a soil and water science professor involved in studying Pima County's sludge-use program. "The metal content of Tucson sludge is relatively low," Pepper said. "There isn't as much impact from heavy industry." [57]

"I've been eyeball deep in sewer sludge disposal on agricultural land for years," said Kirk Brown, a soil science professor at Texas A&M University. "Some sludge you could use for 50 years before having problems—not New York City's." Brown's assessment was confirmed by Ian Michaels, a spokesman for the New York City Department of Environmental Protection, who estimated that the city had 2,000 unregulated companies discharging industrial waste into the sewers, but admitted that his department had "no way of knowing how many . . . there are." Michaels said half of New York's 14 sewage treatment plants were built in the 1930s, and only 11 meet modern treatment standards. [58]

Despite this information, Ronald Bryce began spreading New York sludge on his farm in Bowie on April 5, 1994. Town residents complained that the state allowed him to spread millions of pounds of sludge before receiving any test results on the incoming material. Tests on the April shipment were finally completed in July, showing that the New York sludge contained petroleum hydrocarbons at 14 to 22 times the level at which state regulations require a cleanup from oil and gasoline spills. [59] The tests also showed fecal coliform bacteria at 33.5 times the limit allowed under federal law.

"That sounds more like untreated sludge," said Laura Fondahl, an engineer at the EPA's San Francisco office. "It couldn't be land-applied—it would have to go to a municipal landfill, a dedicated sludge-only landfill, or to a treatment plant. Those are binding rules." [60] Nevertheless, Bryce was allowed to resume spreading on his farmland in August 1994.

When Push Comes to Sludge

After Merco's rejection in Oklahoma, it turned to an alternate site—the Mexican border town of Sierra Blanca (population 500), one of the poorest towns in one of the poorest counties in Texas. Once again, citizens quickly mobilized to protest Merco's plans to spread sludge on desert grazing land—nine miles from a planned repository for nuclear waste from power plants in Maine and Vermont.

To placate the town, Merco offered money to buy a new fire engine, donated $10,000 to the school board, set up a scholarship fund, threw barbecues, handed out Christmas turkeys, and promised $50,000 a year to the local community development corporation. Merco executives also contributed $5,000 to Texas Governor Ann Richards, whose appointees on the water commission approved Merco's permit in record time.

"These host community benefits are considered normal in these types of projects," explained Merco representative Kelly Sarber.[61]

Critics, however, noted that the money Merco was spending in Austin and Sierra Blanca was a drop in the bucket compared to the $168 million the company was receiving from New York City.

Local supporters of the plan included George Fore, ranch manager of the Merco site and President of the "Texas Beneficial Use Coalition," a Merco front group. Fore accused opponents of behaving irrationally: "It's like that [salsa sauce] commercial. When the cowboys find out the stuff they have is from New York City, they want to string someone up. It's the same way with land application. People get particularly bothered when they find out you're bringing sludge out here from the big city."[62]

Critics, however, expressed more visceral objections. "I've smelled cow manure, the rice paddies in Vietnam they use human manure to fertilize. That's a different smell," said Sierra Blanca resident Leonard Theus. "This is like a chemical smell."[63]

In February 1994, several opponents of the sludge farm said they had received anonymous death threats. Bill Addington, leader of an anti-sludge citizens' group called "Save Sierra Blanca" blamed Merco for a recent fire in which his family's lumber company had burned to the ground, a claim that Merco attorney Jon Masters described as "absolutely ludicrous."[64]

In August 1994, EPA tests of Merco sludge in Sierra Blanca showed 35 times the safe level of fecal coliform bacteria. "We don't perceive it as a problem," responded Masters. "The fecal coliform testing is erratic in its results."[65]

"The Smell of Money"

The town's sludge war hit the national airwaves in 1994 when it was featured on *TV Nation,* a satiric show hosted by investigative film-maker Michael Moore. *TV Nation* accompanied a trainload of New York sludge cake ("rich and moist like most finer cakes") from New York to Sierra Blanca, where Merco representative Kelly Sarber led a tour of the farm site. "There's been a lot of thought and there's a lot of integrity in how we're doing this, and the proof is in the pudding," Sarber quipped. Asked about the smell, another Merco employee smiled. "It's the smell of money," she said.[66]

The cheap humor turned serious as the camera cut to the Washington office of Hugh Kaufman. "This hazardous material is not allowed to be disposed of or used for beneficial use in the state of New York, and it's not allowed to be disposed of or used for beneficial use in Texas either," Kaufman said. "What you have is an illegal 'haul and dump' operation masquerading as an environmentally beneficial project, and it's only a masquerade. . . . The fishes off of New York are being protected, the citizens and land of New York are being protected, and the people of Texas are being poisoned. Something is rotten in Texas."

TV Nation aired bitter complaints from local residents interviewed on the dusty streets of Sierra Blanca. "You can smell it all over, and I don't see why New York has any right to dump their shit on us," one woman said angrily. Another said, "We've gotten a lot of allergies. People who have never had allergies in their lives have come up with a bunch of stuff like that."[67]

Soon after the show aired, Merco filed a lawsuit seeking $33 million in damages from Kaufman and *TV Nation*'s producer, Sony Entertainment Pictures, Inc., accusing them of "defamatory and disparaging statements . . . made with actual malice and a reckless disregard for the truth." The lawsuit complained that Merco had spent about $600,000 in direct public relations efforts to establish good will in Texas, half of which had been lost as a result of the program. Hugh Kaufman counter-sued for $3 million, accusing Merco of ties to organized crime, violating Texas and New York laws and interfering with a federal investigation.[68]

In the past, Kaufman has blown the whistle on toxic contaminations of Love Canal and Times Beach, Missouri. Under the Reagan administration, he took on EPA Administrator Anne Burford, who was forced to resign after being found in contempt of Congress for not turning over documents. Burford's assistant administrator, Rita

Lavelle, served four months in jail for lying to Congress about diverting superfund money for political purposes.

"This issue is much bigger," Kaufman said, "because this is obstructing a criminal investigation of companies affiliated with organized crime involved in the illegal disposal of waste with an illegal contract at great taxpayer expense. The Burford-Lavelle thing was just using superfund for political shenanigans—determining which site would be cleaned up or not cleaned up based on politics."

In Sierra Blanca, Kaufman said, "We're talking about government basically taking a dive for organized crime during an open criminal investigation."[69]

Victimless Grime?

Chemicals, pesticides, acids, heavy metals, radioactivity—to some extent these risks can be quantified. However, assessing the health threat from the human disease pathogens inhabiting sewage sludge defies the capabilities of current science. This is especially true given the ability of mutating microbes to withstand antibiotics, and growing concerns over newly emerging diseases such as ebola virus, mad cow disease, killer e-coli and hanta virus.

In 1993, a team of researchers at the University of Arizona published an article titled "Hazards from Pathogenic Microorganisms in Land-Disposed Sewage Sludge." Their study found that "significant numbers" of dangerous human disease organisms infect *even treated sewage sludge*. "Thus, no assessment of the risks associated with the land application of sewage sludge can ever be considered to be complete when dealing with microorganisms."[70]

The viruses, bacteria, protozoa, fungi and intestinal worms present in sewage and sludge is mindboggling. Many of the pathogens cause diseases that sicken, cripple and kill humans including salmonella, shigella, campylobacter, e-coli, enteroviruses (which cause paralysis, meningitis, fever, respiratory illness, diarrhea, encephalitis), giardia, cryptosporidium, roundworm, hookworm, and tapeworm. Sludge pathogens can move through many environmental pathways —direct contact with sludge, evaporation and inhalation, contaminated groundwater, contamination of rodents burrowing in sludge, and uptake through the roots of crops.[71]

Already, victims have begun to emerge. In Islip, New York, 25-year-old Harry Dobin ran a coffee truck at a Long Island Railroad station 1000 feet away from a sludge composting site. In July 1991 he began suffering health problems. Doctors treated him for asthma, arthritis, Weggener's disease, Lyme disease, kidney disorder and bronchitis. Finally in January 1992 when he could no longer breathe, they performed a lung biopsy and discovered *Aspergillus fumigatus*, a common byproduct of sludge composting. By the time the disease was diagnosed, it was unstoppable, spreading to his spine, his legs, and finally his heart, leading to his death on September 23, 1992.[72] Other residents of Islip complained of chronic coughing, nausea and other reactions. A study by the state Department of Health found that neighborhoods downwind of the composting plant had four times the average background level of *Aspergillus*. State officials concluded that "the study did not find that the higher concentration of mold spores increased health problems . . . [but] such a connection might, in fact, be present . . . further study was needed to come to a definitive conclusion."[73]

Outside Sparta, Missouri, a tiny rural town whose sewage plant began operations in the late 1980s, dairy farmer Ed Roller began having problems with his cows in 1990. They were falling sick and dying, and no veterinarian or university scientists could tell him why. The death and disease continued until late 1993 when the farm declared bankruptcy. Someone suggested to Roller that his cows could be victims of sludge which was dumped on a nearby field in 1989-1991, and suggested he read journalist Ed Haag's articles on the topic which had recently appeared in two farm magazines.

Eventually Roller initiated scientific soil tests. "We found lots of heavy metal contaminants. The field where the sludge was dumped ran into our fields." They tested a dead cow and found "lead, cadmium, fluoride in the liver, kidneys, bones and teeth." Roller hired an attorney. His situation is especially difficult because the landowner who accepted the sludge is a public official in Sparta, and sits on the board of Roller's bank. As of 1995, the Roller case was still pending, and Ed's father was experiencing health problems suspected to result from his exposure to sludge.

"I can't believe what's happening," Roller said. "There are very few places to turn. . . . I don't want a government agency to cover this up."[74]

In Lynden, Washington, dairy farmers Linda and Raymond Zander began to lose cows a year after sludge was spread on an adjoining farm. "We noticed . . . lameness and other malfunctions," said Linda Zander. Tests found heavy metals in soils at the sludge disposal site and in water from two neighborhood wells that serve several families. Since then, Raymond Zander has been diagnosed with nickel poisoning, and several family members show signs of neurological damage which they believe is linked to heavy metal poisoning including zinc, copper, lead and manganese. Sixteen neighboring families have experienced health problems ranging from flu symptoms to cancer. Linda Zander formed an organization called "Help for Sewage Victims," and began to hear similar stories of sickness and death from farmers near sludge sites in Virginia, Pennsylvania, North Carolina, Georgia and other parts of the country.

Sludge is often marketed to farmers as "free fertilizer," but environmental consultant Susan Cook, who tested the Zanders' water supply, warned that "farmers may be happy initially but the problems don't show up overnight. It was nearly two years before Ray and Linda realized what was happening."[75]

In fact, says toxicology professor Karl Schurr of the University of Minnesota, "some of the same chemicals found in sewage sludge were also employed by Cesare Borgia and his sister Lucrezia Borgia in Italy during the 1400s to very slowly poison their opponents."[76]

Let Them Eat Cake

As horror stories like these have begun to leak out, advocates of sludge farming are responding. "There is no doubt, among sludge scientists in general, that their long and arduous efforts to convince society of the safety of sludge have been set back a few years," wrote Gene Logsdon in *BioCycle* magazine. "One good effect . . . is that it should become easier . . . to get funds to mount education programs." Logsdon advocated "funding a road show" starring scientist-advocates like Terry Logan "and a star-studded supporting cast of wastewater treatment plant operators. Put another way, this is a job for a creative advertising agency. If the nuclear industry can convince the public that 'nuclear energy means clear air,' then improving the image of sludge would be, pardon the pun, a piece of cake."[77]

As we go to press, the "biosolids" PR blitz is picking up steam. The Water Environment Federation met in July 1995 to examine the "public debate on biosolids recycling in all parts of North America . . . critique local media footage . . . share special strategies, tactics, and materials developed for targeting specific audiences and analyze their region's successes and failures." *Sludge* newsletter reported that Charlotte Newton of Powell Tate PR, whose firm has received EPA tax dollars to push sludge farming, advocated getting tough with opponents. "Attack them in a way that does not demonize them. . . . You can't play to those who act weirdest," she recommended.[78]

One measure of the success of the WEF's "Biosolids Public Acceptance Campaign" is that major food companies and associations are reversing their long-standing opposition to sewage sludge. Until recently, for instance, the National Food Processors Association—the main lobby group representing the food industry, with members such as Del Monte, Heinz and Nestlé—strongly opposed accepting and selling sludge-grown fruits and vegetables. In the wake of the PR blitz from WEF and EPA, that opposition is waning.

In 1992 the tomato and ketchup conglomerate Heinz responded to a consumer inquiry about sludge by writing, "Heinz Company feels the risk of utilizing municipal sludge, which is known to be high in heavy metals such as cadmium and lead, is not a health risk which we need to take. Root crops such as potatoes, carrots and other vegetables which are grown under the ground can take up unacceptable high levels of heavy metals. . . . It should be noted that once the lead levels are present in the soil they stay there for an indefinite period of time. . . . We have at times dropped suppliers who have used the municipal sludge on their crop land."[79]

In 1995, however, a Heinz representative said they were reconsidering their policy. Other companies are following suit. Chris Meyers, a PR representative for the huge Del Monte company, explained that his company's "long-standing position . . . to avoid using raw agricultural products grown on soils treated with municipal sludge" was likely to change. "The EPA has asked the National Academy of Sciences (NAS) to conduct an extensive study of the outstanding safety issues. Del Monte is an active supporter of this study, which we hope will facilitate sludge use in the future."[80]

Once "biosolids" are accepted as a crop fertilizer, the powerful National Food Processors Association lobby will "strongly oppose" any labeling of food grown on sludge land. According to NFPA representative Rick Jarman, consumers don't need to know whether their food has been grown in sludge.[81]

Currently, "certified organic" farmers are prohibited from using sludge on their crops, but the sludge industry is pushing for acceptance by organic farming organizations, and this will be a battleground for industry PR in the future. The amount of farm acreage dedicated to organic farming is currently very small. However, said Brian Baker of California Certified Organic Farmers, "imagine what great PR it would be for the sewage sludge promoters to say that sludge is so clean it can even be certified organic—what a way to 'greenwash' sewage sludge!"[82]

CHAPTER NINE

Silencing Spring

The big corporations, our clients, are scared shitless of the environmental movement. . . . The corporations are wrong about that. I think the companies will have to give in only at insignificant levels. Because the companies are too strong, they're the establishment. The environmentalists are going to have to be like the mob in the square in Rumania before they prevail.

FRANK MANKIEWICZ
Vice-Chairman, Hill & Knowlton PR

More than any other modern American, author Rachel Carson is credited with giving birth to populist ecological awareness. *Silent Spring,* her bombshell 1962 best-seller, gave a dramatic, prophetic and factual account of massive agrichemical poisoning from the chemical industry's sales ($300 million a year in 1962) of DDT, lindane, heptachlor and other dangerous toxins.[1] Written with the goal of shocking the public, government and industry into action, it sowed seeds of consciousness that burst forth eight years later when some twenty million Americans interrupted their "business as usual" to participate in the first Earth Day, April 22, 1970—a day of protests, marches, rallies, concerts and teach-ins on the environmental crises wrought by industrialism. After years of public activism, DDT and other chemicals that Carson warned about were banned or restricted from use within the United States.

Silent Spring also created a crisis—a PR crisis—for the powerful agricultural chemical industry which had emerged after World War II based in large part on the military's widespread use of DDT and its development of 2,4-D and 2,4,5-T herbicides. The agrichemical industry hit back at Carson with the PR equivalent of a prolonged carpet bombing campaign. Even before her book was published, Velsicol chemical company tried unsuccessfully to intimidate its publisher into changing it or canceling publication. The National Agricultural Chemical Association doubled its PR budget and distributed thousands of book reviews trashing *Silent Spring*.[2] Monsanto chemical company published *The Desolate Year,* a parody in which failure to use pesticides causes a plague of insects that devastate America. About 5,000 copies were sent out to book reviewers, science and gardening writers, magazine editors and farm journalists. The argument was picked up by Walter Sullivan of the *New York Times*, who wrote, "By stating her case so one-sidedly, Rachel Carson forfeits persuasiveness. . . . She also lays herself open to parody. Some unsung hero of the chemical industry has written for Monsanto magazine an article entitled, *The Desolate Year*."[3]

A rising young PR executive named E. Bruce Harrison was appointed "manager of environmental information" for the manufacturers of agricultural pesticides. He was assigned to coordinate and conduct the industry's attack on the book. In their campaign to discredit Carson, Harrison and his cohorts used "crisis management" including emotional appeals, scientific misinformation, front groups, extensive mailings to the media and opinion leaders, and the recruitment of doctors and scientists as "objective" third party defenders of agrichemicals.

Today, agrichemical poisoning of our soil, wind, water, food and bodies is a worldwide environmental health threat. Supermarket surveys find that most foods in the US are routinely contaminated with one or more pesticide residues, and in Third World countries the use of dangerous chemicals is even more widespread. The US ban on DDT hasn't stopped it from being manufactured and used elsewhere, and global use is now at an all-time high. Everyone on the planet has scores of pesticides and other chemical contaminants stored in body fat and organs, a toxic biological cocktail whose full consequences are as yet unknown. Evidence is emerging that DDT and other organochlorine pesticides mimic hormones, triggering sexual and physiological abnormalities in humans and animals.[4]

Rachel Carson succumbed to cancer on April 14, 1964, never seeing herself venerated as the founder of modern environmentalism. However, her old nemesis E. Bruce Harrison is alive and thriving. He even has his own book out, a PR how-to guide titled *Going Green: How to Communicate Your Company's Environmental Commitment*.[5]

Going, Going Greenwash

In 1973 Harrison established his own PR company, drawing in clients such as Monsanto and Dow Chemical, who were among the sponsors of the campaign against *Silent Spring*. In 1990 he declared "green PR" to be the sole specialty of his firm, and in 1993 The PR trade publication *Inside PR* named him a "PR All Star." His award stated that by writing *Going Green* Harrison had "confirmed his status as the leading [PR] thinker on environmental issues" and as a continuing "pioneer in the field."[6]

The E. Bruce Harrison Company now has offices in DC, Dallas, Austin, New York, and San Francisco, and recently opened a new office in Brussels, Belgium that will, in the words of *Inside PR,* "help its transnational clients work through the complexity" of Europe's new environmental regulations. The company employs more than 50 staff and nets $6.5 million dollars annually working for about 80 of the world's largest corporations and associations, including Coors, Clorox, R.J. Reynolds, the American Medical Association and Vista Chemical. Harrison's clients include corporate front groups like the Global Climate Coalition (which opposes environmental action to prevent global warming) and the Coalition for Vehicle Choice (which opposes emission-control regulations for automobile manufacturers).[7] He has even received taxpayer funding from one of his clients, the federal Environmental Protection Agency (EPA).[8]

In the perverse world of corporate public relations, propagandizing and lobbying *against* environmental protection is called "environmental" or "green" PR. "Greenwashing" is a more accurate pejorative now commonly used to describe the ways that polluters employ deceptive PR to falsely paint themselves an environmentally responsible public image, while covering up their abuses of the biosphere and public health. In the years since the publication of *Silent Spring,* corporate public relations experts have learned how to tame and turn aside the activism that it spawned. Today a virulent, pro-industry, *anti*-environmentalism is on the rise, propelled by some of the same industries and PR practitioners who battled Rachel Carson. PR experts—at Burson-Marsteller, Ketchum, Shandwick, Bruce Harrison and other firms—are waging and winning a war against environmentalists on behalf of corporate clients in the chemical, energy, food, automobile, forestry and mining industries.

US businesses spend an estimated $1 billion a year on the services of anti-environmental PR professionals and on "greenwashing" their corporate image.[9] *O'Dwyer's PR Services* termed the environmental struggle "the life and death PR battle of the 1990s."[10] It is a battle that is being waged on many fronts: television, the printed press, grade school classrooms, community meeting halls, the boards of directors of mainstream environmental groups, journalism conferences, and talk radio.

The PR industry's strategy for pacifying the environmental movement reflects its well-researched understanding of public opinion in the United States. Polls indicate that the vast majority of people today believe that human actions are damaging the natural environment they live in. Market researchers say that somewhere between 75 percent to 95 percent of US citizens consider themselves to be "green." More than 20 million Americans translate these concerns into contributions of time and money to environmental organizations.

Public opinion contrasts strongly with that of corporate executives. According to a survey by E. Bruce Harrison, 99.9 (!) percent of business executives agree with the statement: "Overall, the quality of the environment in your country is improving." Obviously business leaders are a minority whose opinions run contrary to the mainstream of American thought, but they are able to determine government policy thanks to a carefully-planned, long-term strategy. Harrison says "top management" realizes that the vast majority of green Americans are "disconnected" from environmental reality, but communications specialists can now "quantify the sources of misperceptions that need to be addressed."[11]

Good Cop/Bad Cop

"Environmental PR" seeks to fix these "misperceptions" by convincing the public that ecological crises don't exist, that corporations are really protecting and improving the natural environment, and that environmental activists who criticize and attack industry are "eco-terrorists," fear mongers, and the latest incarnation of the communist menace. Over the past decades anti-environmental PR practitioners have refined a combination of "good cop, bad cop" techniques—a two-pronged strategy that skillfully creates and exploits divisions within the environmental movement. This strategy of "divide and conquer" coopts and compromises mainstream environmental organizations, while simultaneously orchestrating extremist attacks against grassroots activists and others not willing to "behave respectably" in exchange for industry cash.

On the one hand, the "good cop" strategy seeks to create "partnerships" between businesses and environmental groups for mutual image-building and financial profit. On the other hand, "bad cop" tactics include smear campaigns, lawsuits, and the creation of astro-turf pro-industry groups that foment hatred and physical harassment of green activists.

The anti-environmental campaign is most obvious in the fringe activities of radical right-wing organizations calling themselves the "Wise Use" movement. Supported by corporate sponsors, Wise Use is loudly agitating against laws and regulations that constrain the rampant exploitation of natural resources. The Wise Use movement and its allies have few scruples about using slanders and misleading information to discredit environmentalists. According to Rush Limbaugh, "Environmentalists fall into two categories, socialists and enviro-religious fanatics."[12] To discredit environmentalists, Hill & Knowlton PR distributed a phony memo on Earth First! letterhead, calling for acts of violence "to fuck up the mega machine."[13] Kathleen Marquardt of Putting People First was awarded "best newcomer" at the 1992 Wise Use Leadership Conference. Upon accepting her award, Marquardt said: "Here is our enemy—the Sierra Club, the Nature Conservancy, the Humane Society." According to Marquardt, the Humane Society is a "radical animal rights cult . . . a front for a neo-pagan cult that is attacking science, health and reason."[14]

Industry's "good cop/bad cop" strategy explains why many of the same companies that are funding *anti*-environmental extremists are also pouring money into mainstream environmental groups. Joe Lyford, Jr. reports in *Propaganda Review* that corporate sponsors of the World Wildlife Fund, Nature Conservancy, Defenders of Wildlife, Natural Resources Defense Council, Environmental Defense Fund, Audubon Society and National Wildlife Federation also funded about one-quarter of the 37 organizations described in the *Greenpeace Guide to Anti-Environmental Organizations.*[15] Frank Boren, former president of the Nature Conservancy and a board member of ARCO Petroleum, advocates corporate cooptation of mainstream environmental organizations. As he told his colleagues, "One good thing about that is that while we're working with them, they don't have time to sue us."[16]

Company collaborations with environmental groups provide another benefit to corporate PR professionals: the opportunity to glean valuable knowledge from green critics of the companies they represent. "Companies must have some vehicle for knowing what the intelligent public thinks about their products and processes," says Joanna Underwood, president of the New York-based INFORM, an environmental research organization. "If they want to understand sophisticated outside views of environmental issues affecting their companies, they would do well to have someone in the room." [17]

Green Backers

In *Going Green,* E. Bruce Harrison declares that environmental activism is dead and that its death presents an opportunity to redefine environmentalism in pro-business ways. The "activist movement that began in the early 1960s, roughly when the use of pesticides was attacked in the book *Silent Spring,* . . . succumbed to success over a period roughly covering the last 15 years." [18]

As defined by Harrison, "success" boils down to money and access to power in the nation's capitol. After the first Earth Day in 1970, Harrison points out, ecological activism transformed itself from a popular grassroots *movement* into competing, professionally-run nonprofit enterprises—a multi-million dollar environmental *bureaucracy,* maintaining expensive offices in downtown Washington and divorced from its activist roots and any meaningful grassroots accountability. The executive directors of the big eco-lobbies command six-figure salaries. The mainstream environmental organizations are tightly run by boards which more and more include representatives from Fortune 500 companies, including PR firms. These green groups have turned their back on their local supporters, who are little more than recipients of cleverly worded junk mail funding appeals.

Going Green says that despite their formal nonprofit status, today's big environmental groups are first and foremost business ventures. Harrison advises his PR clients that the green groups primarily want to "stay in the greening business," and that their real goal "is not to green, but to ensure the wherewithal that enable it to green." The managers of the big green groups are primarily concerned with raising money from individuals, foundations and increasingly from corporations. To do so they have chosen to maintain a "respectable" public image and are very willing to sit down with industry PR executives to cut deals. This puts the mainstream environmental groups right where industry wants them, in a position to be compromised through industry partnerships and funding.

Some of the biggest and best-known green organizations—the Izaak Walton League, the National Wildlife Federation, and the National Audubon Society among them—are receiving support, recognition and large cash contributions from corporate polluters.

In exchange, the corporate benefactors have been able to buy a green image that is worth literally millions in the consumer marketplace. Harrison's PR firm spends much of its time helping its Fortune 500 clientele to build issue coalitions, partnerships and alliances with carefully chosen pro-business environmentalists.

Package Deals

As an example of an ideal partnership, E. Bruce Harrison points to the marriage between McDonald's restaurants and the Environmental Defense Fund (EDF). After the Citizens Clearinghouse on Hazardous Waste organized a national grassroots campaign against McDonald's use of plastic foam containers, EDF Executive Director Fred Krupp barged in, negotiated a highly-publicized settlement, and began an ongoing "partnership" with the fast-food behemoth. Krupp gained a "victory" which the EDF highlights prominently in its fundraising activities. Bragging about this achievement helped EDF raise over $17 million dollars in 1993, and pay Fred Krupp his salary and benefit package worth more than $200,000 a year.[19]

Harrison provides a bottom-line assessment of the deal: "In the late 1980s, the company slipped into its worst sales slump ever—and the anti-McDonald's drive of the [grassroots] green activists was at least partly blamed. . . . Krupp saw the golden arches of McDonald's, the nation's fast food marketing king, as a sign of opportunity. . . . Krupp was ready to deal, and so was McDonald's."[20]

EDF's mission, Krupp said, is not to attack corporations but "to get environmental results." He told the *New York Times*, "Being willing to consider new ways to regulate and being willing to talk with business in a businesslike way is not the same as being in favor of halfway compromises."[21]

The main beneficiary of the agreement, however, has been McDonald's, which saw its environmental reputation soar. Opinion polls now give McDonald's one of the highest environmental ratings of any US corporation. To celebrate the 25th anniversary of Earth Day in 1995, McDonald's announced that the fast-food giant would be printing recycling messages on millions of its bags and cups. EDF assists McDonald's in fooling the public into believing that something significant has occurred.[22]

Meanwhile, McDonald's remains a massive corporate polluter. It continues to hire and underpay an unorganized work force that sells greasy, fatty food grown with pesticides on factory farms, sold by an international franchise that destroys community economic diversity, advertised with billions of dollars that target children using bigger-than-life millionaire sports celebrities. When a tiny group of London environmental activists had the audacity to leaflet McDonald's and publicly criticize its destructive policies, the fast food giant sued them under Britain's reactionary libel laws to prevent even this small mention of the truth from undermining the company's cultivated image.[23]

In *Losing Ground,* author Mark Dowie cites the EDF-McDonald's arrangement as an example of "high-level capitulations" which unfortunately "allow companies like McDonald's to look a lot greener than they are. The corporate exploitation of so-called 'win/win' compromises has been relentless. Companies compete through paid and free media to out-green one another. That, of course, is life on the corporate food chain; it's predictable and understandable. But the environmentalists' complicity and their own PR-driven tendency to turn compromise into false triumph illuminates the desperation and impending moral crisis of the mainstream organizations."[24]

At the grassroots level, meanwhile, thousands of citizens are engaged in genuine environmental activism, facing off in their communities against the waste dumpers, wanton developers and pesticide pushers. These grassroots activists are being left high and dry by the big green groups, which soak up almost all the environmental money from green philanthropists and small donors alike, while providing little or no support to the legitimate footsoldiers of the environmental movement.

Big green operations like EDF claim that the best way to be effective is to look for common ground with businesses and eschew the politics of citizen empowerment and confrontation. According to Harrison, however, the aggressive tactics of grassroots activists are the greens' strongest weapons. Harrison writes that "Greening and the public-policy impact of greenism are being propelled by what I refer to as the 'AMP Syndrome'—a synergy of Activists + Media + Politicians. . . . Activists stir up conflict, naming 'victims' (various people or public sectors) and 'villains' (very often, business interests). The news media respond to conflict and publicize it. Politicians respond to media and issues, moving to protect 'victims' and punish 'villains' with legislative and regulatory actions."[25]

The Good Guys Guise

"There has recently been a spurt of corporate advertising about how corporations work to clean the environment," writes Jerry Mander, author of *In the Absence of the Sacred.* "In fact, it is a fair rule of thumb that corporations will tend to advertise the very qualities they do not have, in order to allay a negative public perception. When corporations say 'we care,' it is almost always in response to the widespread perception that they do *not* care."[26]

Some of the industrial polluters with the worst records have devised "public education" campaigns that enable them to placate the public while they continue polluting. The agrichemical conglomerate Monsanto, for example, has given away hundreds of gallons of its Round-Up™ herbicide through "Spontaneous Weed Attack Teams" (SWAT) for spraying in inner-city neighborhoods to make them "cleaner and safer places to live." Monsanto's PR also touts Round-Up™ as a boon to endangered species, pointing out that the herbicide "is used in Kenya, Africa, to keep grasses from short circuiting electric fences that protect the endangered black rhino."[27]

Dow Chemical's environmental PR campaign began in 1984 with the goal of making "Dow a more highly regarded company among the people who can influence its future." Dow's reputation was still suffering from its manufacture of napalm bombs and Agent Orange defoliants that devastated much of Vietnam. The company mailed glossy "Public Interest Reports" to 60,000 opinion makers: scientists, the media, legislators, regulators, employers, customers and academics. Illustrated with numerous high-quality photographs, the "Public Interest Reports" touted Dow's programs in the area of environment and five other "good works" categories.[28]

In 1986 a poll by the *Washington Journalism Review* found that business editors rated Dow's PR efforts tops among Fortune 500 chemical companies. As a member of the Chemical Manufacturers Association, Dow participates in Responsible Care, a PR program where each chemical company evaluates its own environmental performance. Its advertising slogan reinforces the message: "Dow helps you do great things." As a result of this systematic campaign, *American Demographics* listed Dow in 1993 as one of the 10 US firms with the best environmental reputations among consumers.[29]

"Many people use [Dow] as an example of doing the right thing. There is hardly a discussion of pollution control and prevention among American industries that fails to highlight Dow and the strides it has made," writes Jenni Laidman in the *Bay City Times* of Saginaw, MI. Laidman notes that Dow garners all this praise even though the company "is still a leading polluter in the state and the nation. . . . fish caught downstream from Midland [Dow's home base in Michigan] remain inedible, according to state fish advisories."[30]

Sometimes a change of name is all it takes to improve a company's image. Waste Management, the nation's largest waste disposal company, has paid an estimated $45 million since 1980 for admitted and alleged violations of environmental laws. Recently the company changed its name to WMX, Inc., and began advertising itself as a provider of "environmental services."

In addition to coopting environmental moderates, corporate PR firms are helping companies set up "community advisory panels" (CAPs) to strengthen their image in neighborhoods that host industrial facilities. Dow Chemical is one of the companies that has pioneered the establishment of CAPs. "I would give it three years and you'll see [CAPs] all around. They will be an integral part of doing business in all major industries," said A.J. Grant, president of Environmental Communication Associates in Boulder, Colorado. "You've got to have a marketing department, you've got to have accounting, and you'll have to have community interaction in the form of a CAP."[31]

According to Joel Makower, editor of *The Green Business Letter,* CAPs "differ in makeup, style, and function," but "a typical CAP consists of 12 to 15 people, including activists, homemakers, community leaders—a representative sampling of just plain folks—as well as company representatives." CAPs create a forum for dialogue between the company and the community, but the nature of the dialogue is carefully modulated to emphasize emotions and image-shaping rather than issues of substance.

As an example of their PR effectiveness, Makower relates the following anecdote: "Members of one CAP, unbeknownst to the company, appeared voluntarily before a local hearing to testify why the company should be allowed to site an incinerator in their backyard. You can't buy that kind of help at any price."[32]

Shifting the Blame

If corporations are not despoiling our natural environment, then who *is* to blame? According to corporate-sponsored PR campaigns, the answer is obvious. *You* are. In place of systemic analysis and systemic solutions to social problems, they offer an individualistic and deeply hypocritical analysis in which "all of us" are to blame for our collective "irresponsibility." If we would all just pick up after ourselves, they nag, the problems would go away.

Gregg Easterbrook, the author of *A Moment on the Earth,* concludes that the acts of individuals are the root of many environmental problems. He wrote in the *New York Times* magazine, "Though environmental orthodoxy holds that Third World deforestation is caused by rapacious clear-cutters and ruthless cattle barons, penniless peasants seeking fuel wood may be the greatest threat to our forests." [33] He conveniently fails to mention that "penniless peasants" are *forced* to colonize rainforests and cut down trees for firewood after being driven from their traditional lands by "rapacious clearcutters and ruthless cattle barons."

In the US, the Keep America Beautiful campaign (KAB) is industry's most organized proponent of the belief that individual irresponsibility is at the root of pollution. About 200 companies, including McDonald's, fund KAB to the tune of $2 million a year. According to the *Greenpeace Guide to Anti-Environmental Organizations*, most of the companies that support KAB "manufacture and distribute aluminum cans, paper products, glass bottles and plastics that account for about a third of the material in US landfills." KAB's message to consumers is that *they* are responsible for this trash, and that they must solve this problem by changing their habits. [34]

Since the early 1970s, Greenpeace reports, KAB has used more than half a billion dollars worth of donated advertising time and space to encourage guilty consumers to "put litter in its place." Of course, since the responsibility for litter rests with individuals, KAB leadership strongly *opposes* a national bottle bill that would place a deposit on glass and metal drink containers. In effect, KAB is a PR front group for industries that refuse to be responsible for the trash they generate in the course of doing business. [35]

The Selling of Earth Day

On April 22, 1995, the major Washington-based environmental organizations celebrated Earth Day's 25th anniversary with a celebrity-studded free concert in the national capital. In the intervening quarter century these groups had raised and spent billions of dollars in pursuit of environmental reform initiatives. In the White House they had as Vice-President Al Gore, a mainstream environmental leader with a best selling book of his own to prove it. In the countryside opinion surveys consistently indicated that a solid majority of Americans strongly supported environmental protection initiatives.

Despite these trappings of accomplishment, the 25th anniversary celebration was a hollow shell of the once vigorous environmental movement. Rather than stimulating a new wave of activism, it dramatized the failure of its national leaders and their policies of "compromise and respectability."

The first Earth Day in 1970 began when Wisconsin Senator Gaylord Nelson, a staunch conservationist, borrowed the idea for a student environmental teach-in from the tactics of anti-war organizers. Nobody *owned* the first Earth Day; the marches, demonstrations and protests mushroomed almost spontaneously, manifesting the power of aggressive, 1960s-style activism. Many of its organizers saw the common systemic roots of both the war against Vietnam and ecological destruction. Denis Hayes, a national student coordinator, spoke passionately to the first Washington, DC, Earth Day rally: "Our country is stealing from poorer nations and from generations yet unborn. . . . We're tired of being told we are to blame for corporate depredations. . . . institutions have no conscience. If we want them to do what is right, we must *make* them do what is right."[36]

The term "corporate greenwashing" hadn't yet been coined, but the problem already existed. "Political and business leaders once hoped that they could turn the environmental movement into a massive anti-litter campaign," shouted Hayes in his historic speech. "Industry has turned the environmental problem over to its public relations men. . . . We have learned not to believe the advertising."[37]

Two decades later, however, Gaylord Nelson himself helped turn Earth Day into a corporate commodity. Since losing his 1986 bid for re-election, Nelson has been a lobbyist and consultant with the Wilderness Society, a prestigious mainstream environmental group that accepts funding from WMX, Archer Daniels Midland and other multinationals.[38] In 1991, Nelson and environmental business consultant Bruce Anderson created an umbrella organization titled "Earth Day USA" to orchestrate and fundraise for the event's 25th anniversary. Unlike previous Earth Day organizations, however, Anderson and Nelson encouraged corporations to buy into their "official" Earth Day, without any standards to screen out major corporate polluters. Anderson justified this approach by arguing that "we're all to blame, every one of us. If a business says they want to improve their environmental record, it's not up to Earth Day USA to be the judge and jury of their past behavior. Confrontation is the old way. We have to work together hand-in-hand, arm-in-arm, or we're wasting time, fiddling while the planet burns."[39]

Nelson agreed. Greenwashing, he said, is no problem at all, "not even on the map. If a corporation is moving to be green, that's just fine. Many of today's corporate leaders participated in [the first] Earth Day in college; it turned them into environmentalists. I'm glad to see corporations joining in. If they try to coopt Earth Day, they'll just help spread environmental propaganda."[40]

Nelson also defended Earth Day USA's shocking decision to hire Shandwick PR—a leading *anti-environmental greenwasher*—to help plan, coordinate and execute the twenty-fifth Earth Day celebration. "I have no concerns about that," Nelson said. "They are a PR firm. They represent all kinds of people. Its like hiring a lawyer. If he represents a murderer or a crooked businessman, that's what lawyers do. Am I not to hire him?"[41]

Of course, PR firms are *not* law firms, although practitioners promote the comparison to dignify their profession and to rationalize their work for unsavory clients. Bruce Anderson made the decision to hire Shandwick "at a greatly reduced fee" after a breakfast meeting in Washington, DC, with company executive Allen Finch. Anderson said he was impressed with Allen Finch's attitude. "I see [his] commitment to Earth Day USA expanding every day. He looks at it the same way I do: Earth Day is an incredible gift with a potentially tremendous impact."[42]

No doubt Allen Finch *did* see Earth Day as a tremendous "gift," much the way a fox would relish managing the chicken coop. Finch's work for Shandwick includes personally representing one of the oldest, most notorious anti-environmental front groups, called the Council for Agricultural Science and Technology (CAST). Founded in 1972, CAST is funded by hundreds of companies invested in genetically-engineered foods, agricultural chemicals, food additives and corporate factory farming, including Dow, General Mills, Land O'Lakes, Ciba-Geigy, Archer Daniels Midland, Monsanto, Philip Morris, and Uniroyal.[43] According to *O'Dwyer's PR Services*, Allen Finch personally works to establish CAST as "the source for public policy-makers and news media on environmental issues."[44]

CAST is a classic industry front group claiming "to provide current, unbiased scientific information concerning food and agriculture." In fact, for over two decades CAST has vigorously and publicly defended and promoted pesticide-contaminated foods, irradiated fruits and vegetables, and the use of hormones and drugs on farm animals. The hundreds of industry and university researchers who belong to CAST are often on the receiving end of large grants and other payments from the same agribusiness corporations that subsidize CAST.

When Earth Day USA hired Shandwick, its other PR clients included Ciba-Geigy, Chase Manhattan Bank, Ford Motor Company,

Hydro-Quebec, Monsanto, Pfizer, Procter & Gamble, Purina Mills, and Sumitomo Bank. Shandwick's net receipts totalled over $11 million in 1992 for "environmental public affairs services."[45] As an example of these services, Shandwick cites its success in helping the Western Livestock Producers Alliance "win its battle against raising grazing fees on public lands"—handing the environmental movement one of the biggest defeats it suffered in the 103rd Congress.[46]

In 1994 Shandwick PR claimed that "we're helping companies . . . maximize green market opportunities, mitigate environmental risks and protect the bottom line," with "access to the corridors of power at the federal level and every state capital, local business community and newsroom."[47]

With Allen Finch on board, Earth Day USA began meeting with the Clinton White House and various corporations to make April 22, 1995, the biggest eco-publicity blast of all time, with a prominent role for corporate contributors. What about decisions by previous national Earth Day groups to screen large corporate contributions? According to board member Jerry Klamon, that approach was *passé*: "We would work with companies others probably wouldn't, because we see the need for the 'carrot' approach. These companies need to be nurtured and brought along." Klamon's St. Louis group accepted funding from Monsanto, and relied on the donated PR work of Allen Finch's St. Louis affiliate. "We need to use tactics that people are habituated to following," Klamon said. "These PR people are obviously good at penetrating the American consciousness."[48]

Earth Day USA raised hundreds of thousands of dollars from businesses, including clients of Allen Finch's PR firm. Gifts of $15,000 or more came from Procter & Gamble, Honeywell, Ralston Purina, Kinkos, Pillsbury and AT&T.[49] For $20,000 a company could become an Earth Day USA sponsor. Further negotiations could buy permission to use the official Earth Day USA logo. An internal Earth Day USA memo contemplated the spin-off of a second organization called "the Earth Day Corporate Team," consisting of "environmental leaders within corporations in the United States . . . organized as a separate nonprofit corporation," but with its board of directors dominated by the leaders of Earth Day USA. The Team would "enhance the fundraising opportunities for Earth Day USA and the other members of the Earth Day Family." To protect its own image, Earth Day USA would "retain some independence from its corporate arm to preserve the innocence and inclusiveness of the Earth Day spirit."[50]

In the end, the "inclusive," pro-corporate strategy of Finch, Anderson and Nelson fell apart when media coverage disclosed the corporate greenwashing behind Earth Day USA. Unwanted publicity led to internal dissension and the eventual breakup of the organization's board of directors. Efforts to involve the Clinton White House in raising millions of dollars from corporations to fund a huge event on the DC mall also fell apart under reporters' scrutiny.[51]

Begging for Mercy

The whimpering demise of Earth Day USA epitomized the crisis that had come over the environmental movement by 1995. The "good cop" strategy of lulling environmentalists to sleep had proven a smashing success. With the election of a Republican majority in Congress, the national green organizations found themselves effectively cut out of the loop, just another remnant of a dying liberalism. The new Congress moved quickly to eviscerate the past legislation and regulations that had been the green lobbies' major accomplishments. The professional environmental lobbyists—cut off from the grassroots they had abandoned—were unable to turn up any significant heat on legislators. In desperation, some environmentalists drafted a pleading petition addressed to the political architect of their demise, former professor of environmentalism Newt Gingrich.[52]

In fact, the corporate victory was so complete that the public relations industry was quietly advising its corporate clients to refrain from gloating. The February 1995 issue of *O'Dwyer's PR Services* said "green PR people" should "ride the Republican fueled anti-environmental backlash wave as far as possible. . . . Green PR pros are salivating at the chance to prove their worth to clients. They are ready to navigate the thicket of regulations in DC, select those most annoying to clients, and convince lawmakers to dump them." But *O'Dwyer's* warned, "they should not be greedy because overreaching may come back to haunt them once the sun sets on the pro-business Republicans and greenies are again on the rise."[53]

Similar advice came from Michael Kehs, head of Burson-Marsteller PR's worldwide environmental practice: "Don't appear greedy by complaining how much compliance with green laws costs . . . That could jeopardize years of good works and careful corporate positioning. The business community enjoys the upper hand. . . . There is a new contract on the street. And although the word 'environment' is never mentioned, many observers believe it's less a contract with America than a 'contract on environmental busybodies.' . . . There is no better time to extend an olive branch."[54]

In this milieu, the Earth Day 1995 release of *A Moment On The Earth: The Coming Age of Environmental Optimism*, a 745-page exercise in sophistry by Gregg Easterbrook, seemed like dirt in the face of the losing green lobbyists.[55] "Cancel your plans for doomsday, planet earth is alive and well," screamed the book's full page *New York Times* advertisement.[56] Easterbrook's one-sided and factually deformed tract promoted his pollyannish doctrine of "ecorealism." While defensively proclaiming himself a liberal and an environmentalist, he provided the PR greenwashers with their best manifesto to date, written by an "objective" journalist.[57]

Easterbrook's own mother died of breast cancer after working in the notorious Hooker Chemical plant that produced the toxic wastes buried at Love Canal, yet *A Moment on the Earth* claims that all major environmental crises are virtually solved or never really existed in the first place. It argues that corporate capitalism has embraced environmental and social responsibility and will soon end all pollution, and accuses environmentalists of denying these "facts" in order to sustain their fear-based fundraising campaigns.[58]

Ironically, Easterbrook's book was completed just before the anti-environmentalists seized Congress and began dismembering the various regulations that he claimed had guaranteed an ecological utopia.

In an Earth Day column in the April 21, 1995 *New York Times*, Easter-brook's naïveté showed as he publicly pleaded with industry to call off its lobbyists' assault on environmental regulations. "Has all the apparent progress in the chemical industry been merely a public-relations ploy?" Easterbrook wondered with apparently genuine consternation.[59]

Notwithstanding the advice from *O'Dwyer's* to "avoid overreach-ing," the PR industry was already positioning itself for a no-holds-barred assault on the greens—the "bad cop" component of its good cop/bad cop strategy. Now solidly in the political driver's seat, pol-luting corporations could relax in their efforts to coopt and partner with environmental groups. *PR News*, an industry publication, acknowledged that "since Earth Day more than 20 years ago, a gen-eration of PR executives have become accustomed to donning the green hat." But now, it advised, the rise of anti-environmentalism "presents an opportunity for PR executives at corporations and firms to play the advocate role not for . . . corporate environmentalism," but for the rabidly anti-environmental "Wise Use" groups.[60]

In fact, Hill & Knowlton, Burson-Marsteller, Edelman PR, Shand-wick, Fleishman-Hillard, Bruce Harrison and other greenwashers had been working for Wise Use all along. But now, they could come out of the closet, since their tactics of cooptation had the real greens on the run.

Crafty Alliances

The *Washington Post* reported that even a decade ago, Burson-Marsteller's DC office alone had five PR specialists concentrating only on designing coalitions for clients.[61] As one PR executive explained it, these astroturf coalition designers "are building allies and neu-tralizing the opposition." James Lindheim, Burson-Marsteller's former director of worldwide public affairs, put it this way: "Don't forget that the chemical industry has many friends and allies that can be mobilized . . . employees, shareholders, and retirees. Give them the songsheets and let them help industry carry the tune."[62]

Sometimes the public catches on. A group called "Citizens to Pro-tect the Pacific Northwest and Northern California Economy" was formed in 1993 by timber company executives, who mailed out 1.5 million form letters asking people to send back a signature card if they agreed with the group's goals. State leaders were then appointed. When asked what he was going to do, the group's Wash-ington state co-chair replied: "I haven't been brought up to date on what their agenda is going to be." A *Seattle Post-Intelligencer* editorial put it this way: "To hire a press agent to cook up a campaign, pay all that campaign's bills and then claim that the campaign 'was founded by more than 100 prominent community leaders in Oregon, Washington, and Northern California' is too crafty by half."[63]

More recently, National Audubon Society board member Leslie Dach was embarrassed when *O'Dwyer's Washington Report* noted that his PR firm, Edelman, was organizing publicity and security for the June 1995 "Fly-In for Freedom," the Wise Use movement's annual lobby event in the nation's capital, sponsored by the Western States Coalition. Dach attempted to distance himself from the event by stating that he personally "never had any involvement with the Coalition." Actually, he epitomizes the dual "good cop/bad cop" strategy that coopts environmental groups like Audubon on the one hand, and wages war against them on the other.[64]

Dach handled PR for Democratic presidential candidate Michael Dukakis and is now an executive vice-president of Edelman PR and the General Manager of their DC operations. Edelman's right-wing contingent includes Michael Deaver who, like Dach, is also an Edelman Executive VP. Deaver was the PR genius behind Ronald Reagan and helped develop the 1994 Republican "Contract with America." Edelman is a leading anti-environmental greenwasher. According to *O'Dwyer's PR Services,* "the firm's executives have a broad range of environmental expertise and have managed numerous issues surrounding Superfund, the Clean Water Act, the Resource Conservation and Recovery Act, wetlands preservation and public lands."[65] Edelman's client, the Alliance for America, is an industry-subsidized network of 650 anti-environmental companies and associations that are the backbone of the Wise Use movement. At the 1995 "Fly-in for Freedom," Edelman helped the Alliance target the Endangered Species Act for elimination.

No More Mr. Nice Guy

Wise Use is the brainchild of Alan Gottlieb and Ron Arnold, respectively founder and director of the Bellevue, Washington-based Center for the Defense of Free Enterprise—the "premier think tank and training center for the Wise Use movement," according to the *Greenpeace Guide to Anti-Environmental Organizations.* The founding funders of the Center include the timber firms Georgia-Pacific, Louisiana-Pacific, Boise Cascade, Pacific Lumber and MacMillan Bloedel, along with companies like Exxon and DuPont. The Wise Use agenda is simple. Says Arnold, "We intend to wipe out every environmental group, by replacing it with a Wise Use group."

The public relations industry has been closely involved with Wise Use since its founding, according to Joyce Nelson, the author of *Sultans of Sleaze: Public Relations and the Media.* Nelson writes that 36 of the corporations that are known to fund the Wise Use movement in the United States were clients of the PR firm Burson-Marsteller in the 1980s, the period during which industry began to pour money into organizing grassroots anti-environmentalism.[66]

To recruit and mobilize its troops, Wise Use relies on standard PR techniques of astroturf organizing. "Pro-industry citizen activist groups can do things the industry can't," explained Arnold. In a candid talk to the Ontario Forest Industries Association, Arnold elaborated on the benefits of a citizen front group strategy: "It can form coalitions to build real political clout. It can be an effective and convincing advocate for your industry. It can evoke powerful archetypes such as the sanctity of the family, the virtue of the close-knit community, the natural wisdom of the rural dweller, and many others I'm sure you can think of. It can use the tactic of the intelligent attack against environmentalists and take the battle to them instead of forever responding to environmentalist initiatives. And it can turn the public against your enemies."[67]

The first Wise Use conference, held in 1988, was supported by a variety of special interests including Exxon and the National Rifle Association. The highlight of the conference was the presentation of Alan Gottlieb's "Wise Use Agenda," which listed goals such as:

- rewriting the Endangered Species Act to remove protection from "non-adaptive species" like the California Condor;

- immediate oil drilling in the Arctic National Wildlife Refuge;

- opening up all public lands to mineral and energy production, including national parks and wilderness areas;

- turning the development of national parks over to "private firms with expertise in people moving, such as Walt Disney";

- imposing civil penalties against anyone who legally challenges "economic action or development on federal lands."

The 1990 conference, funded by Chevron, Exxon, Shell Oil and Georgia-Pacific, featured a talk by Reed Irvine of Accuracy in Media and Accuracy in Academia. Titled "Red Into Green," Irvine's talk claimed that environmentalism is the latest incarnation of socialism.[68]

Irvine's groups are bankrolled by Dresser Industries, Chevron, Ciba-Geigy, Exxon, IBM, Kaiser Aluminum and Chemical, Union Carbide, Phillips Petroleum, Mobil Foundation and Texaco Philanthropic Foundation, among others.[69]

Also at that conference, the right-wing Mountain States Legal Foundation gave three seminars on "Suing Environmental Organizations." Mountain States Legal Foundation is funded by companies including Amoco, Exxon, Ford, Texaco, Phillips Petroleum, Chevron and the Coors Foundation. "Our intent is to sue environmental groups whenever there is a legal reason to do so," Arnold said. "We feel that whenever any environmental group tells lies that have an economic harm against anybody, that is a civil tort, and under US law they should be vigorously prosecuted in civil court."[70]

And if lawsuits fail, some anti-environmentalists urge even stronger tactics. Former Interior Secretary James Watt (who in 1996 pleaded guilty to trying to influence a Federal grand jury) told a gathering of cattlemen in June 1990, "If the troubles from environmentalists cannot be solved in the jury box or at the ballot box, perhaps the cartridge box should be used."[71]

CHAPTER TEN

The Torturers' Lobby

*If I wanted to lie, or if we wanted to lie, if we wanted to exaggerate,
I wouldn't use my daughter to do so. I could easily buy other people
to do it.*

SAUD NASIR AL-SABAH
Kuwait's Ambassador to the United States and Canada

On October 10, 1993, the Bogotá newspaper *El Tiempo* reported
with satisfaction on President Clinton's remarks at a ceremony for
Colombia's new ambassador to the United States. The President
praised Colombia as a "valued trading partner" and "one of our
strongest allies, not only in the effort to free the world of the scourge
of narcotics trafficking, but also in our common desire to see democracy flourish and the rule of law prevail throughout the region."

"More than any nation in this hemisphere, Colombia has suffered
at the hands of the drug traffickers," Clinton said. "The courage your
people have demonstrated at all levels, from the President to the
prosecutor, to the policeman on the street and the soldier in the field,
merits our respect and thanks."

The following day, a group of "soldiers in the field" killed three
peasants—two men and one woman—and dumped their bodies in
front of the Catholic bishop's residence in Tibú in Colombia's San-
tander region. The bishop, Monsignor Luis Madrid Merlano, con-
demned the killings and the fact that soldiers displayed the bodies
in the street for three hours before allowing them to be removed.
In response to the Colombian army's accusation that the peasants
had been subversive guerrillas, Madrid Merlano noted that "the
owner of the farm where they worked told me that they had been
employed there for more than 20 months, and the woman who was
killed was the trusted cook of the household."[1]

Colombia's "policemen in the street" and "soldiers in the field" commit similar atrocities on literally a daily basis. The country's dismal human rights record prompted Amnesty International to publish a special 1994 report titled *Myth and Reality,* which held government forces responsible for most of Colombia's human rights violations. Similar reports have come from human rights organizations, including Americas Watch and the Inter-American Human Rights Commission of the Organization of American States. The Andean Commission of Jurists, a human rights organization with offices in Bogotá, has compiled data showing that Colombia's police and armed forces were responsible for 70 percent of the country's twelve political murders *per day* during 1993. Human rights groups estimate that there are at least 300,000 internal refugees in Colombia today and about 50,000 more who have fled to Ecuador. Of 264 unionists assassinated worldwide from January 1990 to March 1991, over half were Colombian, according to the International Confederation of Free Trade Unions in Brussels.

There is an almost surreal absurdity in Clinton's kind words of "respect and thanks" to the intellectual authors and physical perpetrators of these crimes—particularly since Clinton's words came packaged in a speech in which he also declared, "All who abuse human rights, regardless of their ideology or position, must be punished severely and swiftly." But President Clinton was simply expressing a common illusion in the United States—the notion that Colombia's human rights problems are side-effects of the country's "war on drugs." As Marcela Salazar of the Andean Commission of Jurists observes, this perception is the result of careful PR positioning by the government of Colombia. "They present themselves as victims and say, 'Things are very difficult for us, we are confronting the drug traffickers, and sometimes there are problems,' " Salazar says. "They have presented a good image for themselves, and they even say that they are in the vanguard of the struggle for human rights, but we have to look at their actual practice." [2]

From Villain to Victim

Until a decade ago, the government of Colombia didn't pay much attention to its international image, but in the mid-1980s it began to show concern about its growing reputation as a compliant haven for the world's largest drug empire. An opinion poll in 1987 showed that 76% of Americans thought the Colombian government was corrupt, and 80% wanted sanctions imposed. [3] The country's image suffered an additional blow in 1991 when the government stopped extradition of drug traffickers to the US and negotiated an in-country "surrender" of Pablo Escobar, the head of the notorious Medellín drug cartel. At the time, Escobar was facing nine indictments in the US for drug trafficking and murder. Under the terms of the surrender, he was picked up by a government helicopter and flown to a luxury jail dubbed the "Hilton prison" by US Congressman James Traficante. Escobar's mountaintop jail came equipped with jacuzzi, air conditioning, three huge bedrooms and a guest room, walk-in closets and private baths, phone and fax machines, a soccer field, a game room, and a panoramic view of the Medellín valley. He was also allowed to designate his own prison guards, and although police were banned from entering the "prison," well-placed bribes enabled Escobar to "escape" and "surrender" at will.[4]

To clean up its badly-soiled image, the Colombian government turned to the Sawyer/Miller Group, a top media consulting firm. Sawyer/Miller built its early career managing political campaigns for Democratic Party candidates including Senators Daniel Patrick Moynihan, Ted Kennedy and John Glenn, as well as 1984 vice-presidential candidate Geraldine Ferraro. In the mid-1980s, the firm shifted from election campaigning to "issue management" for corporations and international clients.[5]

After conducting opinion polls to evaluate the public's opinion of Colombia, Sawyer/Miller concluded that the country's image was so negative that an attempt to improve it through positive publicity would be dismissed as obvious propaganda. Instead, the firm devised a multi-stage campaign: first, reposition Colombia in the public mind from villain to victim. Then, turn the victim into a hero, and then a leader in the war on drugs.[6]

In 1991 alone, Colombia poured $3.1 million into the campaign, which began with newspaper ads and TV commercials targeted at Washington policymakers. The commercials showed stark images of a bullet-riddled car, a coffin and mourners. A voice-over recited a list of prominent Colombians murdered by drug traffickers, and asked viewers to "remember the Colombian heroes who are dying every day in the war against drugs."[7] Another ad attempted to swing the focus away from Colombia's role as drug supplier to the US role as consumer. It showed a young woman snorting a line of cocaine, with a caption that said, "Drug User or Drug Terrorist? How can we also consider her a drug terrorist? After all, this young American has never built a bomb or fired a gun. But, because of her cocaine habit, she is directly supporting the drug terrorists who are tearing apart our country. . . . We—and she—have to win this war together."

"Look at the press clips from then on," bragged Sawyer/Miller's Jack Leslie. "News stories, columns, editorials, all start talking more and more about demand."[8]

In addition to advertising, Sawyer/Miller pumped out pamphlets, video news releases and letters to editors signed by Colombian government officials. All requests from US journalists for interviews with Colombian officials were channeled through Sawyer/Miller. Sympathetic reporters got quick access, while critical journalists were turned away. Sawyer/Miller also organized meetings between Colombian government officials and newspaper editorial boards, pitching favorable stories and stressing Colombia's value as a US trading partner. Following a meeting with *New York Times Magazine* editor Warren Hoge, the *Times* ran a lengthy, factually flawed profile glorifying Colombian President César Gaviria Trujillo—whose election campaign, in fact, had been heavily funded by drug cartels. After the article appeared, the Colombian embassy bought reprint rights and sent thousands of copies to journalists around the United States.[9]

Another Sawyer/Miller ad featured a line-up of dead or jailed drug leaders. "These men once ran the world's largest drug empire," said the text. "They murdered thousands, terrorized a democratic nation and turned the profits of cocaine into lives of luxury. . . . No country has paid a higher price in the war on drugs than Colombia. That war isn't over—but every day brings evidence that democracy can triumph over drugs." The ad put a favorable spin on Colombia's handling of Pablo Escobar, claiming that "Escobar is out of business and in jail. His prison is like many in the US—ringed by barbed wire and electric fences. A Colombian Army battalion surrounds it. Soon Pablo Escobar will be tried for his crimes."[10]

In fact, the Colombian Army's frequent *collaboration* with drug traffickers is common knowledge in Colombia. *Justicia y Paz,* a Colombian human rights organization comprising 55 religious congregations, has documented the links between drug cartels and army-supported "paramilitary groups" to carry out covert death squad activities as part of Colombia's decades-long guerrilla war. "They use very savage methods, such as cutting off people's arms and legs with chainsaws," said a *Justicia y Paz* researcher, speaking anonymously for fear of personal retribution.[11]

As Colombia's image graduated from "victim" to "hero" in the war on drugs, the government's acts of brutality and repression were cast as "tough but necessary measures." In 1991, Colombia began a "judicial reform" known as the system of "faceless justice." In cases brought before the faceless courts, judges are kept hidden behind a partition that renders them invisible to defendants and their attorneys. Special electronic equipment is used to disguise the judge's voice. Prosecuting attorneys and witnesses may also have their identities kept secret, and defendants are even denied access to information about the legal process and the evidence that has been brought against them. The system is supposedly aimed at protecting Colombian judges from intimidation and assassination by "narcoterrorists," and received glowing praise in December of 1993 by *60 Minutes,* which ran a segment extolling the bravery of the Colombian judges who serve on the faceless courts. Cecilia Zarate, a Colombian woman active with human rights groups in the United States, had a different opinion: "Secret judges, secret witnesses, secret evidence—this is really scary. In Latin culture, people have a vivid historical memory of the killings, tortures and injustices that went on under this type of system during the Spanish Inquisition. It's horrible that they should be bringing this back, really horrible."

The Center for Investigation and Popular Education (CINEP), a highly respected Jesuit organization which monitors human rights conditions in Colombia, examined the system of faceless justice and discovered that 584 of the 618 persons prosecuted under these special courts during the first six months of 1992—that is, 94 percent—were persons engaged in social protests or civic organizing, while only 6 percent consisted of drug-trafficking or guerrilla cases.

After workers with the state-owned telephone system went on strike, for example, the government charged that the disruption of phone service constituted terrorism and arrested 13 union leaders. Other union members became victims of unofficial violence. The government used a strategy of "implausible denial" to account for the death of Telecom union member Jose Joaquin Caicedo Angulo. After he was strangled, gasoline was poured on his body, and he was set on fire. The government's investigation into his death concluded that he had committed suicide. Later that year, a car bomb claimed the life of another Telecom worker, a technician named Gonzalo Garcia. The government listed his murder as "unsolved."

"These official 'explanations' serve two functions," said Jack Laun, a Wisconsin attorney who has been active for many years in Colombian human rights groups. "Before the international community, they enable the Colombian government to represent itself as innocent of crimes committed by its agents. To the victims of those crimes, on the other hand, they send a very different message. The government is announcing to the workers of Telecom, 'We can kill you with impunity, and whatever we say about it afterwards will be believed.' "[12]

Meanwhile, Colombia's justice system remained notoriously lax with drug dealers. Pablo Escobar's death in a 1994 shootout merely transferred power from his hands to a rival cocaine cartel in Calí, with no appreciable impact on the drug trade. After Ernesto Samper replaced Gaviria as president of Colombia, investigators discovered that Samper had received campaign contributions from the Calí cartel. Samper attempted to counter this revelation by launching a highly-publicized crackdown on the druglords, but journalist Steven Gutkin noted that "cartel leaders may actually prefer to be behind bars for a while. . . . More than a thousand underlings in the drug trade have already taken advantage of indulgent anti-narcotics legislation, either surrendering or cutting deals after being arrested. The average sentence has been three years, far less than the punishment for carrying an unlicensed gun. . . . No one expects a significant decrease in the amount of illicit drugs entering the United States. . . . The government must come through with meaningful prison sentences—not public relations ploys to appease the United States."[13]

Flacking for the Fascists

Governments that murder and jail their critics don't particularly need to worry about maintaining an attractive image among their own people. Their public relations efforts are targeted primarily at an international audience—in particular, to corporations, policymakers and news media responsible for shaping trade and foreign aid policies.

"Contrary to common assumptions, propaganda plays an important role—and certainly a more covert and sophisticated role—in technologically advanced democratic societies, where the maintenance of the existing power and privileges are vulnerable to popular opinion," writes Australian scholar Alex Carey. He cites a study by Robert Brady of PR during the first half of the twentieth century, which shows that "broadly speaking the importance of public relations . . . decreases as one moves away from countries with long and deep-seated liberal, democratic and parliamentary institutions."

> Brady argues that Italy and Japan had the least experience of democratic institutions and therefore produced the least competent propaganda. In Germany, where there had been greater, though still limited experience of democratic institutions, "National Socialist propaganda

was by all means better organized . . . more vociferous and more versatile than the propaganda of either Italy or Japan." At the other end of the scale, that is among countries with the longest experience of liberal, democratic institutions, "public relations propaganda . . . in the United States . . . is more highly coloured and ambidextrous than it has ever become, even in England."[14]

In 1933, the Nazis turned for guidance to Ivy Lee, the US pioneer of public relations. Lee's firm was hired for $25,000 per year by the German Dye Trust, I.G. Farben, which invited him to visit Germany and meet Hitler along with propaganda minister Joseph Goebbels and other Nazi government officials. Lee's 28-year-old son, James Lee, went to work for Farben in Berlin for $33,000 a year. An employee of Lee's firm drafted a report suggesting that Joachim von Ribbentrop, the German general who later became Hitler's foreign minister, "undertake a definite campaign to clarify the American mind" by speaking "over the radio to the American people" and writing "a considered article for an important American publication."[15]

Max Ilgner, the I.G. Farben official who hired Lee, was a member of the Nazi "Circle of Experts of the Propaganda Ministry." After World War II he was convicted as a Nazi war criminal by the Nuremberg Military Tribunals. According to the Nuremberg prosecution, "Farben's foreign agents formed the core of Nazi intrigue throughout the world. Financed and protected by Farben, and ostensibly acting only as businessmen, Farben officials carried on propaganda, intelligence, and espionage activities indispensable to German preparation for, and waging of, aggressive war."

In 1934, Ivy Lee's work for Germany brought him before the US House Special Committee to answer charges that he was a Nazi propagandist. Lee claimed that his meeting with Hitler was "just as a personal matter, to size him up," and said he had advised the Germans to abandon their persecutions of the Jews. These rationalizations failed to satisfy Congress, which in 1938 passed the Foreign Agents Registration Act (FARA) requiring anyone who engages in US political activities on behalf of a foreign government to register with the Criminal Division of the Justice Department. Under FARA, it is illegal for a foreign interest or agent to make political contributions, or for a US government official to act as a foreign agent.[16]

In practice, however, FARA is virtually toothless. "Many lobbyists do not even bother to register, and those who do provide only the minimum required information," writes author Susan Trento. "When violations are discovered, little action is taken."[17]

Banana Republicans

Many of the big spenders on Washington lobbying and PR are governments with severe human rights abuses including Taiwan, South Korea, Pakistan, Mexico and Saudi Arabia. In 1992, the Washington-based Center for Public Integrity published a study titled "The Torturers' Lobby," showing that Washington lawyers and lobbyists, many of whom served as top political advisors to Presidents Reagan, Bush and Clinton, were raking in more than $30 million a year by helping repressive governments improve their images. PR giant Hill & Knowlton topped the list, with $14 million in receipts from countries with documented records of abuse, torture and imprisonment, including Kuwait, Indonesia, Israel, China, Egypt and Peru. China, of course, uses strict media censorship and political prisons to control its population. In 1989 it carried out the infamous massacre of hundreds of pro-democracy students in Tiananmen Square. Other examples cited by "The Torturers' Lobby" included:

- Turkey, which got $800 million in US aid despite being charged by the State Department with widespread human rights abuses, spread $3.8 million around to capitol influence-peddlers, including $1.2 million to Hill & Knowlton.

- Guatemala, whose genocide against its indigenous population is described in the autobiography of Nobel prize-winner Rigoberta Menchu, laid out $650,000 for Washington lobbying. During 1991–92, while hundreds of Guatemalans were executed for political reasons, fees totalling $220,000 went to the Washington firm of Patton, Boggs & Blow, whose partners included Democratic National Committee Chairman Ron Brown (President Clinton's Commerce Secretary).

- Nigeria's military government spent $2.6 million from 1991–92, over $1 million of which went to Burson-Marsteller subsidiary Black, Manafort, Stone & Kelly, one of the top five firms in the "torturers' lobby." In addition to Nigeria, the firm collected another $1.2 million in fees from the Republic of Kenya and Angola's UNITA rebels.[18]

In some cases, "The Torturers' Lobby" showed that countries were spending a large part of their foreign aid from the United States to subsidize Washington lobbyists. Nigeria's $2.6 million in lobbying fees, for example, represented nearly a third of its $8.3 million in US aid. "The system stinks," said Makau Mutua, director of Harvard Law

School's Human Rights Project. "It's morally objectionable, all this influence-peddling. There's no doubt several of these countries couldn't afford these lobbyists without the help of the American taxpayers." [19]

Everybody Needs Some Bodies Sometime

Some PR firms argue that they are ethically *obligated,* like attorneys, to accept virtually any client who can afford to pay. Reagan-era powerhouse Gray & Company's clients included the murderous "Baby Doc" Duvalier in Haiti. In her biography of Robert Keith Gray, author Susan Trento says the company's rationalizations to explain working for Haiti "utilized an Orwellian logic that would be dazzling if it weren't so appalling." According to company executive Adonis Hoffman, "The government of Haiti, rank it wherever you will, . . . is entitled to make its position known in Washington to the US government, and has the right to try to tell its side of whatever the story is to the media and to the American public. In order to do that, they are going to have to retain a firm that knows how to do those kinds of things. . . . By definition, people who hire lobbyists and PR people have problems, they have fears, and they have needs."

Trento comments sarcastically, "It was as if one of the most brutal dictators of the twentieth century were a poor lost soul seeking his inner child and Gray & Company a benevolent, kindly therapist." [20]

In his pre-Clinton days, Ron Brown also personally represented the Duvalier government while working for Patton, Boggs & Blow in the early 1980s. Duvalier finally fled Haiti in 1986 to escape a popular uprising, and power passed through the hands of a quick succession of unpopular governments until December 16, 1990, when Haiti held the first democratic elections in the country's history. Jean-Bertrand Aristide, a radical Catholic priest, received 67 percent of the vote in a field of 23 candidates, and assumed office on February 7, 1991. Eight months later, however, soldiers led by Lieutenant-General Raoul Cédras and Colonel Michel François surrounded the presidential palace, seized Aristide and sent him into exile. During Aristide's exile, some 4,000 Haitians were killed by the Cédras regime. "Boat people" from Haiti began fleeing in large numbers to the United States and other neighboring countries. The United States and the Organization of American States declared a trade embargo against the military regime. [21]

Cédras and François responded with a smear campaign against Aristide. After expelling him from the country, they rummaged through Aristide's diaries and personal effects in search of incriminating evidence. Predictably, this "investigation" concluded that Aristide was a "psychotic manic-depressive with homicidal and necrophiliac tendencies."[22] The junta transmitted these charges to the US news media through an array of hired lobbyists and PR representatives, including George Demougeot, who also represented a US apparel firm with an assembly plant in Haiti, and Stephen A. Horblitt and Walter E. Faunteroy of Creative Associates International Inc.[23] Another employee in the PR campaign was Darryl Reaves, a one-term Florida state representative who worked to arrange interviews and Capitol Hill connections for François and Cédras. Reaves avoided publicity for himself, telling reporters, "I don't exist." When one journalist inquired too deeply, he responded with obscenities and vague threats that he would have the reporter arrested.[24]

The regime's most visible lobbyist, however, was Robert McCandless. In addition to the junta, McCandless represented a group of businessmen headed by Gregory Brandt, whose interests in Haiti included cooking oil, cars, tomato paste and coffee. In March of 1992, McCandless accepted $85,000 from the junta as part of a $165,000 contract. In his FARA filing, McCandless said he would be working "to direct favorable PR to Provisional Government and unfavorable PR against former President Aristide. . . . Eventually, . . . try to get aid in money and in kind."[25] In the spring of 1992, the Treasury department ordered McCandless to stop representing the Haitian government on grounds that he was breaking the embargo, but he continued to do so on what he claimed was now a "pro bono" basis.[26]

McCandless circulated position papers and editorials in Washington. In an August 13, 1992, memo, he rehashed the Haitian military's claim that Aristide was a "tyrant and a cruel and oppressive ruler," and characterized the US trade embargo as "a policy of genocide" that would cause the deaths of "hundreds of thousands of innocent Haitians." As a "suggested compromise," McCandless proposed to end the crisis by letting Aristide return to Haiti—not to resume office, but to face trial before a "blue-ribbon citizens' panel" on charges of embezzlement, inciting mob violence, torture and murder.[27]

In his PR work for the provisional government, McCandless cashed in on his friendship with conservative syndicated columnist Robert Novak, who obliged by visiting Haiti at McCandless' invitation and writing a series of columns in support of the junta. In a 1993 article titled "Why So Hard on Haiti's Military?" Novak accused the Clinton administration of "uncharacteristic rigidity" for refusing "to consider a negotiated settlement of exiled Haiti President Jean-Bertrand Aristide's return to power or even to hear conflicting advice. . . . Warnings about Haiti began even before Clinton took office, when Washington lawyer Robert McCandless offered his invaluable contacts with the Haitian military and police to seek a solution. . . . McCandless again has offered the president use of his relationship with François and Cédras to seek a peaceful solution."[28]

The Bush and Clinton administrations expressed support for Aristide as Haiti's elected president, but behind the scenes the junta had powerful allies in the CIA and in the offices of conservative US Senators Jesse Helms and Robert Dole. Its attacks on Aristide's character received extensive media attention when Helms organized a "classified briefing" with Brian Latelle, the CIA's intelligence officer for Latin America. The briefing, at which Latelle used a forged letter to document his false claim that Aristide suffered from psychological disorders, was promptly leaked to Novak at the *Washington Post*.[29] Helms followed up by delivering a newsmaking tirade against Aristide on the floor of the Senate, labeling him a "psychopath" and claiming that Aristide had incited followers to murder his opponents.

With Friends Like These . . .

Ironically, the most effective PR work against Aristide may have come from his "friends in high places." Throughout the crisis, the US sponsored negotiations that forced Aristide to make repeated concessions. When Aristide failed to comply, US officials attacked his "intransigence," portraying his obstinacy as the primary obstacle to peace.

Gregory Craig, a well-connected Washington attorney, was a key player in shaping the Clinton policy. A former Yale classmate of the Clintons, Craig was hired in 1992 to represent the interests of Fritz Mevs, Sr., a Miami resident who made his fortune with a sugar monopoly under the dictatorship of François "Papa Doc" Duvalier. Mevs, along with his sons and other family members, have been called the "mini-Mafia" of Haiti. They reportedly shared the military's disdain for Aristide. A report by the National Labor Committee, a labor education group representing 23 national unions, claimed that Mevs was one of the chief organizers of the coup and that the Mevs family made money smuggling cement in violation of the embargo.[30]

Mevs contacted Craig to discover what measures he should take to protect his interests as the Bush administration considered freezing assets of backers of the coup. After determining that the US government had no proof of Mevs family complicity in the coup, Craig agreed to become the family's personal lobbyist in Washington. Using his Clinton connections, Craig played a key role in shaping US policy toward Haiti after Bush left office.[31]

The Bush and Clinton administrations vacillated for two years before finally taking action, while the junta's defenders repeated and refined their charge that Aristide was "just as bad or worse." The Clinton administration finally sent troops in to Haiti in September 1994 to impose a settlement that granted a full amnesty to the junta. After two years in exile, Aristide was allowed to resume office with barely 16 months remaining in his term, under an agreement that forbade him from running for re-election.

The true significance of Aristide's return to Haiti received a frank assessment from Major Louis Kernisan of the US Defense Intelligence Agency, who led the retraining of Haiti's "new, reformed" police force. "You're going to end up dealing with the same folks as before, the five families that run the country, the military and the bourgeoisie," Kernisan said. "They're the same folks that are supposed to be the bad guys now, but the bottom line is you know that you're always going to end up dealing with them."[32]

Them vs. Us

The latter half of the twentieth century has been marked by growing disillusionment as the American people have learned of the gulf that separates official rhetoric from the actual conduct of US foreign policy. This disillusionment has led to a set of attitudes that on the surface seem paradoxical. On the one hand, the people of the United States donate billions of dollars each year to overseas charitable causes, and although attitudes about most aspects of US foreign policy tend to vary with the times, surveys of public opinion consistently show a deep concern abut the plight of needy people in other countries. According to one survey, 89% of the American people feel that "wherever people are hungry or poor, we ought to do what we can to help them."[33] Only 5% feel that fighting world hunger is "not important." Eliminating world hunger and poverty rank far ahead of "protecting American business abroad" and even ahead of "defending our allies' security" as an international concern.[34]

On the other hand, the public's attitude toward *government* foreign aid programs has been thoroughly negative since at least the early 1970s, when pollsters began taking surveys on that question. When asked to volunteer their views of "the two or three biggest foreign-policy problems facing the nation," respondents regularly identify "reducing foreign aid" as one of their top concerns.[35] According to the Gallup polling organization, a sharp difference has emerged between the attitudes of the general public and the attitudes of people that pollsters (somewhat misleadingly) designate as "opinion leaders"—i.e., heads of business, the professions, politicians, the news media and labor union officials. With respect to *economic* aid, over 90 percent of "opinion leaders" support it, but the general public favors such aid by only a thin margin. Most people see foreign aid as helpful to the economies of recipient countries, but not to the United States. Moreover, they perceive it as benefitting the rich more than the poor, and 75 percent feel that it gets the US "too involved in other countries' affairs."[36] Public support for *military* aid is even weaker. Although it still receives the support of a two-to-one majority among "opinion leaders," roughly the same majority within the general public *opposes* military aid. Moreover, four out of five Americans believe that military aid "lets dictatorships repress their own people," and five out of six believe that it "aggravates our relations with other countries" and "gets us too involved in their affairs."[37]

At the same time, the field of foreign policy offers a fertile breeding-ground for propaganda. Most efforts at molding public opinion target the portion of the public which is undecided, uninformed or vaguely informed about an issue, and foreign countries are by definition faraway places inhabited by people whose language and customs are unfamiliar and different from ours. It is no accident that the US public relations industry first rose to prominence as a result of the Creel Committee's propaganda efforts during World War I. Every successive war has brought new innovations and growth in both the technique and scope of public relations.

Wartime propaganda has a long history, going back to Attila the Hun. The classical rhetorical model is crude but effective. "Before ordinary human beings can begin the organized killing known as 'war,' they must first 'kill' their opponents psychologically," observes Vincent Kavaloski. "This is the ritual—as old as civilization itself—known as 'becoming enemies.' The 'enemy' is described by our leaders as 'not like us,' almost inhuman. They are evil. They are cruel. They are intent on destroying us and all that we love. There is only one thing the 'enemy' understands—violence. This 'logic of the enemy image' leads to one inescapable conclusion: the enemy must be killed. Indeed, destroying the enemy is an heroic act, an act of salvation and purification."[38]

Author John MacArthur notes, for example, that during World War I, the French and British seized on Germany's conquest of Belgium for propaganda purposes. The British-sponsored Bryce Committee claimed that German "murder, lust and pillage prevailed over many parts of Belgium on a scale unparalleled in any war between civilized nations during the last three centuries." The committee's claims, which were never documented or corroborated, included allegations that German soldiers had publicly raped Belgian girls, bayonetted a two-year-old child, and mutilated a peasant girl's breasts. The London *Times* claimed that a witness had seen Germans "chop off the arms of a baby which clung to it's mother's skirts"—a story which was embellished further when the French press published a drawing showing German soldiers eating the hands.[39]

One of the striking features of war in the late half of this century has been the degree to which it has become closely integrated with sophisticated public relations, to the degree that military strategy itself has been transformed. For propaganda reasons, war has been redefined using new terminology—as a "police action" or "limited engagement." The dead have become "casualties," "missing in action" or the result of "collateral damage" and "friendly fire."

The Vietnam War contributed substantially to the military's new emphasis on propaganda and psychological warfare. The war's planners realized that the use of US troops to accomplish traditional military objectives—capturing and holding territory—backfired when the US presence inspired anti-American nationalism among the Vietnamese. As the conflict dragged on, the steady stream of soldiers returning in body bags fed anti-war sentiment at home. Future wars, the planners concluded, should avoid extended placements of US troops on foreign soil. Instead, they proposed two alternative strategies: (1) brief blitzkriegs using overwhelming force to quickly and decisively defeat the enemy; and (2) replacing US forces with foreign proxies, special operations forces and mercenaries to engage the enemy using guerrilla tactics of unconventional warfare. In either case, the psychological war for "hearts and minds" took precedence over the conventional war for terrain and physical assets.

Lightning Wars

The 1983 US invasion of Grenada, a tiny island nation with a population of 160,000 and a per capita income of $390 per year, marked the adoption of the new military doctrine. Following a violent coup within Grenada's leftist government, the Reagan administration seized the opportunity to return Grenada to the fold of capitalism by sending an invasion force of 6,000 US troops to storm the island. Grenadan troops, outnumbered, outgunned and demoralized by the recent coup, offered little resistance. "With the equipment we have, it's like Star Wars fighting cavemen," said one soldier.[40] Three days after the troops landed, the fighting was essentially over.

Unlike the invasion of Normandy Beach during World War II, the invasion of Grenada took place without the presence of journalists to observe the action. Reagan advisors Mike Deaver and Craig Fuller had previously worked for the Hannaford Company, a PR firm which had represented the Guatemalan government to squelch negative publicity about Guatemala's massive violence against its civilian population. Following their advice, Reagan ordered a complete press blackout surrounding the Grenada invasion. By the time reporters were allowed on the scene, soldiers were engaged in "mop-up" actions, and the American public was treated to an antiseptic military victory minus any scenes of killing, destruction or incompetence. In fact, as former army intelligence officers Richard Gabriel and Paul Savage wrote a year later in the *Boston Globe,* "What really happened in Grenada was a case study in military incompetence and poor execution." Of the 18 American servicemen killed during the operation, 14 died in friendly fire or in accidents. To this day, no one has been able to offer a reliable estimate of the number of Grenadans killed. Retired Vice-Admiral Joseph Metcalf III remembered the Grenada invasion fondly as "a marvelous, sterile operation."[41]

After reporters protested the news blackout, the government proposed creating a "National Media Pool." In future wars, a rotating group of regular Pentagon correspondents would be on call to depart at a moment's notice for US surprise military operations. In theory, the pool system was designed to keep journalists safe and to provide them with timely, inside access to military operations. In practice, it was a classic example of PR crisis management strategy—enabling the military to take the initiative in controlling media coverage by channeling reporters' movements through Pentagon-designated sources.[42]

The first test of this "pool system" came on December 20, 1989, when President Bush sent US troops into Panama to oust General Manuel Noriega. Until his fall from official grace earlier that year, Noriega had been a longtime informant for the CIA and US Drug Enforcement Agency. As vice-president, in fact, Bush himself had personally honored Noriega for his assistance to US anti-drug efforts.

For that reason alone, the invasion of Panama required careful management to keep the media from raising embarrassing questions.

Once again, the invasion was carried out with blinding speed. The Pentagon held the National Media Pool captive on a US base in Panama for the first five hours of the fighting, by which time the heaviest action was already over. Outside of Pentagon pictures spoon-fed to journalists, little real information reached the American public. In El Chorrillo, the desperately poor neighborhood in Panama City where General Manuel Noriega's headquarters were located, at least 300 civilians died in the attack and resulting crossfire, some burned alive in their homes. Aside from the victims and US Army film crews, however, no one was allowed to observe the attack. The media dutifully reported the Pentagon's claim that only 202 civilians and 50 Panamanian soldiers died in the entire invasion, even though estimates from other sources ranged as high as 4,000 civilian deaths.[43]

Dirty Little Wars

Central America's revolutionary movements were too strong to be dislodged with a weekend war like the ones in Grenada and Panama. A longer-term, more sophisticated strategy was needed—one that kept US troops out of the line of fire while enabling the Pentagon to confront "the enemy." The strategy that carried the day in Washington became known as the doctrine of "low-intensity conflict." As Sara Miles observed in her landmark 1986 analysis,

> Its name comes from its place on the "intensity spectrum" of warfare which ascends from civil disorders, through classical wars, to nuclear holocaust. . . . "This kind of conflict is more accurately described as revolutionary and counterrevolutionary warfare," explains Col. John Waghelstein, currently commander of the Army's Seventh Special Forces. He warns that the term "low-intensity" is misleading, as it describes the level of violence strictly from a military viewpoint. In fact, Waghelstein argues, this type of conflict involves "political, economic, and psychological warfare, with the military being a distant fourth in many cases." In perhaps the most candid definition given by a US official, Waghelstein declares that low-intensity conflict "is total war at the grassroots level."[44]

The 1979 Sandinista revolution, which overthrew the Somoza dictatorship in Nicaragua, rang alarm bells in Washington. The Somoza family had ruled the country for 45 years after coming to power by murdering its enemies. It was notorious for corruption and violence, but it was also considered an unwavering ally of the United States.

Anastasio Somoza was also one of the first Latin American dictators to recognize the value of a good flack, hiring the Mackenzie and McCheyne PR firm in New York, along with lobbyist William Cramer, a former Republican congressman from Florida. In 1978, Somoza's last full year in power, Mackenzie and McCheyne received over $300,000 in fees from the Somoza government. As the revolution gained momentum, Mackenzie and McCheyne partner Ian Mackenzie was dispatched to counter negative reports characterizing the dictator as corrupt, authoritarian, crude, cruel and overweight. "The president is totally different from what people think," Mackenzie said. "He is intelligent, most capable, warm-hearted. He is loyal and strong with his friends, compassionate with his enemies. . . . By the sheer law of averages, Somoza has to have done some good. Even Mussolini did some good for Italy." As an example of the freedom that existed under the Somoza regime, Mackenzie pointed to Nicaragua's opposition newspaper, *La Prensa*.[45]

Two months later, *La Prensa* editor Pedro Joaquin Chamorro was gunned down in the street by Somoza's business partners, triggering a paralyzing nationwide strike demanding Somoza's resignation. Somoza hired a new flack, paying $7,000 per month for the services of Norman L. Wolfson of the New York PR firm of Norman, Lawrence, Patterson & Farrell. As Somoza's air force was decimating Nicaraguan cities with aerial bombings during its final campaign of terror, Wolfson—who didn't speak Spanish—complained to whoever would listen that reporters were trying to "knock down" Somoza and had not "been entirely fair."[46] (Wolfson's memoir of his experience, titled "Selling Somoza: The Lost Cause of a PR Man," appeared in the July 20, 1979, issue of William Buckley's conservative *National Review*, which was on sale at newsstands on July 19, the day Somoza fled the country. In it, Wolfson describes his client as "a spoiled brat who had evolved into middle age, a know-it-all who asked for advice and couldn't take it, a boor, a rude, overbearing bully" who fantasized about crushing the genitals of journalists.)[47]

By the time Somoza fled Nicaragua, his family had accumulated wealth estimated at $400 to $500 million. Meanwhile, half the country's population was illiterate. One in three infants born to poor Nicaraguans died before the age of one. More than 20,000 Nicaraguans suffered from advanced tuberculosis. The victorious Sandinistas launched ambitious, popular vaccination and education programs. They also broke new ground in foreign policy, seeking alliances with Cuba and the Soviet Union. A line in the country's new national anthem—"We fight the yankees, enemies of humanity"—showed just how far they intended to take Nicaragua from the Somoza days of dependence and fealty to the United States.

The "low-intensity" strategy aimed at undermining the Sandinistas was an ambitious concept, uniting Vietnam-era counterinsurgency with civic action initiatives, psychological warfare, public relations activities and civilian "development assistance" projects traditionally considered beyond the sphere of military responsibilities. On the economic level, the US pressured international financial institutions to cut off loans to Nicaragua and imposed a debilitating trade embargo. On the political front, the US promoted carefully stage-managed elections in El Salvador and Honduras. Psychological operations against Nicaragua ranged from sabotage attacks to radio propaganda broadcasts. On the military level, US strategy was designed to avoid the commitment of US ground troops, while doing everything possible to create the *fear* of a US invasion.

The US also brought together Somoza's dispersed National Guard and reorganized it into what became known as the *contra* army. At first the *contras* had no political leadership, so the White House recruited a group of disaffected Nicaraguan businessmen and scripted speeches to help them pose as the *contras'* "civilian leadership." The civilian leaders included Edgar Chamorro, a Managua advertising executive who later became disaffected with the cause. Chamorro complained bitterly in his 1987 book, *Packaging the Contras: A Case of CIA Disinformation,* that the US had used him as a civilian figurehead for an army over which he had no real control.

The CIA paid Chamorro a salary of $2,000 per month plus expenses for his work, which included bribing Honduran journalists and broadcasters to write and speak favorably about the *contras* and to attack the Nicaraguan government and call for its overthrow. "Approximately 15 Honduran journalists and broadcasters were on the CIA's payroll, and our influence was thereby extended to every major Honduran newspaper and radio and television station," Chamorro said.[48]

In 1983, the Reagan Administration began a series of major military maneuvers in Honduras, coordinated with *contra* units and the Salvadoran military. The maneuvers were carefully staged to create the impression that they were preludes to a US invasion of Nicaragua. In reality, as Miles observed,

> The maneuvers were not a preparation or cover for the war: *they were the embodiment of the war. . . .* Fears that the Administration *may* be

threatening to invade have been an integral part of the plan at the psychological level. . . . The first goal . . . was to squeeze the economy by forcing a massive diversion of resources into defense. . . . Next came psychological operations to feed on the conflict: leaflets distributed throughout the country urged Nicaraguan youths to escape the "totalitarian Marxist draft"; radio stations of the Nicaraguan Democratic Force (FDN) in Honduras urged revolt against "the communists who spend our national treasure on bullets instead of food."[49]

The Reagan administration faced a scandal in 1984 with the disclosure that the CIA had produced a training manual for the *contras* titled *Psychological Operations in Guerrilla Warfare.* The strategy outlined in the text include recommendations for selective assassination of Nicaraguan government officials. Critics charged the CIA with encouraging indiscriminate assassination of civilians. Miles observed, however, that the actual intent of the document was more subtle:

There is a conscious effort to reduce the presence of the civilian government, to remove successful social programs and the ideological influence that comes with them. . . . In practice, this means the targeted torture and assassination of teachers, health workers, agricultural technicians and their collaborators in the community. This is not, as many critics charge, "indiscriminate violence against civilians." . . . Rather, the violence is part of a logical and systematic policy, and reflects the changing pattern of the war.[50]

The War At Home

The most pressing concern of all for the Reagan administration was the need to win the support of the US people for its policies in Central America. "I think the most critical special operations mission we have today is to persuade the American people that the communists are out to get us. If we can win this war of ideas, we can win everywhere else," explained Michael Kelly, Deputy Assistant Secretary of the US Air Force. "Psychological operations, ranging from public affairs on the one end, through black propaganda on the other end, is the advertising and marketing of our product."[51]

"Public affairs" is the government's term for "public relations"— a rather pointless change in terminology adopted to get around a 1913 law which specifically enjoins federal government agencies against engaging in public relations activities. The law also forbids the White House from using ads, telegrams, letters, printed matter or other media outside "official channels" to influence members of Congress regarding legislation. Rules against CIA involvement in domestic US politics are even more severe. It is against the law for the CIA to operate domestically, except in narrowly-defined circumstances such as cooperating with an FBI investigation. In 1982, however, reports of the secret CIA war in Nicaragua led Congress to pass the Boland Amendment, ending military aid to the *contras* and barring the Reagan administration from any further attempts to overthrow the Sandinistas.

In response, Reagan dispatched CIA Director William Casey in January 1983 to set up a "public diplomacy" machine that journalists Robert Parry and Peter Kornbluh describe as "America's first peacetime propaganda ministry . . . a set of domestic political operations comparable to what the CIA conducts against hostile forces abroad. Only this time they were turned against the three key institutions of American democracy: Congress, the press, and an informed electorate. . . . Employing the scientific methods of modern public relations and the war-tested techniques of psychological operations, the administration built an unprecedented bureaucracy in the [National Security Council] and the State Department designed to keep the news media in line and to restrict conflicting information from reaching the American public."[52]

As head of the operation, Casey appointed Walter Raymond, Jr., a 20-year veteran of the CIA's clandestine overseas media operations—described by one US government source as the CIA's leading propaganda expert. According to *Washington Post* editor Ben Bradlee, Raymond's involvement in the campaign symbolized "the wholesale integration of intelligence and PR at the National Security Council."[53] During the Iran/Contra scandal, Congress investigated the Reagan administration's domestic propaganda operations and found that Raymond's name appeared on Oliver North's calendar more than that of any other White House staff member or government employee. A chapter detailing these domestic activities was drafted for the investigating committee's Iran/Contra report, but House and Senate Republicans successfully blocked even a paragraph of the draft from being included in the committee's final report. As a result, the CIA's domestic propaganda activities in violation of its charter have received almost no public scrutiny.

A Little Help from Our Friends

As the PR apparatus was taking shape in August 1983, Casey summoned a group of top public relations executives to a full-day, hush-hush strategy meeting. Four of the five PR executives at the meeting with Casey were prominent members of the Public Relations Society of America, the industry's leading professional association. All five were members of "PR Seminar," a 37-year-old highly secretive gathering of about 120 senior corporate PR executives. All PR Seminar proceedings are "off the record," and members are threatened with a lifetime ban if they reveal any details of PRS to the press. The members who met with Casey were:

- Kalman B. Druck, retired president and founder of Harshe-Rotman & Druck. He was national president of the PRSA in 1972 and has long been one of its most outspoken and prominent members.

- Kenneth Clark, vice-president for corporate communications of Duke Power Co., and a former national treasurer of PRSA.

- Kenneth D. Huszar, a senior vice-president of PR giant Burson-Marsteller, the largest PR firm in the world.

- William I. Greener, Jr., senior vice-president of corporate relations at G.D. Searle. Greener had served previously as deputy press secretary for President Gerald Ford and then as assistant secretary of public affairs for the Department of Defense under Donald Rumsfeld in the late 1970s.

- James Bowling of Philip Morris, a highly experienced Washington hand who later went on to work for Burson-Marsteller. In 1985 Bowling became chairman of the Public Affairs Council, the leading public affairs industry trade association.[54]

According to Druck the atmosphere at the meeting was emotionally supercharged. It began in the morning with a briefing in front of a large map of Latin America. Aides from the CIA and National Security Council painted a frightening picture of subversion spreading throughout Central America and asked for advice to help pin "white hats" on the *contras* and "black hats" on the Sandinistas. At the aides' request, the PR executives brainstormed some 25 ideas, which were presented on an easel while Casey took copious notes.

Their advice boiled down to two principal suggestions. First, "that the administration follow the lead of modern-day corporations by setting up a classic corporate communications function within the White House." Second, to dramatize the *contra* cause, they proposed that the White House set up "a private sector-funded public education program," headed by a prominent individual, "to launch a highly-publicized national fund drive."[55]

Following this advice to the letter, the White House brought together a coalition of "retired" military men and right-wing millionaires to support the "Nicaragua Freedom Fund," chaired by Wall Street investment executive William Simon. Contributors included familiar right-wing figures like TV evangelist Pat Robertson, Colorado beer baron Joseph Coors, oil magnate Nelson Bunker Hunt, singer Pat Boone, and *Soldier of Fortune* magazine. The Fund claimed to raise over $20 million through activities such as a $250-a-plate "Nicaraguan refugee" dinner in April 1985 attended by Casey and Simon and featuring a speech by Reagan. In reality, the Fund was a propaganda front, spending almost as much money as it raised. An audit of the "refugee dinner" showed it had raised $219,525 but costs totaled $218,376, including $116,938 in "consulting fees."[56]

The main purpose of the Nicaraguan Freedom Fund was to divert attention from the *covert* channels through which *real* money flowed to the *contras* in violation of the Boland Amendment. One of those channels was a specialized PR firm, International Business Communications, which pleaded guilty in 1987 to fraud by using a tax-exempt foundation to raise funds to arm the *contras*. It had been a profitable business, according to the Iran/Contra congressional investigating committee, which concluded that IBC had kept about $1.7 million of the $5 million it channeled to the *contras*.[57]

The other part of the PR plan—setting up a "communications function within the White House"—put Raymond at the head of a newly-created "Office of Public Diplomacy for Latin America and the Caribbean." "Public diplomacy" was simply another synonym for public relations. In its first year alone, reported Parry and Kornbluh, the activities of the OPD included "booking more than 1,500 speaking engagements, including radio, television, and editorial board interviews; publishing three booklets on Nicaragua; and distributing materials to 1,600 college libraries, 520 political science faculties, 122 editorial writers, and 107 religious organizations. Special attention was given to prominent journalists."[58] In 1985, for example, a memo by OPD staffer Otto Reich described using a "cut-out" (someone whose tie to the OPD was concealed) to set up visits by *contra* leader Alfonso Robelo to news organizations including Hearst Newspapers, *Newsweek,* Scripps-Howard Newspapers, the editorial board of the *Washington Post, USA Today,* CNN, the "MacNeil-Lehrer Report," the "Today Show" and CBS Morning News.[59]

In private memos to the National Security Council, the OPD boasted also of having "killed" news stories that contradicted the

Reagan administration's public position on Nicaragua, using tactics that included intimidation and character assassination of journalists. Using $400,000 raised from private donors, the OPD funded organizations such as Accuracy In Media, a right-wing organization that vigorously attacked journalists who criticized Reagan's foreign policy. In July 1985, the OPD itself helped spread a scurrilous story that some American reporters had received sexual favors from Sandinista prostitutes in return for writing slanted stories.[60]

The OPD assigned five Army experts from the 4th Psychological Operations Group to find "exploitable themes and trends" and used opinion polling to "see what turns Americans against Sandinistas." A variety of publicity stunts and news stories were staged to achieve this objective. In 1984, for example, the White House leaked information to the press to create a mythical "MIGs Crisis." The story, which claimed that Nicaragua was about to receive a delivery of Soviet fighter planes, was prominently played on the TV news, with "special bulletins" interrupting regular programming. Although it was later proven false, the MIGs story helped create the public perception that Nicaragua posed a military threat to the US, and also diverted attention away from elections which had been held earlier that week in Nicaragua. Despite widespread praise from a large contingent of international observers, Nicaragua's first free elections—in which the Sandinistas received 67 percent of the vote—were summarily dismissed as a "sham" by the Reagan administration.[61]

The White House used classic "enemy-image" propaganda to paint the Sandinistas as the embodiment of evil—"a second Cuba, a second Libya"—while describing the *contras* as "the moral equivalent of our founding fathers." White House Communications Director Patrick Buchanan claimed that "Iranian, PLO, Libyan and Red Brigade elements" were "turning up in Managua" and warned that "if Central America goes the way of Nicaragua, they will be in San Diego."[62] The Sandinistas were accused of drug trafficking, terrorism, persecuting Jews, building secret prisons, and beating Catholics in the street for attending mass.[63]

To push the terrorism charge, the White House used Neil Livingstone, a self-proclaimed "expert on terrorism" and senior vice-president with the public relations firm of Gray & Company. In fact, considerable circumstantial evidence suggests that Gray & Company was itself connected to secret arms and money shipments connected with the Iran/Contra affair.[64] In addition to a web of incriminating financial transactions, the evidence includes the September 24, 1985, shooting of Glenn Souham in Paris. Souham was the son of New York PR counselor Gerard Souham, a frequent White House visitor whose firm was affiliated with Gray & Company. Glenn had talked openly to friends of working with a certain "lieutenant colonel" at the National Security Council and of suddenly making more money than ever before. Although the killing received almost no attention in the major news media, *O'Dwyer's PR Services* came to the conclusion that "young Souham, because of his international social and business connections, was enticed into Iran-Contra arms dealing" and that his indiscriminate bragging to friends led to his assassination.[65]

The Smell of Success

By the late 1980s, the Sandinistas' image in the United States was so negative that to describe Nicaragua as anything *other* than a "totalitarian dungeon" was considered commie-symp heresy. Reporters stationed in Nicaragua discovered that they had to trim their sails accordingly. "In the first couple of years I was here," said Judy Butler, a journalist living in Managua, "there was an interest, at least on the part of some reporters, to try to write about what they saw in Nicaragua, within the framework of what would be acceptable to their editors. Increasingly, their stories were changed in the States and the reporters started carrying telexes around to show that what got published was not what they had written. Now, they don't even bother."[66]

The final nail in the Sandinista coffin was the National Endowment for Democracy (NED), founded by the same White House executive order that launched the Office of Public Diplomacy. Funded by Congress, the NED provides money for "democracy promotion" and "civic training" in foreign countries abroad. As Nicaragua geared up for elections in 1990, President Bush sent $9 million in NED money, including a $4 million contribution to the campaign of opposition presidential candidate Violeta Chamorro.

Bush almost needn't have bothered. By 1990 a decade of war, combined with the US blockade of trade and investment, had reduced Nicaragua to a bleeding hell-hole. Economists debated whether "shattered" was a strong enough word to describe the state of the Nicaraguan economy, which suffered an inflation rate of 20 *thousand* percent in 1988. To curb inflation, the Sandinistas had adopted a series of drastic economic measures, driving up unemployment and slashing free food and health programs to the poor. The unpopular military draft, rationing, and a general feeling of exhaustion all contributed to the Sandinistas' growing unpopularity, and the Chamorro opposition won the elections handily.

In the United States, revelations of White House Iran/Contra operations brought congressional investigations, lawsuits and convictions which were later overturned. The Office of Public Diplomacy was disbanded in 1988, after the US Comptroller General concluded that it had "engaged in prohibited, covert propaganda activities designed to influence the media and public to support Administration Latin American policies."[67]

The PR officials involved in helping Casey design the plan also came under scrutiny, when another member of the Public Relations Society of America, Summer Harrison, filed a complaint with the PRSA's Ethics Board. Under PRSA's code of ethics, members are supposed to "strictly" adhere to government rules. After meeting to assess Harrison's charges, however, the Ethics Board issued a terse announcement stating that its members had not violated the code and that "there was no basis for further examination." Harrison complained about improprieties and conflicts of interest in the ethical review process. In response, the committee took up charges against *Harrison,* claiming that her complaint had violated a provision of the ethics code which says PRSA members may not "intentionally damage the professional reputation or practice of another practitioner." Rather than answer the charge, Harrison resigned in disgust from the PRSA.[68]

The Mother of All Clients

On August 2, 1990, Iraqi troops led by dictator Saddam Hussein invaded the oil-producing nation of Kuwait. Like Noriega in Panama, Hussein had been a US ally for nearly a decade. From 1980 to 1988, he had killed about 150,000 Iranians, in addition to at least 13,000 of his own citizens. Despite complaints from international human rights group, however, the Reagan and Bush administrations had treated Hussein as a valuable ally in the US confrontation with Iran. As late as July 25—a week before the invasion of Kuwait—US Ambassador April Glaspie commiserated with Hussein over a "cheap and unjust" profile by ABC's Diane Sawyer, and wished for an "appearance in the media, even for five minutes," by Hussein that "would help explain Iraq to the American people."[69]

Glaspie's ill-chosen comments may have helped convince the dictator that Washington would look the other way if he "annexed" a neighboring kingdom. The invasion of Kuwait, however, crossed a line that the Bush Administration could not tolerate. This time Hussein's crime was far more serious than simply gassing to death another brood of Kurdish refugees. This time, *oil* was at stake.

Viewed in strictly moral terms, Kuwait hardly looked like the sort of country that deserved defending, even from a monster like Hussein. The tiny but super-rich state had been an independent nation for just a quarter century when in 1986 the ruling al-Sabah family tightened its dictatorial grip over the "black gold" fiefdom by disbanding the token National Assembly and firmly establishing all power in the be-jeweled hands of the ruling Emir. Then, as now, Kuwait's ruling oligarchy brutally suppressed the country's small democracy movement, intimidated and censored journalists, and hired desperate foreigners to supply most of the nation's physical labor under conditions of indentured servitude and near-slavery. The wealthy young men of Kuwait's ruling class were known as spoiled party boys in university cities and national capitals from Cairo to Washington.[70]

Unlike Grenada and Panama, Iraq had a substantial army that could not be subdued in a mere weekend of fighting. Unlike the Sandinistas in Nicaragua, Hussein was too far away from US soil, too rich with oil money, and too experienced in ruling through propaganda and terror to be dislodged through the psychological-warfare techniques of low-intensity conflict. Waging a war to push Iraq's invading army from Kuwait would cost billions of dollars and require an unprecedented, massive US military mobilization. The American public was notoriously reluctant to send its young into foreign battles on behalf of any cause. Selling war in the Middle East to the American people would not be easy. Bush would need to convince Americans that former ally Saddam Hussein now embodied evil, and that the oil fiefdom of Kuwait was a struggling young democracy. How could the Bush Administration build US support for "liberating" a country so fundamentally opposed to democratic values? How could the war appear noble and necessary rather than a crass grab to save cheap oil?

"If and when a shooting war starts, reporters will begin to wonder why American soldiers are dying for oil-rich sheiks," warned Hal Steward, a retired army PR official. "The US military had better get cracking to come up with a public relations plan that will supply the answers the public can accept."[71]

Steward needn't have worried. A PR plan was already in place, paid for almost entirely by the "oil-rich sheiks" themselves.

Packaging the Emir

US Congressman Jimmy Hayes of Louisiana—a conservative Democrat who supported the Gulf War—later estimated that the government of Kuwait funded as many as 20 PR, law and lobby firms in its campaign to mobilize US opinion and force against Hussein.[72] Participating firms included the Rendon Group, which received a retainer of $100,000 per month for media work, and Neill & Co., which received $50,000 per month for lobbying Congress. Sam Zakhem, a former US ambassador to the oil-rich gulf state of Bahrain, funneled $7.7 million in advertising and lobbying dollars through two front groups, the "Coalition for Americans at Risk" and the "Freedom Task Force." The Coalition, which began in the 1980s as a front for the contras in Nicaragua, prepared and placed TV and newspaper ads, and kept a stable of fifty speakers available for pro-war rallies and publicity events.[73]

Hill & Knowlton, then the world's largest PR firm, served as mastermind for the Kuwaiti campaign. Its activities alone would have constituted the largest foreign-funded campaign ever aimed at manipulating American public opinion. By law, the Foreign Agents Registration Act should have exposed this propaganda campaign to the American people, but the Justice Department chose not to enforce it. Nine days after Saddam's army marched into Kuwait, the Emir's government agreed to fund a contract under which Hill & Knowlton would represent "Citizens for a Free Kuwait," a classic PR front group designed to hide the real role of the Kuwaiti government and its collusion with the Bush administration. Over the next six months, the Kuwaiti government channeled $11.9 million dollars to Citizens for a Free Kuwait, whose only other funding totalled $17,861 from 78 individuals. Virtually all of CFK's budget—$10.8 million—went to Hill & Knowlton in the form of fees.[74]

The man running Hill & Knowlton's Washington office was Craig Fuller, one of Bush's closest friends and inside political advisors. The news media never bothered to examine Fuller's role until after the war had ended, but if America's editors had read the PR trade press, they might have noticed this announcement, published in *O'Dwyer's PR Services* before the fighting began: "Craig L. Fuller, chief of staff to Bush when he was vice-president, has been on the Kuwaiti account at Hill & Knowlton since the first day. He and [Bob] Dilenschneider at one point made a trip to Saudi Arabia, observing the production of some 20 videotapes, among other chores. The Wirthlin Group, research arm of H&K, was the pollster for the Reagan

Administration. . . . Wirthlin has reported receiving $1.1 million in fees for research assignments for the Kuwaitis. Robert K. Gray, Chairman of H&K/USA based in Washington, DC had leading roles in both Reagan campaigns. He has been involved in foreign nation accounts for many years. . . . Lauri J. Fitz-Pegado, account supervisor on the Kuwait account, is a former Foreign Service Officer at the US Information Agency who joined Gray when he set up his firm in 1982."[75]

In addition to Republican notables like Gray and Fuller, Hill & Knowlton maintained a well-connected stable of in-house Democrats who helped develop the bipartisan support needed to support the war. Lauri Fitz-Pegado, who headed the Kuwait campaign, had previously worked with super-lobbyist Ron Brown representing Haiti's Duvalier dictatorship. Hill & Knowlton senior vice-president Thomas Ross had been Pentagon spokesman during the Carter Administration. To manage the news media, H&K relied on vice-chairman Frank Mankiewicz, whose background included service as press secretary and advisor to Robert F. Kennedy and George McGovern, followed by a stint as president of National Public Radio. Under his direction, Hill & Knowlton arranged hundreds of meetings, briefings, calls and mailings directed toward the editors of daily newspapers and other media outlets.

Jack O'Dwyer had reported on the PR business for more than twenty years, but he was awed by the rapid and expansive work of H&K on behalf of Citizens for a Free Kuwait: "Hill & Knowlton . . . has assumed a role in world affairs unprecedented for a PR firm. H&K has employed a stunning variety of opinion-forming devices and techniques to help keep US opinion on the side of the Kuwaitis. . . . The techniques range from full-scale press conferences showing torture and other abuses by the Iraqis to the distribution of tens of thousands of 'Free Kuwait' T-shirts and bumper stickers at college campuses across the US."[76]

Documents filed with the US Department of Justice showed that 119 H&K executives in 12 offices across the US were overseeing the Kuwait account. "The firm's activities, as listed in its report to the Justice Department, included arranging media interviews for visiting Kuwaitis, setting up observances such as National Free Kuwait Day, National Prayer Day (for Kuwait), and National Student Information Day, organizing public rallies, releasing hostage letters to the media, distributing news releases and information kits, contacting politicians at all levels, and producing a nightly radio show in Arabic from Saudi Arabia," wrote Arthur Rowse in the *Progressive* after the war. Citizens for a Free Kuwait also capitalized on the publication of a quickie 154-page book about Iraqi atrocities titled *The Rape of Kuwait,* copies of which were stuffed into media kits and then featured on TV talk shows and the *Wall Street Journal.* The Kuwaiti embassy also bought 200,000 copies of the book for distribution to American troops.[77]

Hill & Knowlton produced dozens of video news releases at a cost of well over half a million dollars, but it was money well spent, resulting in tens of millions of dollars worth of "free" air time. The VNRs were shown by eager TV news directors around the world who rarely (if ever) identified Kuwait's PR firm as the source of the footage and stories. TV stations and networks simply fed the carefully-crafted propaganda to unwitting viewers, who assumed they were watching "real" journalism. After the war Arthur Rowse asked Hill & Knowlton to show him some of the VNRs, but the PR company refused. Obviously the phony TV news reports had served their purpose, and it would do H&K no good to help a reporter reveal the extent of the deception. In *Unreliable Sources,* authors Martin Lee and Norman Solomon noted that "when a research team from the communications department of the University of Massachusetts surveyed public opinion and correlated it with knowledge of basic facts about US policy in the region, they drew some sobering conclusions: The more television people watched, the fewer facts they knew; and the less people knew in terms of basic facts, the more likely they were to back the Bush administration."[78]

Throughout the campaign, the Wirthlin Group conducted daily opinion polls to help Hill & Knowlton take the emotional pulse of key constituencies so it could identify the themes and slogans that would be most effective in promoting support for US military action. After the war ended, the Canadian Broadcasting Corporation produced an Emmy award-winning TV documentary on the PR campaign titled "To Sell a War." The show featured an interview with Wirthlin executive Dee Alsop in which Alsop bragged of his work and demonstrated how audience surveys were even used to physically adapt the clothing and hairstyle of the Kuwait ambassador so he would seem more likeable to TV audiences. Wirthlin's job, Alsop explained, was "to identify the messages that really resonate emotionally with the American people." The theme that struck the deepest emotional chord, they discovered, was "the fact that Saddam Hussein was a madman who had committed atrocities even against his own people, and had tremendous power to do further damage, and he needed to be stopped."[79]

Suffer the Little Children

Every big media event needs what journalists and flacks alike refer
to as "the hook." An ideal hook becomes the central element of a
story that makes it newsworthy, evokes a strong emotional response,
and sticks in the memory. In the case of the Gulf War, the "hook"
was invented by Hill & Knowlton. In style, substance and mode of
delivery, it bore an uncanny resemblance to England's World War I
hearings that accused German soldiers of killing babies.

On October 10, 1990, the Congressional Human Rights Caucus
held a hearing on Capitol Hill which provided the first opportunity
for formal presentations of Iraqi human rights violations. Outwardly,
the hearing resembled an official congressional proceeding, but
appearances were deceiving. In reality, the Human Rights Caucus,
chaired by California Democrat Tom Lantos and Illinois Republican
John Porter, was simply an association of politicians. Lantos and
Porter were also co-chairs of the Congressional Human Rights Foundation, a legally separate entity that occupied free office space valued at $3,000 a year in Hill & Knowlton's Washington, DC office.
Notwithstanding its congressional trappings, the Congressional
Human Rights Caucus served as another Hill & Knowlton front group,
which—like all front groups—used a noble-sounding name to disguise its true purpose.[80]

Only a few astute observers noticed the hypocrisy in Hill & Knowl-
ton's use of the term "human rights." One of those observers was
John MacArthur, author of *The Second Front,* which remains the best
book written about the manipulation of the news media during the
Gulf War. In the fall of 1990, MacArthur reported, Hill & Knowlton's
Washington switchboard was simultaneously fielding calls for the
Human Rights Foundation and for "government representatives of
Indonesia, another H&K client. Like H&K client Turkey, Indonesia
is a practitioner of naked aggression, having seized . . . the former
Portuguese colony of East Timor in 1975. Since the annexation of
East Timor, the Indonesian government has killed, by conservative
estimate, about 100,000 inhabitants of the region."[81]

MacArthur also noticed another telling detail about the October
1990 hearings: "The Human Rights Caucus is not a committee of
congress, and therefore it is unencumbered by the legal accouter-
ments that would make a witness hesitate before he or she lied.
. . . Lying under oath in front of a congressional committee is a
crime; lying from under the cover of anonymity to a caucus is merely
public relations."[82]

In fact, the most emotionally moving testimony on October 10 came from a 15-year-old Kuwaiti girl, known only by her first name of Nayirah. According to the Caucus, Nayirah's full name was being kept confidential to prevent Iraqi reprisals against her family in occupied Kuwait. Sobbing, she described what she had seen with her own eyes in a hospital in Kuwait City. Her written testimony was passed out in a media kit prepared by Citizens for a Free Kuwait. "I volunteered at the al-Addan hospital," Nayirah said. "While I was there, I saw the Iraqi soldiers come into the hospital with guns, and go into the room where . . . babies were in incubators. They took the babies out of the incubators, took the incubators, and left the babies on the cold floor to die." [83]

Three months passed between Nayirah's testimony and the start of the war. During those months, the story of babies torn from their incubators was repeated over and over again. President Bush told the story. It was recited as fact in Congressional testimony, on TV and radio talk shows, and at the UN Security Council. "Of all the accusations made against the dictator," MacArthur observed, "none had more impact on American public opinion than the one about Iraqi soldiers removing 312 babies from their incubators and leaving them to die on the cold hospital floors of Kuwait City." [84]

At the Human Rights Caucus, however, Hill & Knowlton and Congressman Lantos had failed to reveal that Nayirah was a member of the Kuwaiti Royal Family. Her father, in fact, was Saud Nasir al-Sabah, Kuwait's Ambassador to the US, who sat listening in the hearing room during her testimony. The Caucus also failed to reveal that H&K vice-president Lauri Fitz-Pegado had coached Nayirah in what even the Kuwaitis' own investigators later confirmed was false testimony.

If Nayirah's outrageous lie had been exposed at the time it was told, it might have at least caused some in Congress and the news media to soberly reevaluate the extent to which they were being skillfully manipulated to support military action. Public opinion was deeply divided on Bush's Gulf policy. As late as December 1990, a *New York Times/CBS News* poll indicated that 48 percent of the American people wanted Bush to wait before taking any action if Iraq failed to withdraw from Kuwait by Bush's January 15 deadline. [85] On January 12, the US Senate voted by a narrow, five-vote margin to support the Bush administration in a declaration of war. Given the narrowness of the vote, the babies-thrown-from-incubators story may have turned the tide in Bush's favor.

Following the war, human rights investigators attempted to confirm Nayirah's story and could find no witnesses or other evidence to support it. Amnesty International, which had fallen for the story, was forced to issue an embarrassing retraction. Nayirah herself was unavailable for comment. "This is the first allegation I've had that she was the ambassador's daughter," said Human Rights Caucus co-chair John Porter. "Yes, I think people . . . were entitled to know the source of her testimony." When journalists for the Canadian Broadcasting Corporation asked Nasir al-Sabah for permission to question Nayirah about her story, the ambassador angrily refused.[86]

Front-line Flacks

The military build-up in the Persian Gulf began by flying and shipping hundreds of thousands of US troops, armaments and supplies to staging areas in Saudi Arabia, yet another nation with no tolerance for a free press, democratic rights and most western customs. In a secret strategy memo, the Pentagon outlined a tightly-woven plan to constrain and control journalists. A massive babysitting operation would ensure that no truly independent or uncensored reporting reached back to the US public. "News media representatives will be escorted at all times," the memo stated. "Repeat, at all times."[87]

Deputy Secretary of Defense for Public Affairs Pete Williams served as the Pentagon's top flack for the Gulf War. Using the perennial PR strategy of "good cop/bad cop," the government of Saudi Arabia played the "heavy," denying visas and access to the US press, while Williams, the reporters' friend, appeared to intercede repeatedly on their behalf. This strategy kept news organizations competing with each other for favors from Williams, and kept them from questioning the fundamental fact that journalistic independence was impossible under military escort and censorship.

The overwhelming technological superiority of US forces won a decisive victory in the brief and brutal war known as Desert Storm. Afterwards, some in the media quietly admitted that they'd been manipulated to produce sanitized coverage which almost entirely ignored the war's human cost—today estimated at over 100,000 civilian deaths. The American public's single most lasting memory of the war will probably be the ridiculously successful video stunts supplied by the Pentagon showing robot "smart bombs" striking only their intended military targets, without much "collateral" (civilian) damage.

"Although influential media such as the *New York Times* and *Wall Street Journal* kept promoting the illusion of the 'clean war,' a different picture began to emerge after the US stopped carpet-bombing Iraq," note Lee and Solomon. "The pattern underscored what Napoleon meant when he said that it wasn't necessary to completely suppress the news; it was sufficient to delay the news until it no longer mattered." [88]

Mexican Standoff

For Hill & Knowlton, the Kuwaiti account was a sorely-needed cash cow, appearing at a time that the PR giant was suffering from low employee morale amid controversies surrounding some of its sleazier clients. When the Kuwaiti money dried up at the end of the war, Hill & Knowlton went into a precipitous decline. A series of layoffs and resignations at its Washington office, including a mass walkout of two dozen employees, reduced the staff from 250 to about 90. Clients began deserting the company, and rival PR firm Burson-Marsteller stepped in to take its place as the world's largest PR firm.

During the US debate over passage of the North American Free Trade Agreement (NAFTA), Burson-Marsteller spearheaded a PR campaign for the government of Mexico that, in dollar terms, made Hill & Knowlton's campaign for Kuwait look small by comparison. Mexican business interests and the country's ruling Institutional Revolutionary Party (PRI) spent over $50 million on PR and lobbying in the US alone to guarantee NAFTA's passage.[89] And these expenditures in turn were small change compared to the spending on spin control that went into the PRI's dubious victory in Mexico's 1994 elections. By the mid-1990s, advertising giant Young & Rubicam, Burson-Marsteller's parent corporation, was raking in yearly Mexican revenues of over $100 million. Analysts estimate that the PRI and its wealthy supporters spent well over $1 billion to win the 1994 elections, compared to only $3.6 million spent by its left-wing opposition. The money went not only to reel in voters, but also to reassure US and other foreign investors that 1994's elections were "clean and honest" in contrast to the blatant electoral frauds of the past, and that the investment climate in Mexico would remain "favorable"—i.e., low wages, access to prime markets, no environmental restrictions, and prompt payment on the national debt.

To judge from the party line that prevailed in the US press during the early 1990s, Mexico was in the midst of an impressive economic renaissance—seemingly proving the wisdom of the country's "free market" policies under president Carlos Salinas de Gortari. What the press missed, however, was the country's growing social inequality.

Since the inauguration of Salinas in 1988, Mexico's 200 most powerful families had exponentially increased their wealth, thanks to
lucrative government contracts, insider trading on Mexico's stock
market, and bargain-basement purchases of over 900 formerly state-
owned enterprises. This transfer of public wealth into private hands
created a country which in 1992 ranked fourth in the world in the
number of billionaires—including extremely influential behind-the-
scenes billionaire drug traffickers such as Carillo Fuentes with an estimated net worth of $25 billion. (By way of comparison, the world's
two "richest" men, according to *Forbes,* are William Gates, with $12.9
billion and Warren Buffett, with $10.7 billion.)[90]

While *"los ricos"* were growing richer, real wages for the majority of Mexicans plummeted in the 1980s and 1990s, and an increasing number of small farmers and Indians were forced to abandon
their subsistence landholdings. As social scientists and government
critics point out, this is the real reason why rebels calling themselves
the "Zapatista Army of National Liberation" rose up against the Mexican government on New Year's day, the day that NAFTA went into
effect. In the face of the Zapatista uprising, the facade of Mexico's
"economic miracle" crumbled almost instantly. A series of other incidents contributed to the country's collapsing image: A Catholic Car-
dinal was killed by drug traffickers in the Guadalajara airport,
apparently with collusion from police and government officials. Several billionaire businessmen were kidnapped for ransom of up to
$100 million. During the 1994 election campaign, an assassin killed
Donaldo Colosio, the PRI's candidate for president, and opinion polls
showed that the majority of the Mexican people believed the assassination was the work of the PRI itself. Later that summer, the head
of the PRI was assassinated as well, in what investigative reporters
said was an internal party feud. Responding to these events, foreign
investment slumped and the peso was devalued. The Mexican elite
began transferring billions of dollars out of the country.

Fix the Focus, Not the Problem

Through all these crises, Burson-Marsteller and other Mexican and
transnational PR firms demonstrated their effectiveness by working
behind the scenes—gauging public opinion, counseling government
and corporate leaders, shaping media coverage, and facilitating elite-
to-elite communications. The stakes were high. Currently, 66% of
Mexico's foreign investment comes from the US. To keep this money
flowing, along with sufficient international loans to prevent Mexico

from defaulting on its $150 billion foreign debt, investors demand guaranteed profits and political stability. Since real stability did not exist, Mexico's spin doctors worked to create the *image* of stability. As a Burson-Marsteller official in Mexico euphemistically put it, "our job is to build up the level of confidence of foreign investors, to spotlight the positive economic developments in the country."[91]

Burson-Marsteller's spin on the 1994 election was that the PRI— a notoriously corrupt institution which has used force and fraud to rule Mexico without interruption for nearly 70 years—had "reformed." This effort at spin control, targeted in particular at international investors, reached all the way into the Clinton White House. Nine days before the election, Burson-Marsteller client Santiago Oñate, representing the Mexican Office of the President, met with several of President Clinton's closest advisors, including Cabinet Chief Leon Panetta and National Security Council Director Anthony Lake. At the end of the meeting, Clinton's advisors reassured Oñate that the White House didn't believe that there was "any crisis in Mexico, but rather just the normal anxiety that represents the transition to a competitive democracy." Meanwhile, the Mexican Businessmen's Council, another B-M client, was reassuring US investors that the PRI would cleanly win the elections—just as the polls indicated—and that Mexico's investment climate would remain stable. Back in Mexico City another B-M client, the Secretary for Commerce and Industrial Development, worked to arrange a press conference featuring "Indian leaders" from Chiapas who denounced the Zapatista rebels as "violent radicals."[92]

The elections were held on August 21, and as expected, the PRI swept the field, gaining the presidency and retaining overwhelming control over the national legislature. The US government and international press described the elections as the "cleanest in Mexico's history," ignoring widespread evidence of voter fraud, registration manipulation, intimidation, bribery, illegal financial donations, partisan misuse of government resources, distorted media coverage, and misleading polling techniques. As in 1988, the PRI and government-appointed election officials refused to allow outside observers to compare computer tallies with the actual packets of marked ballots from the country's 90,000 voter precincts.[93]

In the aftermath of the elections and a massive collapse of Mexico's inflated economy, civil unrest intensified, with street demonstrations, riots, strikes, road blockades, seizures of city halls, and even armed conflicts. Leaders of the Zapatista guerrillas vowed to continue civil resistance until new, democratic elections are held under a National Constituent Assembly.

To re-establish "stability," the Mexican army has apparently adopted a strategy of "low-intensity conflict" reminiscent of the wars of attrition that decimated Central America during the 1980s. This strategy has been studied by Global Exchange, an international organization which sponsors frequent delegations to Chiapas, the poverty-stricken department in southern Mexico where the Zapatista rebels remain entrenched. In June 1995, a delegation to southeastern Chiapas observed "large-scale deployment of troops in the areas of conflict, the systematic destruction of the means of community-based self-sufficiency, the creation of divisions through selective rewards and punishments, and the gradual dismantling of independent bases of community organization," tactics which appear to be "governed by political, economic and psychological objectives."[94]

As the world moves toward the end of the twentieth century, it seems to have solved many of its image problems but few of its real ones. Foreign policy planners have developed a frightening sophistication in their ability to combine military strategies with propaganda and psychological manipulation, but they have failed to eliminate starvation, disease, economic exploitation and violence—the root causes of international conflict. During the 1980s and early 1990s, the United States seemingly won every war it waged, but the untamed uprising in Chiapas suggests that these wars may have been mere preliminary skirmishes in a broader war that we have been losing. The low-intensity conflicts in Nicaragua and El Salvador have given way to a new conflict in which the stakes are larger and the battles are closer to our own national borders. While US planners remain obsessed with images and oblivious to the real human needs of the poor, Latin America and the rest of the Third World will remain a hotbed of revolutionary ferment, fueled by the desperation of people for whom dying in battle appears preferable to dying of hunger. In a very real sense, the Third World War has already begun—but thanks to clever public relations, it simply hasn't been announced.

CHAPTER ELEVEN

All the News That's Fit to Print

It's to the point where Brit Hume, the ABC correspondent at the White House, plays tennis with George Bush. Tom Friedman of the *New York Times* is very close to Jim Baker. You find these relationships are so close that reporters don't challenge the subjects of their stories, they just tell you what the government is saying. In other words, they have become stenographers for power and not journalists.

JEFF COHEN
Executive Director, Fairness & Accuracy In Reporting (FAIR)

If popular culture is any guide at all to the imagination of the American people, there is something sacred about the news. Journalists, along with private detectives and police, seem to occupy a special place as the ministers of truth and wisdom in our society. The archetypal image for all three professions is the "little guy" with the common touch—picture Columbo, Lou Grant or Phil Marlowe—dressed in cheap clothes, cynical, smoking a cigar, fond of a drink at the local tavern, working odd hours, bothering people, persistent, smart beneath that rumpled exterior, piecing together clues, finding contradictions, relentless and inquisitive, refusing to let go of an investigation until the truth is exposed and the villains receive their just punishment. This image of the journalistic profession has been the backdrop for a number of popular plays, novels, films and television shows, including "Citizen Kane," "His Girl Friday," "Meet John Doe," "The Front Page," "The Paper" and "Murphy Brown." Of course mild-mannered reporter Clark Kent is the alter-ego of Superman, the ultimate comic-book hero, who spends much of his time rescuing fellow reporters Lois Lane and Jimmy Olsen when their journalistic curiosity gets them into trouble. Hollywood turned to real life in "All the President's Men," in which Robert Redford and Dustin Hoffman portray *Washington Post* reporters Bob Woodward and Carl Bernstein in their investigation of President Nixon's role in the Watergate scandal. The final scene of the movie visually dramatizes the power of the press when the camera zooms in on a clattering newsroom teletype as it prints out a sequence of bulletins from the Watergate affair, culminating in the terse headline: "NIXON RESIGNS."

Today—more than 20 years after Watergate—the saga of Woodward and Bernstein is related in high school textbooks as an example of the power of muckraking journalism. To perpetuate the mythology of the crusading press, many newspaper mastheads carry mottos such as Thomas Jefferson's statement that "the only security of all is a free press." Americans grow up believing that the free press, so cherished and constitutionally protected, is a fierce watchdog of the public interest, and that when societal or political wrongs are splashed across page one of the *New York Times* or aired on *60 Minutes*, our democratic system in some automatic way responds to right the wrongs.

But schoolbooks often fail to mention that Woodward and Bernstein were virtually alone in their dogged pursuit of the Watergate scandal, which occurred in the midst of a presidential election yet had absolutely no impact on the election outcome. According to Project Censored, a phone call from the Nixon White House was all it took to persuade CBS chair William Paley to scale back Walter Cronkite's attempt to do an extraordinary two-part series about Watergate on the *CBS Evening News* before the election. Nixon was re-elected by an overwhelming margin, and wasn't forced to resign until two years after the burglary. Even then, the real "heroes" include a still-unknown whistleblower dubbed "Deep Throat" and Nixon's own arrogance in leaving behind expletive-loaded tape recordings of his self-incriminating involvement in a cover-up. Even Woodward and Bernstein were never able to explain important aspects about the scandal, such as White House motivations behind the Watergate break-in, or Deep Throat's reasons for coming forward.

Hard Pressed

The romantic mythology surrounding the journalistic profession attracts many more would-be reporters than there are jobs available. In reality, as most working reporters readily admit, the profession is a far cry from its image. Reporters are notoriously underpaid and overworked. While researching this book, we encountered one reporter with a small-town daily paper who was earning an annual income of $13,000 in 1994 while working 60-hour weeks—less than he could have earned flipping hamburgers. Sitting below a poster of Rush Limbaugh which the newspaper management had mounted on the wall of his break room, the reporter described how the paper had ordered him and his fellow reporters to falsify time cards so it would appear they were only working 40 hours per week—thus enabling management to violate minimum-wage laws. We contacted a state labor official who assured us that if the reporter kept good records, he could document the fraud and force the paper to pay him for his uncompensated labor. The reporter, however, was afraid that he would be fired if he filed a complaint, and we were left wondering: Is someone who collaborates this easily with covering up his own exploitation even *capable* of investigating and exposing the larger wrongs in his community?

In a democracy, a free and independent press is counted upon to provide the information and opinions that fuel public debate, expose corruption, illuminate major social issues, and enable an informed citizenry to make participatory decisions. Today's reality, however, is ever more distant from this lofty ideal. Journalism is in fact in demise, and its collapse is opening ever more opportunities for PR practitioners to increase their influence in the news room.

To begin with, the media itself is a huge, profitable business, the domain of fewer and fewer giant transnational corporations. "Modern technology and American economics have quietly created a new kind of central authority over information," writes media critic Ben Bagdikian in *The Media Monopoly*, his landmark 1982 exposé. "By the 1980s, the majority of all major American media—newspapers, magazines, radio, television, books, and movies—were controlled by fifty giant corporations. These corporations were interlocked in common financial interest with other massive industries and with a few dominant international banks." Bagdikian concedes that "There are other media voices outside the control of the dominant fifty corporations," but "most are small and localized . . . their diminutive sounds tend to be drowned by the controlled thunder of half the media power of a great society."[1]

When Bagdikian updated his book in 1993, he was alarmed to find that during the ensuing decade media concentration had accelerated so that fewer than 20 giant corporations owned over half of all media. When we interviewed him in August 1995, he said the situation is "worsening so quickly and dramatically that it's hard now to even get a number to compare. Suddenly there are big new actors in the media business, super-giant corporations like Disney, Time-Warner, TCI cable TV, and telephone companies. The magnitude of the players is incredibly large. Increasingly corporate giants and super-giants are working together in joint ventures; for instance, Turner is partly owned by Time-Warner and TCI. Journalism, news and public information have been integrated formally into the highest levels of financial and non-journalistic corporate control. Conflicts of interest between the public's need for information and corporate desires for 'positive' information have vastly increased." [2]

"I generally agree with those who bemoan the decline of journalism for sensationalism and titillation," said Buck Donham, a former newspaper editor who has worked for papers in Arkansas and Hawaii. "I blame at least part of this decline on the trend of large corporations to buy up both major and minor news media. Back in the good old days, most medium or small newspapers were owned by families, some of whom lovingly passed along their publications to the next generation. I worked for one such newspaper, the *Arkansas Gazette,* which at the time was the oldest newspaper west of the Mississippi. The pay was atrocious, $85 a week in 1965, but the prestige of working for such a news organization more than made up for the small salary."

When corporations buy up a local paper, Donham says, standards usually decline:

> They practice what I call 'bottom-line journalism'—which means, to quote the late Don Reynolds, editorial material is the 'gray matter that fills up the space between the ads.' Here's how these corporations work: After buying up a small or medium-sized newspaper with much fanfare, the companies make a lot of noises about local editorial control, promising not to interfere with the editorial content of the publication. They frequently keep on the old editor. Slowly, however, they exert their control, and the editor usually leaves after six months to a year after purchase. They cut the newspaper's staff to the bare minimum it takes to put out the publication on a daily or weekly basis; . . . they stop reinvesting any of the profits in the product and instead ship all profits made back to corporate headquarters; they de-emphasize the news and emphasize advertising and circulation revenue.
>
> After about a year or so, you have an extremely streamlined operation. What remains of the editorial staff is humping so hard just to get the paper out, there is no time to do in-depth or investigative reporting. Needless to say, it makes for superficial journalism and news

by press release. If they don't quit, hard-pressed and bitter reporters resign themselves to covering the superficial and the easy, to relying on press releases or on breaking, easy-to-cover stories, such as the O.J. Simpson case. Reporters simply don't have the time, and after a while, the inclination to do anything in depth.[3]

This environment may be demoralizing to journalists, but it offers a veritable hog's heaven to the public relations industry. In their 1985 book, *PR: How the Public Relations Industry Writes the News,* authors Jeff & Marie Blyskal write that "PR people know how the press thinks. Thus they are able to tailor their publicity so that journalists will listen and cover it. As a result much of the news you read in newspapers and magazine or watch on television and hear on radio is heavily influenced and slanted by public relations people. Whole sections of the news are virtually owned by PR. . . . Newspaper food pages are a PR man's paradise, as are the entertainment, automotive, real estate, home improvement and living sections. . . . Unfortunately 'news' hatched by a PR person and journalist working together looks much like real news dug up by enterprising journalists working independently. The public thus does not know which news stories and journalists are playing servant to PR."[4]

Today the number of PR flacks in the United States outnumbers working journalists, and the gap is widening. A working reporter is deluged daily with dozens if not hundreds of phone calls, letters, faxes and now e-mailed press releases. Pam Berns, the publisher of *Chicago Life* magazine, estimates that her office receives at least 100 PR contacts each and every day. "It's annoying and overwhelming," says Berns.[5]

PR Newswire claims to be "the world's acknowledged leader in the distribution of corporate, association and institutional information to the media and the financial community" for forty years. The firm has 19 offices in the US and distributes some 100,000 news releases a year to some 2,000 newsrooms for more than 15,000 clients. Other PR distribution services specialize in placing stories in newspapers through the mass distribution of PR-written feature articles and opinion pieces which are simply picked up as "real" news.[6] The North American Precis Syndicate, for example, sends camera-ready stories on behalf of most of the top PR firms and most Fortune 500 companies to 10,000 newspapers, almost all of whom reprint some of the material. The stories are designed to promote products, or serve clients' political agendas. "Lobbyists love it," claims NAPS' promotional material. "You generate tons of letters to legislators."[7]

A similar business, RadioUSA, "supplies broadcast quality news scripts to 5,000 radio stations throughout the country. . . . We'll write, typeset, print and distribute broadcast quality scripts . . . We give you usage reports based on station verifications." Hard-pressed radio journalists greet these canned scripts with relief rather than suspicion. "When your job is to come up with hundreds of story ideas every month, RadioUSA helps," says Suzan Vaughn, news director at KVEC in San Luis Obispo, California. Max Kolbe, the news director at KKIN in Aitkin, MN, describes RadioUSA as "a lifesaver on a slow news day."[8]

Even the media itself is getting into the PR distribution act. The Associated Press now makes money distributing electronically digitized PR photos to over 400 newspapers that have agreed to receive them. On June 24, 1994, for example, the *New York Times* ran a prominent article announcing that Federal Express had formally changed its name to "FedEx"—not exactly an earth-shattering exposé. In fact, the story resulted from a PR campaign by FedEx. A photo accompanying the story showed a FedEx jet, and the photo credit simply read "Associated Press." Actually, Federal Express *paid* AP to electronically distribute the PR photo, which was staged and taken by the Federal Express company rather than an AP photographer.[9]

Is It Real Or Is It Memorex?

The use of radio and video news releases is a little-known practice which took hold during the 1980s, when PR firms discovered that they could film, edit and produce their own news segments—even entire programs—and that broadcasters would play the segments as "news," often with no editing. When Gray & Company began producing a radio program for its clients called "Washington Spotlight," the Mutual Radio Network came to Gray and *asked* to carry it. "PR firms would not send out packaged radio and television stories if no one was using them," notes author Susan Trento. "Not only technology, but economics made things easier for PR firms in the 1980s."

Video news releases, known as VNRs, typically come packaged with two versions of the story the PR firm is trying to promote. The first version is fully edited, with voiceovers already included or with a script indicating where the station's local news anchor should read his or her lines. The second version is known as "B-roll," and consists of the raw footage that was used to produce the fully-edited version. The receiving station can edit the B-roll footage itself, or combine it with other footage received from other sources. "There are two economics at work here on the television side," explains a Gray & Company executive. "The big stations don't want prepackaged, pretaped. They have the money, the budget, and the manpower to put their own together. But the smaller stations across the country lap up stuff like this."[10]

MediaLink, a PR firm that distributed about half of the 4,000 VNRs made available to newscasters in 1991, conducted a survey of 92 newsrooms and found that all 92 used VNRs supplied free by PR firms and subtly slanted to sell a clients' products and ideas while appearing to be "real" TV news. On June 13, 1991, for example, the *CBS Evening News* ran a segment on the hazards of automatic safety belts. According to David Lieberman, author of a 1992 article titled "Fake News," the safety belt tape "was part of a 'video news release' created by . . . a lobby group largely supported by lawyers."[11]

"VNRs are as much a public relations fixture as the print news release," stated George Glazer, a senior vice-president of Hill & Knowlton. "In fact, many public relations firms are well into the second generation of VNR technology. We use satellite transmissions from our own facilities almost on a daily basis, and wait eagerly for fiber optics systems to allow us to dial into nationwide networks. . . . With few exceptions, broadcasters as a group have refused to participate in any kinds of standards establishment for VNRs, in part because they rarely will admit to using them on the air. . . . There are truly hundreds of examples of self-denial on the part of broadcasters when it comes to admitting that VNRs are used." Following a beverage-tampering scare on the West Coast, for example, a VNR was mailed out to all three TV stations in the first city to report the problem. All three stations used the VNR in at least one newscast the following day, along with five other stations in the region. When asked later, however, all three stations denied that they had broadcast the material.[12]

In 1985, Trento reports, Gray & Company distributed a VNR featuring a canned interview with one of its clients, the ruthless King Hassan II of Morocco. The segment's airing on CNN provoked a scandal with reporters claiming they had been tricked into airing paid propaganda. An executive at Gray & Company scoffed at the media's hypocrisy: "I used to read in *Broadcasting* the cache of letters from news directors after the story broke about electronic news releases saying, 'How despicable. Never in a thousand years!' And they were people I had talked to who had called me back so that they had the right coordinates on the satellite so that they could take the feed.

They knew exactly who we were. They called us all the time. They asked us for stuff. They told us they couldn't get it. They forgot to turn their downlink on, and could we send them a hard copy FedEx overnight because they'd use it tomorrow night."

"I was personally aggrieved at all this sort of self-righteousness of the media when that story broke," said another Gray & Company executive. "They are free to use it. Not use it. Use it for B-roll. Write their own scripts. Most of them take it straight off the air and broadcast it. Rip and read. Rip and read." [13]

Watching the Detectives

In theory, journalism is a "watchdog" profession, which serves the public by finding and reporting on abuses of power. In practice, reporters live under closer scrutiny than the people they are supposed to be monitoring.

Former *Wall Street Journal* reporter Dean Rotbart has carved a niche for himself within the PR industry by compiling dossiers on his former colleagues so that his corporate clients know how to manipulate individual members of the media. Rotbart's firm—called TJFR Products and Services—publishes this information in high-priced newsletters and delivers customized workshops and reports.

Rotbart told a 1993 meeting of the Public Relations Society of America that his workshops and newsletters help PR professionals know "what a journalist is thinking. . . . One of the services we provide is taking biographies of reporters from all over the country—something like 6,000 bios—in our computer system, and if at any point you get a call from a journalist and don't know who it is, call up and we will fax you that bio within an hour." [14]

These bios are a regular feature in a new Rotbart publication, the *TJFR Environmental News Reporter*. Promotional literature boasts that this $395-a-year PR resource is "tailored to serve the needs of communications professionals who deal with environmental issues. . . . Let us be your eyes and ears when the environmental media convene. . . . Gather vital information on key journalists . . . Who's the boss? . . . How do you break the ice? . . . Not only will you find news on journalists, we'll tell you what they want from you and what strategies you can employ with them to generate more positive stories and better manage potentially negative situations." [15]

The premier issue of Rotbart's newsletter includes a long piece on CNN's Environment Unit, with biographies of all its top staff. It explains, for example, that Peter Dykstra worked for Greenpeace for 11 years and attended Boston University's College of Communi-cations. The issue also contains an interview with Emilia Askari of the *Detroit Free Press*. The accompanying bio explains that Askari is president of the Society of Environmental Journalists and "enjoys all kinds of outdoor activities and tutors illiterate adults with Literacy Volunteers of America." In addition to this information, the story tells PR managers whom to contact if they want to complain about some-thing that Askari writes: "Chain of command: Reports to Bob Camp-bell, assistant city editor."[16]

Some PR firms specialize in tracking specific issues and compil-ing reports on the journalists writing stories. Rowan & Blewitt, a Washington, DC, PR firm, conducted in depth analyses for the dairy industry, analyzing media coverage of the rBGH issue to "help answer these questions: Has the coverage been sensational-istic. . . . Has the coverage favored the anti-[rBGH] views? . . . How does the coverage of [rBGH] compare with the volume of coverage on Alar? Air emissions? . . . Alaskan oil spills?" Detailed charts and graphs examined virtually every story on rBGH over an extended period of time.[17] Another media monitoring firm, CARMA Interna-tional, also worked on the rBGH account and ranked individual reporters based on whether their stories were "favorable" or "unfa-vorable" to rBGH.[18]

The February 1995 issue of the newsletter *Environment Writer* reports on another PR effort to get inside the heads of journalists—laboratory research using 12 real journalists as paid guinea pigs to help develop a PR strategy for DuPont pesticides. DuPont flacks recruited participants by sending an invitation to "selected members of the media," which promised: "This learning endeavor will be used to help DuPont establish new policies regarding pesticides: their use and information important to consumers, the government, farmers and the press. . . . Your ethics as a journalist (and that of your news organization) will not be violated or jeopardized in any way. . . . The goal is to make better pesticide policies."[19]

One participant who asked not to be named said, "They would give us small pieces of paper which would say something like, 'DuPont makes very wonderful chemicals, and no one needs to worry.'" Journalists were then told to develop a storyline based on the information on the slip of paper, while DuPont researchers observed from behind a mirrored window. When their work was done the reporters were handed envelopes that contained $250 cash. "I came out of there and I felt really disgusted that I had to earn money in this kind of way," said one journalist who participated in the study.[20]

PR firms also hire real journalists to participate in training sessions so flacks can hone their skills in handling media situations. In *Sierra Magazine,* reporter Dashka Slater describes her experience working for Robert J. Meyers and Associates, a Houston-based consulting firm that hired her and two other journalists to help ARCO Petroleum practice its PR plan for handling the news media following environmental disasters. In a staged run-through of an oil spill, Slater and the other reporters were assigned to play the part of the "predatory press." Professional actors were brought in to play the part of environmentalists. ARCO employees and government officials played themselves. "The drills give company flacks the opportunity to practice varnishing the truth just in case the mop-up doesn't go as planned," wrote Slater. "Mostly the company and government spokespeople did what they had learned to do in numerous media-training workshops: convey as little information as possible in as many words as possible." In the past 6 years Meyers and Associates have conducted more than 400 such training drills.[21]

A number of firms offer clipping and database services used to monitor the media. For a fee of $1,000 per month, for example, organizations can subscribe to NEXIS/LEXIS, which contains the full text of media stories appearing in a wide range of newspapers, magazines, newsletters and TV and radio programs. A skilled researcher can search for mention of a specific word and obtain articles from hundreds of publications. Clipping services are also available which charge a reading fee to provide virtually instant reports on stories appearing in the media which relate to clients' interest.

To monitor TV coverage, for example, Video Monitoring Services advertises that it "records all news and public affairs programs on local TV stations in more than 130 markets, local radio stations in 14 markets and national broadcast TV, cable TV and radio networks." VMS also monitors stories in more than 20 countries including Australia, Canada, Germany, Israel and Japan. The company notifies its clients immediately which stories it has snagged off the airwaves that correspond to a list of "keywords" the client has provided. The keywords can be "executives, company names, brand names, events, general or specific topics, etc." Such intelligence can assist PR firms in identifying sympathetic or cooperative reporters and editors, pressuring or punishing reporters who file unsympathetic stories, and measuring the impact of coverage upon public opinion.[22]

Careful overnight telephone surveys can also help a corporation decide how, or even whether, to respond to a breaking story on a news program like *60 Minutes*. Before such instant surveys were available, a corporation exposed on national TV for crimes or corruption might feel compelled to immediately hold a news conference. Today, if overnight polling shows that the *60 Minutes* exposé had little impact on viewers, PR consultants advise their clients to simply ignore the report rather than risk drawing attention to it. Surveys can also reveal strategic approaches to crafting a response— perhaps the polling shows some sympathy for the corporation or other opinions that can be exploited in a carefully designed response the next day.

Experts Agree

The advertising industry learned years ago that one of the best ways to influence an audience is to put its message in the mouth of a publicly-trusted expert such as a scientist, doctor or university professor. A whole genre of TV commercials has evolved featuring actors dressed in white laboratory coats who announce that "research proves" their brand is the best product on the market. The PR industry has also mastered the art of using "third party" experts, a ruse which almost never fails to hoodwink supposedly cynical reporters.

Via the internet, for example, public relations representatives "assist" the news media through an on-line service called Profnet, based at the State University of New York in Stony Brook. Journalists in search of information are invited to simply e-mail their request to Profnet, which distributes it to over 800 PR representatives of research institutions in 16 countries. The flacks then find professors or researchers to answer the questions. Needless to say, this "free" information helps shape the spin of the story in a direction the PR representative is trying to promote.[23]

Corporations also fund "nonprofit research institutes" which provide "third party experts" to advocate on their behalf. The American Council on Science and Health (ACSH), for example, is a commonly-used industry front group that produces PR ammunition for the food processing and chemical industries. Headed by Elizabeth Whelan, ACSH routinely represents itself as an "independent," "objective" science institute. This claim was dissected by Howard Kurtz of the *Washington Post* in the March 1990 *Columbia Journalism Review,* which studied the special interests that fund ACSH. Kurtz reported that Whelan praises the nutritional virtues of fast food and receives money from Burger King. She downplays the link between a high fat diet and heart disease, while receiving funding from Oscar Mayer, Frito Lay and Land O'Lakes. She defends saccharin and receives money from Coca-Cola, Pepsi, NutraSweet and the National Soft Drink Association. Whelan attacks a Nebraska businessman's crusade against fatty tropical oils—the unhealthy oils in movie popcorn—while she is in the pay of palm oil special interests. "There has never been a case of ill health linked to the regulated, approved use of pesticides in this country," she claims, while taking money from a host of pesticide makers. And Whelan speaks harshly of mainstream environmentalists, such as the Natural Resources Defense Council. Speaking to the *Bangor Daily News,* Whelan described the NRDC as an "ideologically fueled project" whose "target is the free-enterprise, corporate America system. I think they hate the word 'profit' and they'll do anything that will involve corporate confrontation." [24]

Whelan defends her "scientific" views by saying that her findings have undergone "peer review" by experts among the scientists affiliated with her group. But Michael Jacobson of the Center for Science in the Public Interest dismisses the bona fides of such "peer review" scientists: "They don't exactly publish in leading scientific journals. They publish pamphlets that are reviewed by their professional cronies of the regulated industries. It's science that's forced through a sieve of conservative philosophy."

Journalists rarely check the background of sources, so Whelan and the American Council on Science and Health are often quoted in the news as "scientific experts." For example, in a show hosted by Walter Cronkite titled "Big Fears, Little Risks," Cronkite introduced Whelan as one of "a growing number of scientists who fear that overstating the risk of environmental chemicals is actually threatening the health of Americans." In *Fortune* magazine, Whelan appeared as the source in a story by Ann Reilly Dowd which stated, "A big part of the problem is that America's environmental policy making has increasingly been driven more by media hype and partisan politics than by sensible science. . . . Despite the waves of panic that roll over America each year, some 500 scientists surveyed by the American Council on Science and Health have concluded that the threat to life from environmental hazards is negligible." Neither Cronkite nor Dowd explained that the ACSH is an industry front group.[25]

Rhys Roth of the Northwest Atmosphere Protection Coalition continually goes up against industry "science" as he tries to raise public concern about the greenhouse effect and ozone depletion. Roth says scientists like Whelan—who speaks of the "*allegedly* depleting ozone layer"—are "atmosphere confusionists" who achieve their goal by "simply sowing enough confusion in the minds of Americans about the science behind the greenhouse effect to defuse our collective concern and outrage, rendering us politically mute."[26]

The Truth About Tumors

Whelan and other "experts" use creative manipulation of statistics to obscure the rising rate of cancer in industrialized nations. "We also know there is no cancer epidemic," she says. "Most cancer rates have been constant for decades. . . . What a marvelous time to live, and to be born! We are giving ourselves and our children the gift of better and longer lives."

This claim was repeated by David Shaw of the *Los Angeles Times* in a series of articles examining environmental health risks. Shaw took his information from Resources for the Future (RFF), a pro-industry group that he described as a "think tank that specializes in environmental issues." Shaw quoted RFF vice-president Paul Portney: "If everything is as harmful as we're told, how come we're healthier and living longer . . . than ever before?" Shaw also turned to the National Cancer Institute, a government agency with close ties to the chemical and pharmaceutical industry. According to the Institute, "the age-adjusted mortality rate for all cancers combined except lung cancer has been declining since 1950, except for those 85 and over."[27]

These statistics, however, paint a misleading picture. Research by Samuel Epstein at the University of Illinois School of Public Health, published in the *American Journal of Industrial Medicine,* shows that the incidence of all types of cancer, excluding lung cancer, rose by 29.1 percent during the period from 1950 to 1988. Contrary to the National Cancer Institute's claims, the British medical journal *Lancet* reported in 1990 that the death rate from brain and other central nervous system cancers, breast cancer, multiple myeloma, kidney cancer, non-Hodgkin's lymphoma, and melanoma has been increasing over the past 20 years in persons age 55 and older in the US and five other industrialized nations.[28]

Improved medical care, *not* a decline in cancer rates, has kept cancer mortality rates from jumping dramatically. "The extent to which mortality rates can obscure trends in the incidence of cancer is clearly and tragically demonstrated by childhood cancer statistics," states author David Steinman. According to the National Cancer Institute, deaths from childhood cancers decreased between 1973 and

1987. Yet between 1950 and 1988, the *incidence* of childhood cancers among whites increased 21.3 percent.[29]

Notwithstanding the comforting assurances from industry front groups, most independent scientists recognize that cancer rates are increasing and that industrial chemicals play a critical role in this increase. The National Cancer Institute itself recognizes asbestos, benzene, arsenic, aromatic amines, coal tars, vinyl chloride, chromium and wood dust as carcinogens.[30] A growing body of scientific evidence links pesticides to escalating rates of certain kinds of cancer in farmers.[31] "We are just beginning to understand the full range of health effects resulting from the exposure to occupational and environmental agents and factors," admits a recent NCI report. "Lack of appreciation of the potential hazards of environmental and food source contaminants, and laws, policies and regulations protecting and promoting tobacco use, worsen the cancer problem and drive up health care costs."[32]

Revolving Doors

Media critics note that the media habitually fails to report on itself; it also fails to report on the PR industry. To do so would reveal the extent of its dependency on PR for access, sources, quotes, stories and ideas. According to authors Jeff and Marie Blyskal, "the press has grown frighteningly dependent on public relations people. Outsiders—the reading and viewing public—would have a hard time discovering this on their own because the dependence on PR is part of behind-the-scenes press functioning. . . . Meanwhile, like an alcoholic who can't believe he has a drinking problem, members of the press are too close to their own addiction to PR to realize there is anything wrong. In fact, the press which has a seemingly inborn cynical, arrogant, down-the-nose view of public relations, seems sadly self-deceptive about the true press/PR relationship."[33]

Canned news and industry-supplied "experts" are effective because they appeal to budget-conscious news organizations. When a TV news show airs a video news release, the PR firm that produced the segment pays for all the costs of scripting, filming and editing. Likewise, PR-supplied experts enable reporters to produce authentic-sounding stories with a minimum of time and effort. The public rarely notices the self-serving bias that creeps into the news along with these subtle subsidies.

Sometimes the financial pressures that influence the news are more direct. In Canada, PR giant Burson-Marsteller's work for the

British Columbia timber industry became the subject of investigation by Ben Parfitt, forestry reporter for the daily *Vancouver Sun.* In 1991, however, Burson-Marsteller picked up the *Sun* as a client, and editorial policy shifted. Before Burson-Marsteller went to work for the *Sun,* the paper employed five full-time reporters to cover forestry, fisheries, native affairs, energy and mines, and environment. Today only the environment position remains, and the reporter on that beat has been instructed to cover environmental issues in Greater Vancouver and the lower mainland, an area which is conveniently distant from the Clayoquot Sound, where Burson-Marsteller is helping fell one of the last large areas of intact coastal temperate rainforest in the world.[34]

Parfitt sold an article to another publication, *The Georgia Straight,* that discussed Burson-Marsteller's past history, such as the company's PR work to clean up Argentina's international image at a time when the Argentinean military was murdering thousands of political dissidents. Parfitt also reported that Ken Rietz, a senior Burson-Marsteller employee and timber industry consultant, was a key Watergate conspirator. Following the publication of Parfitt's article, the *Sun* pulled him from the forest beat. "My personal experience in trying to cut through Burson-Marsteller was not greeted with favor by the paper," he says.[35]

Corporate advertisers have enormous power to influence news coverage, despite editors' statements to the contrary. Large corporations pump $100 billion per year in advertising dollars into the coffers of the US media alone. Ben Bagdikian points out that "selecting news in order to make advertising more effective is becoming so common that it has achieved the status of scientific precision and publishing wisdom." PR executive Robert Dilenschneider admits that "the notion that business and editorial decisions in the press and media are totally separate is largely a myth."[36]

Mergers, buyouts and new electronic technologies are all hastening the crumbling of walls that supposedly separate news reporting, advertising, and PR. Two of the biggest global PR firms, Burson-Marsteller and Hill & Knowlton, are owned by two of the biggest advertising conglomerates, respectively Young & Rubicam and the WPP Group. These two PR/advertising giants purchase billions of dollars of media print space, TV and radio time. Their clients include Philip Morris, McDonald's, Ford Motor Company, Johnson & Johnson, AT&T, Pepsi, Coca-Cola, NutraSweet, Revlon, Reebok, and hundreds of other major advertisers.

In 1992 the nonprofit Center for the Study of Commercialism invited some 200 journalists to a Washington, DC, news conference where the Center released a report titled *Dictating Content: How Advertising Pressure Can Corrupt a Free Press*. The scholarly report documented dozens of instances of media self-censorship "imposed by advertisers and advertising-related pressures." Almost none of the invited journalists came to the news conference, and the report was virtually ignored in the news, prompting "Project Censored," a media watchdog project of Sonoma State College, to name *Dictating Content* as one of the ten "best censored" stories of 1992.[37]

Corporations have found that one good way to curry favors with the media is to court individual journalists who have become media celebrities, offering them large sums of money for a brief appearance and talk. During the 1993–94 debate over health care reform, the *National Journal* reported that drug companies and trade associations were "practically throwing money at journalists to get them to speak at their events." Media figures including Fred Barnes of the *New Republic*, Eleanor Clift and Jane Bryant Quinn of *Newsweek*, Dr. Bob Arnot of CBS and Dr. Art Ulene of ABC collected speaking fees ranging from $7,500 to $25,000.[38] More recently, the *Political Finance & Lobby Reporter* noted in June 1995 that "*ABC News'* Cokie Roberts accepted a $35,000 fee for a speech last May to the Junior League of Greater Fort Lauderdale that was subsidized by JM Family Enterprises, a privately-held $4.2 billion company that distributes Toyotas. . . . Roberts refused to discuss her speaking fee. 'She feels strongly that it's not something that in any way, shape or form should be discussed in public,' ABC spokeswoman Eileen Murphy said when *American Journalism Review* reporter Alicia Shephard requested an interview."[39]

Most reporters, of course, never achieve the celebrity status that enables them to cash in on the speaking circuit. Corporate conglomeration and "downsizing" has brought hard times to the newsroom. Many journalists find themselves forced out of their chosen profession when they enter their thirties and find it difficult to support a family, save for retirement and fund college for the kids on a reporter's limited salary. They see former schoolmates and colleagues leaving journalism to earn more money in public relations, and the original dream of becoming another Woodward or Bernstein begins to look naïve and ridiculous. "The revolving door also contributes to the blurred reality projected by the powerhouse PR firms," writes Vermont newspaper reporter John Dillon. "This door not only spins between the government and lobbies but between the press corps and the PR firms. Like Capitol Hill aides who trade in their access and expertise for a lobbyist's salary, burned-out or broke reporters can be tempted by the greener and more lucrative pastures offered by PR companies."[40]

According to author Susan Trento, this revolving door—and the collaboration it fosters among elite groups in Washington—account for much of the gridlock in America's political process. "Nothing seems to change. Nothing seems to get done. Nothing seems to get cleaned up. From Watergate to Koreagate to Debategate to the HUD scandals to BCCI, it seems that the same people are doing the same things over and over, and never getting punished—and no one seems to care. The triangle—the media, the government, and the lobbying and PR firms—protect each other."[41]

The Information Superhypeway

The news media is presently undergoing a technological transformation as the "information superhighway" enters the mainstream of American culture. Its backbone, the internet, began as a military communications system and evolved into an inexpensive, government-subsidized mélange of arcane computerese and loosely-organized data on obscure academic topics ranging from bee migration patterns in Brazil to verb valence structures in Old Saxon. As computer technology brings a user-friendlier version of the internet to a wider spectrum of users, it has become an object of intense corporate interest.

Hyped as the ultimate in "electronic democracy," the information superhighway will supposedly offer "a global cornucopia of programming" offering instant, inexpensive access to nearly infinite libraries of data, educational material and entertainment. In some circles, the hype surrounding the information age has reached evangelical proportions, as its enthusiasts predict a revolutionary new utopian era in which the "the technologies of communication will serve to enlarge human freedom everywhere, to create inevitably a counsel of the people."[42]

Other observers see darker possibilities on the horizon, and point out that similar hype surrounded the introduction of older media technologies such as the telephone, radio and television. Given that a handful of corporations now control most media, media historian Robert McChesney writes that it is "no surprise that the private sector, with its immense resources, has seized the initiative and is commercializing cyberspace at a spectacular rate—effectively transforming it into a giant shopping mall." He predicts "a flurry of competition followed by the establishment of a stable oligopoly dominated by a handful of enormous firms . . . a world of information haves and have-nots, thereby exacerbating our society's already considerable social and economic inequality."[43]

PR firms are jumping on the online bandwagon, establishing "world wide web" sites and using surveys and games to gather marketing and opinion information about the users of cyberspace, and developing new techniques to target and reach reporters and other online users.

The information superhighway is only one of the technologies enabling PR firms to "reach audiences more directly and efficiently than ever before," writes Kirk Hallahan in the Summer 1994 *Public Relations Quarterly.* "Today, with many more options available, PR professionals are much less dependent upon mass media for publicity. . . . In the decade ahead, the largest American corporations could underwrite entire, sponsored channels. Organizations such as Procter & Gamble might circumvent public media altogether and subsidize programming that combines promotional and otherwise conducive messages—news, talk shows, infomercials, or sponsored entertainment or sports. . . . Shows such as 'Entertainment Tonight' stand to become the prototype for programming of tomorrow, in which the source doubles as the deliverer of the message. . . . Channel sponsors will be able to reach coveted super-heavy users . . . with a highly tailored message over which they exert complete control."

Ironically, Hallahan worries that the growing interpenetration of news and advertising is "troublesome" because it weakens the credibility of the traditional news media. "Every time that a newspaper produces an advertorial section that offers free puff pieces to advertisers," he writes, "and every time that a television station presents an infomercial in the guise of programming . . . media organizations cheapen the value of their product. . . . When a news medium covered a story in the past, the information sponsor gained more than mere exposure. The client, product or cause gained salience, stature and legitimacy." That legitimacy will be lost, he warns, if the public ceases to see a difference between news and paid propaganda. "While PR people might circumvent the press occasionally, we aren't going to want to do so all the time," Hallahan writes. "We can't kill the goose that laid the golden egg. A loss of public reliance upon and confidence in the mass media could be devastating."[44]

CHAPTER TWELVE

Taking Back
Your Own Back Yard

The twentieth century has been characterized by three developments
of great political importance: the growth of democracy, the growth
of corporate power, and the growth of corporate propaganda as a
means of protecting corporate power against democracy.

ALEX CAREY
Taking the Risk Out of Democracy

According to PR executive Pamela Whitney, "the key to winning
anything is opposition research." At a PR seminar in December 1994,
she illustrated the point by describing her company's undercover
work for a corporate client who manufactures automobile antifreeze.

Common antifreeze is made of ethylene glycol, whose sweet taste
and smell belies its highly poisonous nature. As little as two tea-
spoons of antifreeze can cause death or blindness, and every year
it claims the lives of children and pets who drink it by accident. In
Europe, antifreeze makers poison-proof their products by adding
"bitterant"—denatonium benzoate, listed in the *Guinness Book of
World Records* as the most bitter substance ever discovered. Adding
it to antifreeze at a price of two cents per gallon will make it taste
so vile that children almost always spit it out the instant it enters
their mouths.

In the United States, however, Whitney's company—National
Grassroots and Communications, Inc.—was hired to discredit an
organization pushing for legislation to require bitterant in antifreeze.
"We set up an operation where we posed as representatives of the

estate of an older lady who had died and wanted to leave quite a bit of money to an organization that helped both children and animals," Whitney said. "We went in and met with this organization and said, 'We want to bequeath a hundred thousand dollars to an organization; you're one of three that we are targeting to look at. Give us all of your financial records. Give us all of your [tax exemption records], give us all of your game plan for the following year, and the states you want to target and how you expect to win. We'll get back to you.' "[1]

Whitney grinned as she boasted, "We got this information and found out she had let her [tax exempt] IRS standing lapse, which put her in not very good standing. Also, we found out that her money came from—surprise, surprise—the companies that make bitterants. Without leaving any fingerprints or any traces we then got word through the local media and killed the bill in all the states."[2]

Whitney told this story before a crowded roomful of PR professionals. It drew no reaction from the rest of the audience, but it shocked *us*. Although Whitney didn't mention the name of the organization she had spied on, we decided to see if we could track it down. A computer search of news articles led us to the "organization," which in reality was just one woman, an Oregon housewife named Lynn Tylczak who said she had started her "Poison Proof Project" after watching a public television documentary that described the use of denatonium benzoate in England, where it was discovered 20 years ago.

Tylczak laughed incredulously when we told her the story we had heard from Pamela Whitney. "She's got a very foolish client," Tylczak snorted. "Her story has got more bullshit than a cattle ranch."

Tylczak said she was suspicious the moment Whitney's spy called claiming that he represented a Texas-based foundation called the "Citadel Trust." In fact, the sting operation "was done so ineptly that I called both Texas and Oregon state officials. . . . After talking to them, I sent her 'trust' a bogus gameplan/budget that hopefully convinced her client to waste lots of time and money."

Contrary to Whitney's claim that her PR firm "killed the bill in all the states" where it was introduced, Tylczak pointed out that a law requiring bitterant in antifreeze was passed by the Oregon state legislature in 1991, and went into effect in May of 1995. "Aside from me, there hasn't been anyone really pushing the issue, so I don't know what she's talking about when she says it was up for passage in other states," Tylczak said. "My goal was to get it passed first in

Oregon and get the kinks worked out here before taking it to other states, and that has happened."

And Tylczak took particular offense at Whitney's claim that her money came from the manufacturers of bitterant. "I volunteered the last six years of my life hoping to prevent serious childhood poisonings," she said. "I spent $50,000 of our family savings on my cause; the 'bitterant manufacturers' she cites donated exactly $100 worth of photocopies and stamps, total. Another interested party donated the legal costs of starting a tax-exempt nonprofit, but I never used it; never organized members, never collected dues, never solicited contributions, never had a paid staff. . . . Did Ms. Whitney know this? She should have. Her client deposed me and subpoenaed all of my personal and financial records almost six months before she gave her speech. Ironically, the only money I have ever received for my efforts was from the antifreeze companies in the form of a deposition fee and settlement. I donated all of this money to a charitable organization; I have not and will not profit from the poisoning of innocent children. I continue to work, unpaid, on their behalf."

You Say You Want a Revolution . . .

Lynn Tylczak is only one example of the new breed of grassroots activists who scare the hell out of corporate America. Most commit to a cause after some personal experience drives them to become involved. Typically they act as individuals or as small groups of citizens who have come together to address a local, immediate threat to their lives, cities and neighborhoods. They are often treated with contempt by the professional environmentalists, health advocates and other public-interest organizations headquartered in Washington, DC. Many times they lack organizing expertise and money. They don't have budgets or polished grant proposals needed to obtain funding from foundations and major donors. But corporations and the US government are spending tens of millions of dollars on PR and lobbying to fight these local community activists whom they derisively label "NIMBYs"—the abbreviation for "Not In My Back Yard."

David Steinman, whose book about pesticide contamination of foods became the target of the stealth PR campaign we describe in Chapter 1, became concerned about what was happening in *his* back yard after discovering that his own body was contaminated with abnormal levels of harmful chemicals.

Our chapter about the nuclear industry originated with Judy Treichel, a woman who lives in Las Vegas, Nevada, and has fought for years to stop nuclear waste from being stored in *her* back yard. Vegas flack Don Williams, who calls his hired pro-nuke PR campaign the "Keep 'em Honest Coalition," refers to Treichel as a "propagandist" and "dedicated nuke-hater" who "has spent much of her adult life screeching that nuke testing should be banned because it is so terrible." When *we* spoke with Judy Treichel, she didn't screech at all. She simply answered our request for information with a well-researched packet of documents that she has spent years tirelessly collecting.

No national environmental group is fighting the dumping of sewage sludge onto farmland, or exposing the risks inherent in the "biosolids" scam. Rural families, whose health or property has been damaged by toxic sludge, are heroes for spending their own time and money while enduring personal attacks from government and corporate PR flacks. Forget the EPA—they're in bed with the sludge industry. The public interest is better served by citizen activists like Jane Beswick of Turlock, California; Jim Bynum of Laredo, Texas; and Linda Zander of Lynden, Washington.

In our own back yard—Madison, Wisconsin—we've seen plenty of inspiring stories of citizen activists—human beings with normal flaws and foibles who have risen to accomplish extraordinary things. Several decades ago, a fourth-generation Wisconsin dairy farmer named John Kinsman was sick and getting sicker. His frustrated doctor suggested that perhaps his problem was toxic poisoning. Kinsman stopped using pesticides and switched to older and proven organic growing methods. His health returned, and his farm grew more profitable as he eliminated the cost of chemicals. He began questioning the ways that commercial and political interests were exploiting farmers. In 1985, Kinsman discovered that Monsanto and other companies were injecting genetically-engineered growth hormone into cows to make them produce more milk. He began picketing the University of Wisconsin to inform students that their favorite campus ice cream was made from hormone test milk. This small protest launched an international struggle which is still ongoing to protect the rights of farmers and consumers.

Nor has Madison's locally-led activism been limited to local issues. During the 1980s, Wisconsin's longstanding "sister state" relationship with Nicaragua evolved into a "municipal foreign policy" that challenged the federal government's war policy in Central America. Over 100 cities around the country followed suit, starting their own sister-city relationships with war-torn Nicaraguan communities. Mark

Falcoff, a PR spokesman for US policy, complained that the worst opposition he faced came from "the loony grandmothers of the US who discovered Nicaragua 'down at my church.' "[3]

In the 1990s, these "loony grandmothers" have proven themselves more persistent and certainly more helpful in their approach to Central American affairs than government "experts" like Falcoff. Cecile Meyer, for example, is a 71-year-old retired social worker who invests her retirement money in a Madison-based project that offers development loans to low-income Nicaraguan communities. "Meyer said she is getting substantial returns—economic ones, ethical ones, even spiritual ones," states the *National Catholic Reporter.* "Meyer is one of a growing number of socially conscious investors from the United States who are aiding reconstruction in postwar Nicaragua through a program called the Nicaraguan Community Development Loan Fund."[4]

These examples don't even scratch the surface of the action that is happening at the local level across the United States. A new citizen-led local movement is reclaiming democracy and directly confronting the PR industry's manipulations. The most visible manifestations of NIMBYism, and its biggest success stories, have been in stopping toxic waste sites and toxin-belching incinerators from invading communities. Author Mark Dowie sees this new wave of grassroots democracy as the best hope for realizing the public's well-documented desire for a clean and healthy environment in sustainable balance with nature. "Today, grassroots anti-toxic environmentalism is a far more serious threat to polluting industries than the mainstream environmental movement. Not only do local activists network, share tactics, and successfully block many dumpsites and industrial developments, they also stubbornly refuse to surrender or compromise. They simply cannot afford to. Their activities and success are gradually changing the acronym NIMBY to NIABY—Not In Anybody's Backyard."[5]

"What if everyone became a NIMBY activist?" asks author Jane Morris in *Not In My Backyard: The Handbook,* "a guide to how your government works, not in theory but in practice." Morris' book does a thorough job of outlining not just the power and potential of NIMBYism, but its downsides and difficulties. Like Dowie, she views the current manifestation of NIMBY activism as a starting-place for the emergence of a revitalized democracy.[6]

Morris, a long-time veteran of non-profit grassroots citizens organizing, describes how "during the course of a NIMBY campaign, your

understanding of government will be profoundly changed and deepened. Just as dramatic will be the transformation of your view about
how each citizen, yourselves included, can be part of a larger change.
. . . NIMBY activism is not an obstruction but a stimulus to finding
lasting solutions instead of temporary and often devastating tech-
nofixes. In NIMBY activism, people take an active role in shaping
their futures and in running their government instead of letting it
run them."

Too Much Democracy?

The term "NIMBY" was originally coined by public relations flacks
as a term of ridicule, but it has become a badge of honor. Dowie
notes that:

> The idea was to discredit their motives and suggest that fighting to
> protect one's health, family, and neighborhood was some kind of
> moral defect or, worse, a social disease. H. Lazier Hickman, Jr, exec-
> utive vice-president of Governmental Refuse Collection and Disposal
> Association, a major promoter of waste incineration, called the NIMBY
> syndrome "a public health problem of the first order. It is a recurring
> mental illness that continues to infect the public." Hickman's solution
> was a "campaign to wipe out this disease." Others saw in NIMBYism
> the threat of anarchy. "More than a century ago de Tocqueville warned
> us of ma be [sic] too much democracy in America," warned Calvin
> Brunner, a consultant to the waste industry. "Because everyone felt
> equal to everyone else, he projected that this would eventually lead
> to anarchy. . . . Is it possible that the NIMBYists will play a large part
> in proving de Tocqueville right in his assertions about democracy
> being [an] untenable form of government?"[7]

This contemptuous attitude toward democracy is the heritage of
Edward Bernays, the father-philosopher of public relations, who saw
corporate "engineering of consent" as a way to eliminate the "chaos"
in democratic society. Democracy is indeed chaotic, messy and
unpredictable—and, most bothersome of all to PR practitioners, it
often produces decisions that their clients are unable to either predict or control.

The difference between "engineered consent" and democracy
parallels the distinction that Australian scholar Alex Carey draws
between "propaganda" and "education." He defines propaganda as
"communications where the form and content is selected with the
single-minded purpose of bringing some target audience to adopt
attitudes and beliefs chosen in advance by the sponsors of the

communications." With education, by contrast, "the purpose is to encourage critical enquiry and to open minds to arguments for and against any particular conclusion, rather than close them to the possibility of any conclusion but one."[8]

The PR professionals who work to manage our opinions and emotions are not doing this because they are evil, but because PR is a financially rewarding business. From their viewpoint they are simply providing a service to their paying customers. If PR poses a threat to democratic values, it is ultimately a manifestation of the deeper contradiction in corporate America—the gap between our dream of governance "by the people, for the people" and the reality of a society deeply divided by unequal access to wealth and power.

As Jerry Mander points out, even enlightened corporate executives are limited in what they can do to implement corporate social responsibility: "No corporate manager could ever place community welfare above corporate interest. . . . US corporate law holds that management of publicly held companies must act primarily in the economic interest of shareholders. If not, management can be sued by shareholders and firings would surely occur. So managers are legally obliged to ignore community welfare . . . if those needs interfere with profitability."[9]

The absolute power of the "bottom line" is understood perfectly well by the rather small percentage of Americans who own and manage large businesses. The need to maximize profit drove antifreeze makers to hire a PR spy so they could fight a law that would save children's lives at a price of only two cents per gallon. Failure to maximize profit is virtual corporate suicide. Companies that ignore this law soon learn their lesson when other, more profitable companies move in to seize their markets using a combination of lower prices and better advertising.

The values that dominate our lives today are corporate, not democratic values. Our system is first and foremost defined by the rules and regulations we follow as employees, customers, and consumers. Public relations firms are themselves corporations which exist to serve the propaganda interests of their clients. And as everyone who works for a corporation knows, democracy does not exist at the workplace. Nor is democracy working in Washington and state capitols where corporate special interests control the political purses that put candidates into office and keep them there.

Public relations exists to manufacture the necessary illusions that bridge the gap between the dream and the reality of American society. In those illusions, however, the dream remains visible. If the PR industry were *only* based on "lies and damn lies," it might be easier to see through its deceptions. But PR's cunning half-truths and "spins" appeal to us and work on us because they come *from* us, from the constant plumbing of the public mind by surveys, opinion polls, focus groups, and information gathered as we apply for bank loans, purchase goods with credit cards, place birth announcements in newspapers, vote, and make phone calls. Every day we as individuals are leaving behind the electronic equivalent of fingerprints and DNA samples that marketing and PR firms lift from the commercial landscape, and refine for use in their efforts to manipulate our minds.

Ultimately, however, the power of PR is limited. It can often redirect public anger and insulate individual corporations or politicians from the consequences of their actions, but as Abraham Lincoln observed, "you can't fool all of the people all of the time."

Fortunately, corporations are not the only institutions that shape our lives. Families are social enclaves organized according to very different rules than the rules governing corporate behavior. No sane person would propose, for example, that a child's value within a family is based on the child's ability to contribute to the unit's profitability. Other alternatives to corporate dominance can be found in varying forms and degrees in the structures of neighborhoods, churches, volunteer organizations and informal networks of friends— all of which constitute fertile soil for the germination and flowering of NIMBY movements.

We don't pretend to possess a magic solution to the problem that PR poses for our society. In truth, any such solution is likely itself to be part of the problem, because real democracy must be the common work and invention of all of us, acting together. The solutions we *do* possess are partial: first, learn to recognize the influence of PR in your life; second, seek out alternative sources of information; third, become personally involved in local efforts to directly address important issues at the community level.

The answers, in short, will be found in fellowship with our neighbors, and in rediscovery of ourselves. Democracy, to be real and continuous, must be lived daily, its values woven into the fabric of society. It cannot be "handed down" or planned from above. Democracy is not like fast food. It can't be standardized, mass-produced, made predictable and "convenient."

Even reining in corporate power will not end propaganda and public manipulation; nothing would. Political leaders and vested interests will always use the most successful techniques available to manipulate human opinion, behavior and public policy in their favor. "Constant vigilance" remains the best watchword for protecting and advancing democracy, and for exposing and avoiding PR manipulation.

Wait a Minute—Maybe We've Been Unfair

As you might expect, the PR industry is constantly vigilant about its own image, and the news that we were writing *Toxic Sludge Is Good For You* created some stir in the PR trade press. The June 19, 1995, issue of *PR News* reported that Ron Levy, president of the North American Precis Syndicate, questioned whether the intention behind our "critical book on PR is to sell copies of the book, rather than to present a balanced view of the public relations profession." Levy wrote that there is a "conflict of interest" between our "moral obligation to tell the truth" and our "interest in writing so the book will sell well." To judge whether we have honored this moral obligation, Levy suggested that readers see whether the book "(a) says only nasty things about the great PR firms, or (b) presents both sides, including how much good the great PR firms are doing . . . to save lives, avoid blindness and other health tragedies, and help people get more happiness out of life." [10]

Actually, we *know* this book doesn't tell the "whole story" about public relations. Many PR practitioners *are* engaged in promotional and publicity campaigns for clinics, schools and deserving charities that benefit the public. The techniques of public relations are not all inherently bad. Everyone at some time uses their skills of persuasion to communicate ideas, sell products, promote a point of view, or "schmooze" socially. But positive uses of PR do not in any way mitigate the undemocratic power of the multi-billion dollar PR industry to manipulate and propagandize on behalf of wealthy special interests, dominating debate, discussion and decision-making. Nor is it our "moral responsibility" as authors to help the public relations industry clean up its own image, which was thoroughly dirty long before we ever set print to paper. The PR industry is equipped like no other industry on earth to publicize its own good works, and if the public image of PR is negative, it can only be because the industry has failed to honor its own advice, as stated by Ivy Lee: "Set your house in order, then tell the public you have done so."

Citizens and individual PR practitioners can use ethical public relations techniques to right social wrongs, clean up the environment, promote minority rights, protect working people and make their communities better. But we consider it an illusion to imagine that PR is a "neutral" technology that can simply be adopted uncritically to achieve socially responsible ends.

There is a danger in this conceit. All the environmental organizations together will never have a budget for public relations equal to that of even a single major manufacturer of pesticides. The polluter will always be able to outspend and outgun the environmentalists, and can bring virtually an unlimited amount of propaganda and lobbypower to an issue, simply by writing a larger check or reaching out to other businesses similarly threatened by reform.

Another danger is that PR campaigns do not invite individuals to become actors on their own behalf, but treat them as a targeted, passive audience. A democratic movement in the best American tradition must emerge from the initiatives of individual citizens acting as true participants in the process, not as the products of a top-down PR campaign.

Is it possible for such a democratic movement to emerge? Was it ever possible in the past? The very existence of the PR industry proves that it *is* possible. The fact that corporations and governments feel compelled to spend billions of dollars every year manipulating the public is a perverse tribute to human nature and our own moral values.

The public relations industry has stolen our dreams, and returned them to us packaged as illusions. It must be our duty to dream more deeply, and to participate in the process of transforming those dreams into reality.

PR Industry Leaders

In 1995 the world's largest public relations firm was Burson-Marsteller, followed by Shandwick and Hill & Knowlton. The following information, gleaned from O'Dwyer publications, gives a brief profile of Burson-Marsteller (B-M) and an idea of its scope:

In 1994, Burson-Marsteller netted just under $192 million dollars of income from its 63 offices in 32 countries. Like most transnational firms it has been "downsizing" its personnel, now at 1,700 employees worldwide. The B-M empire has offices in Argentina, Australia, Belgium, Brazil, Canada, Colombia, Chile, Denmark, England, France, Germany, Hong Kong, Hungary, India, Italy, Japan, Korea, Malaysia, Mexico, Netherlands, Norway, Peoples Republic of China, Poland, Puerto Rico, Russia, Singapore, Slovak Republic, Sweden, Spain, Taiwan, Thailand, and Venezuela.

Burson-Marsteller purchased the Washington-based public affairs/lobby firms of Gold and Liebengood in 1989 and Black, Manafort, Stone & Kelly in 1991. B-M in turn is part of the privately held Young & Rubicam advertising conglomerate, which also owns Cohn & Wolfe and CMF&Z, two other major PR firms. In 1993, Young & Rubicam reported billings of more than $7.5 *billion* dollars.

Burson-Marsteller refuses to release a complete list of current and recent clients, but they are known to include major corporations, business associations, government agencies, right-wing political movements and wealthy individuals, such as the Government of El Salvador, NBC, Philip Morris, the Trump Organization, Jonah Savimbi's UNITA, Occidental Petroleum, Kashmiri American Council, American Airlines, State of Alaska, Genentech, Ford Motor Company, The Times Mirror Company, MCI, National Restaurant Association, Coca-Cola, Government of Italy, British Columbia's timber industry,

Dow Corning, General Electric, Hydro-Quebec, NutraSweet, Government of the Bahamas, AT&T, British Telecom, Chevron, DuPont, IBM, Warner-Lambert, Visa, U.S. Postal Service, Seagram, SmithKline Beecham, Reebok, Procter & Gamble, the Olympic Games, Nestlé, National Livestock, Motorola, Gerber, Eli Lilly, Caterpillar, American Energy Alliance, State Farm Insurance, Sears, Pfizer, NEC, Metropolitan Life, McDonnell Douglas, Government of Kenya, Government of Indonesia, Glaxo, Campbell Soup, Monsanto, Government of Saudi Arabia, Government of Korea, Bombardier/Sea-Doo, Government of Togo, Government of Nigeria, Beretta USA, Hitachi and many hundreds more.

Burson-Marsteller says its international operations are "linked together electronically and philosophically to deliver a single standard of excellence." It claims that "the role of communications is to manage perceptions which motivate behaviors that create business results. We are totally focused on this idea as our mission. . . . [B-M] helps clients manage issues by influencing—in the right combination—public attitudes, public perceptions, public behavior and public policy."

The Top 15 Public Relations Firms in 1994
(Italics Indicates Advertising Agency Ownership)

FIRM	Net Fees Millions
1. Burson-Marsteller *(Young & Rubicam)*	$191.99
2. Shandwick	160.10
3. Hill & Knowlton *(WPP Group)*	139.30
4. Communications International–Porter/Novelli *(Omnicom Group)*	111.72
5. Edelman PR Worldwide	74.90
6. Fleishman-Hillard	73.89
7. Ketchum PR *(Omnicom Group)*	55.40
8. Ogilvy, Adams & Rinehard *(WPP Group)*	39.05
9. Robinson Lake/Sawyer Miller *(Bozell Worldwide)*	37.80
10. The Rowland Company *(Saatchi & Saatchi)*	35.00
11. Manning, Selvage & Lee *(D'Arcy Masius)*	31.60
12. GCI Group *(Grey Advertising)*	31.54
13. Ruder Finn	27.82
14. Financial Relations Board	15.87
15. Cohn & Wolf *(Young & Rubicam)*	14.67
TOTAL NET FEE INCOME	**$1.04 billion**

Information compiled from *O'Dwyer's Directory of PR Firms 1995*

ThE CloRox PR CRisis PlAN

Today, almost every company has in place a "Public Relations Crisis Management Plan" to anticipate and mitigate profit-threatening problems, and the Clorox Company is no exception. Chlorine, the active ingredient in its bleach, has been linked to a variety of health problems, including infertility, impaired childhood development, immune system damage, and cancer. Chlorine is also the basis of many persistent compounds including dioxin, Agent Orange herbicides, PCBs, and climate-destroying CFCs.

In 1991, in the face of a mounting campaign by Greenpeace for a "global phase-out" of chlorine, the Clorox Company turned to Ketchum Public Relations, a premier greenwashing firm. Ketchum's draft plan outlined strategies for dealing with a number of "worst-case scenarios," but failed to plan for the worst of all possible scenarios—the possibility that some conscientious objector would leak the plan to Greenpeace, which in turn provided it to us.

Below are edited excerpts from Ketchum's proposal to help Clorox "present a position that doesn't appear to be self-serving—sometimes using a disarming candor, other times presenting an understandable firmness." As corporations gear up for what one leading public relations advisor predicts will be a "wicked battle" over the chlorine controversy, the following text reveals the rigorous scripting behind their "disarming candor."

CRISIS MANAGEMENT PLAN FOR THE CLOROX COMPANY
1991 Draft Prepared by Ketchum Public Relations

. . . The environmental crises which could affect the Clorox Company can be planned for; strategies to address scenarios flowing from known issues of concern to the public can be established. . . . We have attempted to provide a 'crystal ball' pinpointing some of the issues which could arise over the next year. For each scenario we have suggested different levels of attention and response. . . .

SCENARIO #1:

. . . Greenpeace activists arrive at Clorox corporate headquarters with signs, banners, bull horns and several local television crews and proceed to launch a rally. The demonstrators hang a large banner... They release the results of a new "study" linking chlorine exposure to cancer. Two local network affiliates pick up the piece and go live to their noon news with a remote broadcast. AP Radio and the *San Francisco Chronicle* are on the scene and interview three unsuspecting Clorox employees, on their way to lunch, who agree that the safety of chlorine may be in question. . . .

Objective: Make sure this is a one-day media event. with no follow-up stories, that results in minimal short-term damage to Clorox's reputation or market position.

Strategies:

- Announce that the company will seek an independent, third-party review of the Greenpeace study and promise to report back to the media. . . . (Its primary value will be to cause reporters to question Greenpeace's integrity and scientific capabilities.)
- Reporters are invited into the company, without Greenpeace, for a news conference. . . .
- Team begins alerting key influentials, scientists, government environmental and health officials, and others previously identified as potential allies.
- Names of independent scientists who will talk about chlorine are given to the media. (These lists are assumed to already be on file as per Master Crisis Plan.)
- Regarding the employees who raised concerns . . . employee communications efforts will be improved.
- Survey research firm begins random telephone survey of 500 consumers to assess the impact of the event. Based on the results, available the next morning at 9, team will decide further steps. . . .

SCENARIO #2:

The movement back to more 'natural' household cleaning products is gaining momentum as consumers are eagerly looking for ways they can contribute to a cleaner planet. . . . A prominent newspaper columnist targets the environmental hazards of liquid chlorine bleach in an article, which is syndicated to newspapers across the country. The columnist calls for consumers to boycott Clorox products. Local chapters of Greenpeace take up the cause. . . . A dramatic drop in sales of Clorox products within several weeks. . . . Congress schedules hearings on the environmental safety of liquid chlorine bleach products. . . .

This event is every company's worst nightmare: the company must be prepared to take aggressive, swift action to protect its market franchise. . . . The very future of the product and the company is at stake.

Objective: Restore Clorox's reputation and that of the product as quickly as possible.

Strategy: Use, wherever possible, actual rank and file employees and their families to act as spokespeople to support the company. . . .

- An independent scientist is dispatched to meet with the columnist and discuss the issue.
- Teams of scientists, independent or from Clorox or both, are dispatched . . . to conduct media tours.
- Arrange for sympathetic media, local, state and national governmental leaders, and consumer experts to make statements in defense of the product. . . .
- Advertising in major markets, using Clorox employees and their families who will testify to their faith in the product. . . .
- Advertising campaign: "Stop Environmental Terrorism," calling on Greenpeace and the columnist to be more responsible and less irrational. . . .
- Video and audio news release to affected markets.
- Enlist the support of the union and the national union leadership, since jobs are at stake.
- Determine if and how a slander lawsuit against the columnist and/or Greenpeace could be effective.
- Mass mailings to consumers in affected cities.
- If the situation truly grows desperate, the team agrees to consider the possibility of pulling the product off the market, pending a special review, assuming the review can be done quickly.
- Survey research is conducted daily to measure public reaction, changing attitudes, perceptions, etc.

Moderate Case Event: A nationally syndicated columnist attacks the household use of Clorox bleach as a hazard to the environment and calls for consumers to use 'safer' non-chlorine substitutes. . . . The article is picked up in newspapers in 25 major cities across the U.S., but otherwise generates no news. . . . Although consumers are asking questions, there is no loss of sales.

Objective: Prevent issue from escalating and gaining more credibility.

Strategy: Keep media interest minimal; prevent national or state government action.

Action Plan:
- Employee announcement is posted. . . .
- Media strategy: Reactive/responsive as long as the interest remains light.
- The columnist is briefed on the environmental safety of liquid chlorine bleach.
- Media tours developed, but they rely more on a "Hints from Heloise" approach that only obliquely mentions that chlorine bleaches are useful and safe.

SCENARIO #3:

At least one scientist advisor to the chlorine industry has voiced concern that the National Toxicology Program analysts could conclude that chlorine may possibly be an animal carcinogen. In light of U.S. regulatory policy, a link with cancer could trigger public concern and harsh regulatory action against this important chemical.

Worst Case Event: The final NTP study analysis concludes that chlorine is, indeed, an animal carcinogen. On the same day of the NTP study announcement, Greenpeace holds a satellite news conference in Washington, New York and San Francisco to launch a concerted campaign to eliminate all use of chlorine in the United States. The news conference receives widespread national media coverage. A number of television reporters use a Clorox bottle to illustrate "dangerous" products produced with chlorine. The Environmental Protection Agency decides to reevaluate and severely tighten its regulations on the use of chlorine in manufacturing, causing . . . negative media coverage.

Objective: Working with other manufacturers and the Chlorine Institute, (1) forestall any legislative or regulatory action; and, (2) Maintain-customer and consumer loyalty.

Strategy: Demonstrate company's awareness that people are legitimately frightened and have questions that need answers, its commitment to getting those questions answered as quickly as possible, and its belief that chlorine does not pose a health hazard to people. . . . Where possible, ignore Greenpeace and don't give it credence. . . . Help people understand that Greenpeace is not among the serious players in this issue. . . .

- Through the Chlorine Institute, third-party scientific experts are brought to Washington to testify. . . .

- Because of advance planning, written material for reporters, customers, consumers and employees is in place with the specific target audiences clearly defined.

- Media briefing with key environmental and consumer reporters and with other interested media are held by industry, company, and independent spokespersons.

- Third-spokespeople are scheduled for major television and newspaper interviews.

- Industry generates grassroots letters to legislators calling on them to show restraint. Letters [are] designed to show that Greenpeace's overreaction is not causing widespread consumer concern.

- Through the Chlorine Institute, continue . . . consumer surveys to determine consumer attitudes and concerns and to develop clear, convincing messages.

- A hotline is established for consumers to call if they have questions.

Suggested Reading

Much of the information that we present in this book appeared originally in a newsmagazine titled *PR Watch* that we edit for the Center for Media
& Democracy, a nonprofit organization that monitors the PR industry. (A
brief box describing the Center appears at the end of page 206.) *PR Watch*
is published quarterly and is the only publication in the United States devoted
to analyzing PR propaganda and its impact on our lives. For a sample copy,
send $1 to *PR Watch* at 520 University Avenue, Suite 310, Madison, WI 53703;
phone (608) 260-9713. Also visit our website at www.prwatch.org.

Fairness & Accuracy In Reporting (FAIR) is a national media watchdog
group that focuses awareness on the narrow corporate allegiance of
the media and its under-representation of points of view from women,
minorities and low-income groups. It publishes a magazine, titled *EXTRA!*
For information, contact FAIR, 130 W. 25th Street, New York, NY 10001;
(212) 633-6700.

There are a number of professional and trade publications that report on
the PR industry—*Inside PR, pr reporter, PR News, Public Relations Quarterly,
PR Tactics*—that are available for fairly steep subscription rates. The information in such publications is written to be helpful to the PR industry. One
trade publishing firm—the Jack O'Dwyer Company of New York—stands
above the rest because of the high degree of digging and reporting done
on the industry.

Recently O'Dwyer had lunch with the CEO of a top-ten PR firm, who
began their friendly get-together by asking, "Jack, why does everyone hate
you so much?" The answer, we believe, is that while O'Dwyer's publications provide useful information to the PR industry, O'Dwyer and his staff
are feisty journalists who have not been afraid to step on toes, dig out scandals and criticize the industry.

If you need to track the PR industry on a regular basis, we recommend subscribing to one or more of the O'Dwyer publications. They
include *O'Dwyer's PR Services* (monthly), *Jack O'Dwyer's Newsletter* (weekly),
O'Dwyer's Washington Report (bi-weekly), and the annual *O'Dwyer's*

Directory of Public Relations Firms. For subscription information, contact Jack O'Dwyer, 271 Madison Ave., NY NY 10016; phone (212) 679-2471.

Do you need to know which PR firm or lobbyist is representing whom in Washington, or whether the Coalition for Health Insurance Choices is an insurance industry front group? Then you should probably get the best annual directory to the action inside the Beltway: *Washington Representatives: Who Does What for Whom in the Nation's Capital,* Columbia Books, Inc., 1212 New York Avenue, Washington, DC 20005; phone (202) 898-0662.

Another useful resource, published in 1995 by the nonprofit Advocacy Institute, is titled *By Hook or By Crook: A Guide to Stealth Lobbying Tactics and Counter-Strategies.* Their address is: 1707 L Street NW, Suite 400, Washington, DC 20036; phone (202) 659-8475.

To understand how the PR mind works, and what sort of tactics and strategies are the tools of the trade, we recommend a simple, short textbook, written for PR students, titled *Marketing Public Relations: The Hows That Make It Work,* by Rene A. Henry, Jr. (1995: Iowa State University Press).

Michael Levine is a right-wing Hollywood publicist whose clients include Michael Jackson and Charlton Heston. While we don't recommend his philosophy, we *do* recommend his book, *Guerrilla PR* (1993: HarperCollins, NY), as a useful how-to guide for citizens looking for inexpensive, creative ways to publicize and promote their own causes.

Other Recommended Reading

Censored: The News That Didn't Make the News—and Why: The 1995 Project Censored Yearbook, by Carl Jensen and Project Censored, 1995, Four Walls Eight Windows, NY.

Manufacturing Consent: the Political Economy of the Mass Media, by Edward Herman and Noam Chomsky, 1988, Pantheon Books, NY.

Not In My Backyard: The Handbook, by Jane Anne Morris. 1994, Silvercat Publications, San Diego, CA.

The Powerhouse: Robert Keith Gray and the Selling of Access and Influence In Washington, by Susan Trento, 1992, St. Martin's Press, NY.

PR: How the Public Relations Industry Writes the News, by Jeff & Marie Blyskal, 1985, William Morrow and Company, NY.

Sultans of Sleaze: Public Relations and the Media, by Joyce Nelson, 1989, Common Courage Press, Monroe, ME.

Taking the Risk Out of Democracy: Propaganda In the US and Australia, by Alex Carey, 1995, University of New South Wales Press Ltd, Sydney.

Through the Media Looking Glass: Decoding Bias and Blather in the News, by Jeff Cohen and Norman Solomon, 1995, Common Courage Press, Monroe, ME.

Unreliable Sources: A Guide to Detecting Bias In News Media, by Martin A. Lee and Norman Solomon, 1991, Carol Publishing Group, NY.

Who Will Tell the People: The Betrayal of American Democracy, by William Greider, 1992, Simon & Schuster, NY.

NOTES

Chapter One: Burning Books Before They're Printed

1. Ketchum Public Relations Confidential Memo to CALRAB Food Safety Team, Sept. 7, 1990.
2. *O'Dwyer's Directory of Public Relations Executives 1995,* p. 178.
3. David P. Bianco, ed., *PR News Casebook: 1000 Public Relations Case Studies* (Potomac, MD: Phillips Publishing, 1993), pp. 120-121.
4. David Steinman, *Diet for a Poisoned Planet: How to Choose Safe Foods for You and Your Family* (New York: Harmony Books, 1990).
5. *O'Dwyer's Directory of Public Relations Firms 1994,* pp. 96-97.
6. *O'Dwyer's PR Services Report,* Vol. 8 No. 2, Feb. 1994, p. 42.
7. *O'Dwyer's Directory of Public Relations Executives 1995,* p. 178.
8. Ketchum Public Relations Confidential Memo to CALRAB Food Safety Team, Sept. 7, 1990.
9. Jean Rainey, Memo for Roland Woerner Regarding David Steinman Booking on Today Show. (no date)
10. Elizabeth M. Whelan, American Council on Science and Health, to John Sununu, Chief of Staff, White House, July 12, 1990.
11. Daniel P. Puzo, "The New Naturalism: Controversy Eats at *Diet for a Poisoned Planet,*" *Los Angeles Times,* Nov. 29, 1990, p. 27.
12. Kenneth N. Hall et al., U.S. Dept. of Agriculture, to Food Safety Contacts, Oct. 29, 1990.
13. Ken Miller, "Meltdown in EPA Watchdog Office Puts Millions at Risk, Workers Say," Gannett News Service, May 4, 1995. See also "EPA Reinstatement, Compensatory Damages Awarded Toxicologist Removed by EPA," *BNA Chemical Regulation Daily,* Dec. 11, 1992.

14. *O'Dwyer's Directory of Public Relations Firms 1994,* pp. 124-125.
15. Carol Ward Knox, Morgan & Myers, to dairy industry representatives, Sept. 17, 1992.
16. John F. Berry, "Suit Says Du Pont Co. Pressured Publishers; Author Alleges His History of Family Was Financially Doomed," *Washington Post,* Sept. 22, 1981, p. A2.
17. Interview with Dan Barry.
18. David Helvarg, *The War Against the Greens* (San Francisco: Sierra Club Books, 1994), pp. 365-366.
19. Susan B. Trento, *The Power House: Robert Keith Gray and the Selling of Access and Influence in Washington* (New York: St. Martin's Press, 1992), p. 233.
20. Ibid., p. 196.
21. Ibid., p. 62.
22. James Flynn, Paul Slovic and C.K. Mertz, "The Nevada Initiative: A Risk Communication Fiasco" (unpublished manuscript), May 6, 1993, pp. 6-8.
23. Peoples Bicentennial Commission, *Voices of the American Revolution* (New York: Bantam Books, 1974), pp. 114-116.

Chapter Two: The Art of the Hustle and the Science of Propaganda

1. Edward L. Bernays, *Public Relations* (Norman, OK: University of Oklahoma Press, 1957), pp. 38-39.
2. Ibid., p. 36.
3. Ibid., p. 60.
4. Scott Cutlip, *The Unseen Power: Public Relations: A History* (Hillsdale, NJ: Lawrence Erlbaum Associates, Inc., 1994), p. 51. For a description of press agentry in the early twentieth century, see Neal Gabler, *Winchell: Power and the Culture of Celebrity,* excerpted in *O'Dwyer's PR Services Report,* Dec. 1994, pp. 24-25.
5. Will Irwin, "Press Agent, His Rise and Fall," *Colliers* Vol. 48, Dec. 2, 1991. Quoted in Cutlip, p. 51.

6. Bernays, p. 51.

7. Ibid., pp. 53-55, 63-64.

8. Cutlip, p. 21.

9. Ibid., pp. 47-48.

10. Ibid., p. 58.

11. Ibid., pp. 52-53.

12. Sherman Morse, "An Awakening on Wall Street," *The American Magazine,* Vol. LXII, Sept. 1906.

13. Cutlip, p. 64.

14. Ibid., p. 23.

15. Quoted in Bernays, p. 74.

16. Cutlip, pp. 64-71.

17. Ibid., pp. 121-122.

18. Ibid., p. 144.

19. Ibid., p. 160.

20. Edward L. Bernays, *Propaganda* (New York: 1928), pp. 47-48.

21. Edward L. Bernays, ed., *The Engineering of Consent* (Norman, OK: University of Oklahoma Press), pp. 3-4.

22. Cutlip, pp. 193-214.

23. John T. Flynn, "Edward L. Bernays, The Science of Ballyhoo," *Atlantic Monthly,* May 1932.

24. Cutlip, pp. 170-176.

25. Bernays, *Public Relations,* p. 4.

26. Edward L. Bernays, "What Do the Social Sciences Have to Offer Public Relations?" interview with Howard Penn Hudson for *PR: The Quarterly Journal of Public Relations,* Winter 1956. Reprinted in Edward L. Bernays, *The Later Years: Public Relations Insights, 1956-1986* (Rhinebeck, NY: H&M Publishers, 1986), p. 11.

27. Bernays, *Propaganda,* p. 9.

28. Cutlip, p. 185.

29. Edward L. Bernays, *The Biography of an Idea: Memoirs of Public Relations Counsel Edward L. Bernays* (New York: Simon and Schuster, 1965), p. 652.

Chapter Three: Smokers' Hacks

1. Richard W. Pollay, "Propaganda, Puffing and the Public Interest," *Public Relations Review,* Vol. XVI, No. 3, Fall 1990, p.40.

2. Ibid., p. 41.

3. Ibid., p. 40.

4. Stuart Ewen, *Captains of Consciousness: Advertising and the Social Roots of Consumer Culture* (New York: McGraw-Hill, 1976), p. 160.

5. Pollay, p. 41.

6. Ibid., p. 42.

7. Ibid., p. 50.

8. Scott M. Cutlip, "The Tobacco Wars: A Matter of Public Relations Ethics," *Journal of Corporate Public Relations,* Vol. 3, 1992-1993, p. 26-31.

9. Mike Moore, Attorney General, State of Mississippi in lawsuit filed on May 23, 1994.

10. Cutlip, "The Tobacco Wars," p. 28.

11. Cutlip, *The Unseen Power,* p. 488.

12. Pollay, p. 45-49.

13. Cutlip, *The Unseen Power,* p. 501.

14. Ibid., p. 497.

15. Michael Evans Begay et al., "The Tobacco Industry, State Politics, and Tobacco Education in California," *American Journal of Public Health,* Vol. 83, No. 9, Sept. 1993, p. 1214.

16. Carolyn Henson, "World Health Organizations No Tobacco Day," Associated Press, May 30, 1994. See also Robert Evans, "Third World, Women Boost Smoking Death Forecasts, Reuters wire service, May 30, 1994.

17. Peter H. Stone, "It's All Done With Some Smoke and Some PR," *National Journal,* May 28, 1994, pp. 1244-1245.

18. "Anti-America," *The National Smokers Alliance Voice,* Vol. 2, Issue 4, June/July 1994.

19. John Schwartz, "California Activists' Success Ignites a Not-So-Slow Burn," *Washington Post,* May 29, 1994.

20. "State Official Challenges Tobacco Firm; California Initiative Said to Be Deceptive," *The Washington Post* wire service, June 2, 1994.

21. B. Drummond Ayres, Jr., "Philip Morris on Offensive in California," *New York Times,* May 16, 1994, p. 1.

22. Gaylord Walker, "Smoke Hits the Fan— American Cancer Society Thrilled," PR Newswire, Nov. 9, 1994.

23. Advertising Age/Gallup poll, quoted in "Tobacco Industry's Own Health is the Latest Victim of Marketing Practices," *Inside PR,* April 1994, p. 6.

24. "Tobacco Institute Relies on PR to Help Smoke Out P.C. Police," *O'Dwyer's Washington Report,* Vol. IV, No. 12, June 6, 1994, pp. 1, 7.

25. Bernays, *The Later Years,* p. 115.

26. "3 of 4 Flacks Agree: No Ifs About Butts," *PR Watch,* Vol. 1, No. 4, Third Quarter, 1994, p. 2.

27. Bernays, *The Later Years,* p. 139.

Chapter Four: Spinning the Atom

1. Cutlip, *The Unseen Power,* pp. 508-511.
2. Ibid.
3. Peter Stoler, *Decline and Fail: The Ailing Nuclear Power Industry* (New York: Dodd, Mead & Company, 1985), pp. 27-28.
4. Daniel Ford, *The Cult of the Atom: The Secret Papers of the Atomic Energy Commission* (New York: Touchstone/Simon and Schuster, 1982, 1984), p. 40-41.
5. Stoler, p. 28.
6. David E. Lilienthal, *Change, Hope, and the Bomb* (Princeton, NJ: Princeton University Press, 1963), pp. 97-100.
7. Stoler, p. 16.
8. Ibid., p. 37.
9. Lilienthal, pp. 111-112.
10. Stoler, pp. 41-45. See also Peter Pringle and James Spigelman, *The Nuclear Barons* (New York: Holt, Rinehart & Winston, 1981), pp. 263-272.
11. Stoler, pp. 52-56.
12. Harvey Wasserman, *Energy War: Reports from the Front* (Westport, CT: Lawrence Hill & Co., 1979), pp. 5-6.
13. Stoler, pp. 97-98.
14. Wasserman, p. 6. See also Stoler, p. 99.
15. Stoler, pp. 102-103.
16. Ibid., pp. 39-40.
17. Sheila Harty, *Hucksters in the Classroom* (Washington, DC: Center for Study of Responsive Law, 1979), p. 40.
18. Ibid., pp. 42, 44.
19. Robert L. Dilenschneider, *Power and Influence: Mastering the Art of Persuasion* (New York: Prentice Hall Press, 1990), p. 165.
20. David M. Rubin, "The Public's Right to Know," in *Accident at Three Mile Island: The Human Dimensions,* edited by David L. Sills, C.P. Wolf and Viven B. Shelanski (Boulder, CO: Westview Press, 1982), p. 133.
21. Stoler, pp. 110-113.
22. Dilenschneider, pp. 167-68.
23. Fred Wilcox, ed., *Grassroots: An Anti-Nuke Source Book* (Trumansburg, NY: The Crossing Press, 1980), p. 118.
24. Stoler, p. 2.
25. Flynn et al., "The Nevada Initiative," p. 2.
26. Kent Oram and Ed Allison, "The Nevada Initiative: The Long-term Program: An Overview," unpublished proposal to the American Nuclear Energy Council, Washington, DC, Sept. 1991, pp. 8-9, 12-14, 17.
27. Flynn et al., p. 3.
28. Allen J. Keesler, letter, Oct. 25, 1991.
29. Flynn et al., pp. 4-5.
30. Ibid., pp. 6-7.
31. Ibid., p. 8.
32. Ibid., p. 2.
33. "The Public Relations Behind Nuclear Waste," *Nukem Market Report,* March 1995, pp. 4-5.
34. *Facts on File World News Digest,* Feb. 5, 1988, p. 71G2.
35. "The Public Relations Behind Nuclear Waste," pp. 6-7, 9-10.

Chapter Five: Spies for Hire

1. Interview with Jennifer Lyman.
2. Interview with Dan Barry.
3. Diane Alters, "The Business of Surveillance," *Boston Globe,* July 9, 1989, p. 27.
4. Ibid.
5. Joseph Demma, Michael Slackman and Robert E. Kessler, "High Stakes in Covert War: Spies Used by Animal Rights Foes," *Newsday,* Feb. 5, 1989, p. 7.
6. Seymour D. Vestermark, Jr., ed., *Indicators of Social Vulnerability: Social Indicators in Civil Defense Planning and Evaluation* (McLean, VA: Human Sciences Research, Inc., 1968), pp. iii, xviii.
7. *New York Times,* March 27, 1976, p. 3, col. 1.
8. Seymour D. Vestermark, Jr. and Peter D. Blauvelt, *Controlling Crime in the School: A Complete Security Handbook for Administrators* (West Nyack, NY: Parker Publishing Co., 1978), p. 10, 45, 159, 189, 218, 257, 277.
9. Trento, pp. 93-113.
10. Quoted in *Mormon Spies, Hughes and the CIA* by Jerald and Sandra Tanner (Salt Lake City, UT: Utah Lighthouse Ministry, 1976), p. 13.
11. J. Anthony Lukas, *New York Times Magazine,* Jan. 4, 1976.
12. Tanner, pp. 17, 19, 29.
13. Ibid., pp. 30, 36.
14. "Pagan International: Formed by Public Affairs Strategists Who Resolved Nestlé Boycott," *Business Wire,* May 10, 1985.
15. Paula M. Block, Hazel Bradford and Laura Pilarski, "Forging a Public Affairs Apparatus for Business," *Chemical Week,* June 19, 1985, p. 42.
16. Alters, p. 27.
17. "Pagan International," *Business Wire,* May 10, 1985.
18. "Ex-Nestlé Firm Goes Bankrupt," *O'Dwyer's PR Services,* Nov. 1990, p. 1.

19. Samantha Sparks, "South Africa: US Clergy Group Linked to Shell Oil," Inter Press Service, Oct. 7, 1987.

20. "Ex-Nestlé Firm Goes Bankrupt," p. 1.

21. Jack O'Dwyer, "Study Shows High Cost of Info-gathering," *Jack O'Dwyer's Newsletter,* Aug. 16, 1989, p. 7.

22. "MBD: A Brief Description," internal document, undated.

23. Dilenschneider, p. 96.

24. "MBD: Core Issues Monitored By MBD," internal document, undated.

25. "MBD: A Brief Description," internal document, undated.

26. Interview with Jim Goodman.

27. Interview with Dr. Michael Hansen, Consumers Union.

28. Ibid.

29. Interview with Dr. Richard Burroughs.

30. Interview with Dr. Michael Hansen.

31. Interview with John Kinsman.

32. John Dillon, "Poisoning the Grassroots," *Covert Action,* No. 44, Spring, 1993, pp. 35-36.

33. Ibid.

34. Ibid.

35. Ibid.

36. Interview with John Dillon.

37. John Brady, Direct Impact, to John Seng, Kaufman PR, Jan. 12, 1990.

38. Bill Lambrecht, "Firms Going All Out In Milk Fight," *St. Louis Post Dispatch,* April 7, 1991, p. 1. See also Carol Matlack, "Barnyard Brawl Over Cow Hormone," *National Journal,* April 6, 1991.

39. Demma et al., "High Stakes in Covert War."

40. Interview with Heidi Prescott, May 20, 1995.

41. Lisa McGurrin Driscoll, "A Corporate Spy Story," *New England Business,* Vol. 11, No. 5, May 1989, p. 28.

42. Denise Lavoie, "'Crazy' Invention Grows Into Giant Firm," *Chicago Tribune,* Nov. 22, 1992, Business section, p. 10.

43. Carole Bass, "Animal Activists: Target of Covert Campaign?" *Connecticut Law Tribune,* Dec. 9, 1991, p. 1.

44. Driscoll.

45. Joseph Demma, Robert E. Kessler and Michael Slackman, "Bomb Suspect: 'I Was Set Up,' " *Newsday,* January 27, 1989, p. 3.

46. Driscoll.

47. Ibid.

48. Bass.

49. "Witness Given Money, Cars to Befriend Activist," UPI wire story, Feb. 22, 1989.

50. Bass.

51. Driscoll.

52. Bass.

53. Dan Mangan, "Tax Leins Filed Against Controversial Stratford Private Security Firm," Vol. 31, No. 25, June 15, 1992, p. 7.

54. Carole Bass, "Substitute School Teacher's Double Life as an Informant," *Connecticut Law Tribune,* Dec. 9, 1991, p. 14.

55. Celestine Bohlen, "Animal-Rights Case: Terror or Entrapment?" *New York Times,* March 3, 1989, section B, p. 1. Also see Demma et al., "High Stakes in Covert War."

56. Bass, "Animal Activists: Target of Covert Campaign?"

57. Ibid.

Chapter Six: Divide and Conquer

1. Michael Levine, *Guerrilla PR: How You Can Wage an Effective Publicity Campaign . . . Without Going Broke* (New York: HarperCollins, 1993), p. 46.

2. Jane Meredith Adam, "MADD Founder Lightner Takes Job As Lobbyist for Liquor Industry," *Chicago Tribune,* Jan. 15, 1994, Section 1, p. 3.

3. "Take An Activist Apart and What Do You Have?" *CALF News Cattle Feeder,* June, 1991, p. 9 & 14.

4. Ibid.

5. "Green PR is Dollars and Sense Issue," *O'Dwyer's PR Services Report,* Feb. 1994, p. 6.

6. "Links with Activist Groups Get Results in Environmental PR," *O'Dwyer's PR Services Report,* Feb. 1994, p. 1.

7. Ibid.

8. Ibid., p. 20.

9. Ibid., p. 22.

10. The Public Affairs Council 1993, p. 18-23.

11. Foundation for Public Affairs, *1993-1994 Annual Report,* p. 2.

12. Foundation for Public Affairs, *1992-1993 Annual Report,* p. 5.

13. Foundation for Public Affairs, *Public Interest Profiles 1992-93,* pp. v-x.

14. Conference Call, Annual Conference on Activist Groups and Public Policymaking: Agendas, Strategies, and Alliances With Business, Washington, DC, Oct. 20-21, 1993

15. Ibid.

16. Annual Conference on Activist Groups and Public Policymaking, Oct. 20-21, 1993, Speakers & Registrants.

17. "Taint of Tobacco," *Multinational Monitor,* July/Aug. 1993.

18. News release from the Safe Food Coalition, Nov. 4, 1994.
19. Interview with Carol Tucker Foreman.
20. Sheila Kaplan, "Porter/Novelli Plays All Sides," *Legal Times,* Vol. XVI, No. 27, Nov. 22, 1993, pp. 1, 21-23.
21. Ibid.
22. Press kit from Hill & Knowlton on behalf of Partners for Sun Protection Awareness, 1994.
23. Video News Release, Press kit from Hill & Knowlton on behalf of Partners for Sun Protection Awareness, 1994.
24. "Profiles of Top Environmental PR Firms: Hill & Knowlton," *O'Dwyer's PR Services Report,* Feb. 1994, p. 40.
25. Business for Social Responsibility, *1995 Membership Directory.*
26. Interview conducted by Rob Inerfeld with Craig Cox.
27. Interview conducted by Rob Inerfeld with Bob Dunn.
28. Interview conducted by Rob Inerfeld with Craig Cox.
29. "Corporate 'Do-goodism' Helps Win Consumers' Hearts and Cash," *O'Dwyer's Washington Report,* May 5, 1994, p. 7.
30. Business for Social Responsibility, *1995 Membership Directory.*
31. Interview conducted by Rob Inerfeld with Craig Cox.
32. Anita Roddick, *Body and Soul: Profits with Principles, the Amazing Success Story of Anita Roddick & The Body Shop* (New York: Crown Publishers, 1991), audiotape.
33. Interview conducted by Rob Inerfeld with Jon Entine.
34. Ibid.
35. Ibid.
36. Interview conducted by Rob Inerfeld with Craig Cox.
37. Ibid.
38. Interview conducted by Rob Inerfeld with Jon Entine.
39. Paul Hawken, *The Ecology of Commerce: A Declaration of Sustainability,* (Harper-Business, 1993), p. xiii.

Chapter Seven:
Poisoning the Grassroots

1. Benjamin Franklin, "Information to Those Who Would Remove to America," from Franklin's *Autobiography.* Reprinted in *Great American Essays,* edited by Norman Cousins with Frank Jennings (New York: Dell Publishing, 1967), p. 22.
2. Keith Bradsher, "Gap in Wealth in US Called Widest in the West," *New York Times,* April 17, 1995, p. 1.
3. Bill Clinton, State of the Union address, Feb. 24, 1995.
4. "Grassroots Lobbying Glossary," *Campaigns & Elections,* Dec./Jan. 1995, p. 22.
5. William Greider, *Who Will Tell The People* (New York: Simon & Schuster, 1992), p. 35.
6. Back cover advertisement, *Campaigns & Elections,* Dec./Jan. 1995.
7. Trento, *The Power House,* p. 75.
8. Interview with Matt Reese.
9. "Grasstops: The Ultimate in Corporate Legislative Leverage, Public Policy Services," from Reese Communications Companies.
10. Ibid.
11. Ron Faucheux, "The Grassroots Explosion," *Campaigns & Elections,* Dec./Jan. 1995, p. 20.
12. Greider, p. 11.
13. Ibid., pp. 35-39.
14. Guy Gugliotta, "A Man Who Fertilizes the Grass Roots," *Washington Post,* Aug. 23, 1994, A17.
15. Stephen Engelberg, "A New Breed of Hired Hands Cultivates Grass-roots Anger," *New York Times,* March 17, 1993, pp. 1, 11.
16. Greider, pp. 35-36.
17. Joyce Nelson, *Sultans of Sleaze* (Monroe, ME: Common Courage Press, 1989), pp. 74-75.
18. Dilenschneider, p. 111.
19. Mike Malik speaking at "Shaping Public Opinion: If You Don't Do It, Somebody Else Will," in Chicago, December 9, 1994.
20. Ibid.
21. Ralph Reed speaking on "State-of-the-art Grassroots: The Christian Coalition Model," at Public Affairs Council conference, Sarasota, FL, Feb. 7, 1994.
22. Ibid.
23. Neal Cohen speaking on "Coalitions and Ally Development: The New Imperative In Public Policy Work" at Public Affairs Council conference, Sarasota, FL, Feb. 7, 1994.
24. Michael Dunn speaking on "Charting a Course for Grassroots Success," at Public Affairs Council conference, Sarasota, Florida, Feb. 7, 1994.
25. Ibid.
26. Advertisement, *Campaigns & Elections,* Dec./Jan. 1995, p. 4.

27. John Davies speaking at "Shaping Public Opinion: If You Don't Do It, Somebody Else Will," in Chicago, Dec. 9, 1994.

28. Ibid.

29. Pamela Whitney at "Shaping Public Opinion: If You Don't Do It, Somebody Else Will," in Chicago, Dec. 9, 1994.

30. Ibid.

31. "Public Interest Pretenders," *Consumer Reports,* May, 1994.

32. Ibid.

33. David B. Kinsman, "What's Ahead for Public Affairs Officers in '94," *Impact,* Dec. 1993, p. 2.

34. Eric A. Rennie, "Grassroots: Mobilizing Your 'Extended Family': the Pros and Cons," *Impact,* April, 1994.

35. Kinsman, p. 3.

36. James Fallows, "A Triumph of Misinformation," *The Atlantic,* Vol. 275, No. 1, p. 28.

37. "RX Partners," in promotional information from Beckel Cowan.

38. Robert Hoopes speaking at "Shaping Public Opinion: If You Don't Do It, Somebody Else Will," in Chicago, Dec. 9, 1994.

39. Ibid.

40. "Public Interest Pretenders," p. 317.

41. Thomas Scarlett, "Killing Health Care Reform," *Campaigns & Elections,* October/Nov. 1994, p. 34.

42. Blair Childs speaking at "Shaping Public Opinion: If You Don't Do It, Somebody Else Will," in Chicago, Dec. 9, 1994.

43. Ibid.

44. Robin Toner, "Harry and Louise and a Guy Named Ben," *New York Times,* Sept. 9, 1994.

45. Blair Childs speaking at "Shaping Public Opinion: If You Don't Do It, Somebody Else Will," in Chicago, Dec. 9, 1994.

46. Ibid.

47. Fallows, p. 28.

Chapter Eight:
The Sludge Hits the Fan

1. Nancy Blatt, letter to John Stauber, May 3, 1995.

2. Myron Peretz Glazer and Penina Migdal Glazer, *The Whistle Blowers,* (New York: Basic Books, 1989), p. 135.

3. Interview with Hugh Kaufman.

4. Abby Rockefeller, "Sewage Treatment Plants vs. the Environment" (unpublished document), Oct. 1992, p. 1.

5. Pat Costner and Joe Thornton, "Sewage Treatment Plants," *We All Live Downstream: The Mississippi River and the National Toxics Crisis,* Dec. 1989, p. 35.

6. Debra K. Rubin, Tom Ichniowski, Steven W. Setzer and Mary Buckner Powers, "Clean Water Act Debate Swirls On," *Engineering News-Record,* Vol. 227, No. 14, Oct. 7, 1991, p. 27.

7. Ronald A. Taylor, "Clean-Water Campaign Springs Some Leaks," *US News & World Report,* Dec. 24, 1979, p. 59.

8. Tim Darnell, "Till the Cows Come Home: Rural Wastewater Treatment Plants," *American City & County,* Vol. 106, No. 10, p. 26.

9. Rockefeller, p. 2.

10. Gareth Jones, et al., *HarperCollins Dictionary of Environmental Science,* (New York: HarperPerennial, 1992), p. 372.

11. Stephen Lester, "Sewage Sludge . . . A Dangerous Fertilizer," *Everyone's Backyard,* Oct. 1992, p. 9.

12. Jim Wells et al., "Nuclear Regulation: Action Needed to Control Radioactive Contamination at Sewage Treatment Plants," *GAO Reports* B-255099, June 23, 1994.

13. "In Waste Water, the Talk is About Toxics," *Chemical Week,* Oct. 12, 1977.

14. Costner and Thornton, pp. 35-37.

15. Interview with Hugh Kaufman.

16. "Recycling Sludge Onto Farmlands," *Business Week,* Nov. 7, 1977, p. 84B.

17. "For WPCF: New Directions," *Engineering News-Record,* April 10, 1986, p. 60.

18. "Recycling Sludge Onto Farmlands."

19. Geordie Wilson, "New Name Sought to End Grudge on Sludge, er, Biolife," *Seattle Times,* May 22, 1991, p. A1. Also see "WPCF Reports Strong Support for Name-Change Campaign," *Sludge,* Vol. 16, No. 9, April 24, 1991.

20. "Water Group Plans Earth Day Launch for National Campaign on Biosolids Recycling," *PR Newswire,* April 21, 1994.

21. Geordie Wilson, "Its Name Is Mud, So Sludge Gets a New One," *Seattle Times,* Jan. 31, 1992, p. A1.

22. "WPCF Pins Hopes on Biosolids' to Replace the Term Sludge," *Sludge* Vol. 16, No. 17, Aug. 14, 1991.

23. James W. Bynum, "EPA-Sludge: The Fox Guarding the Chicken House" (unpublished manuscript), May 8, 1995, pp. 3, 14.

24. Debra K. Rubin, "New Name for an Old Group," *Engineering News-Record,* Vol. 227, No. 16, p. 9.

25. "Water Group Plans Earth Day Launch."

26. Paul Hodge, "Trying to Cope With a 600-ton-a-day Sludge Problem, Naturally," *Washington Post*, Jan. 6, 1977.

27. Milwaukee Metropolitan Sewerage District, promotional brochure for Milorganite, 1995.

28. Melvin N. Kramer, Ph.D., executive summary of testimony given Oct. 1, 1992 before the U.S. House of Representatives, Committee on Merchant Marine and Fisheries, Subcommittee on Coast Guard Navigation, Hearing on Ocean Dumping Enforcement and the Current Status of Research Efforts, pp. 1-2.

29. Dianne Dumanoski, "Specialists Debunk Claim of Sludge-Pellet Hazards," *Boston Globe*, July 16, 1992, p. 27.

30. Joseph Zinobile, letter to Environmental Quality Board, Harrisburg, PA, Dec. 27, 1994.

31. Stanford. L. Tackett, "The Myth of Sewage Sludge Safety," delivered at the Municipal Sewage Sludge Conference, State College, PA, May 21, 1994.

32. Stanford L. Tackett, "The Sewage Sludge Scam, " *The Gazette*, Indiana, PA, Oct. 2, 1994.

33. Ibid.

34. Interview with Alan Rubin.

35. Jane Beswick, "Some Interconnected Persons and Organizations in Sludge" (unpublished manuscript), 1994.

36. 1994 Annual Report and Form 10-K of N-Viro International Corporation, p. 1.

37. Ibid., pp. 2-4.

38. William Sanjour, statement to the Georgia State Senate Committee on Natural Resources, Feb. 14, 1990.

39. Patricia L. Deese, et al., *Institutional Constraints and Public Acceptance Barriers to Utilization of Municipal Wastewater and Sludge for Land Reclamation and Biomass Production* (Washington, DC: US Environmental Protection Agency, 1981), pp. 22, 27.

40. Ibid., pp. 3, 33-34.

41. Kelly Sarber, "How to Strategize for Successful Project Development," *BioCycle*, April, 1994, p. 32-35.

42. Ibid.

43. Ibid.

44. Dennis Hevesi, "Investigation Begun Into New York City Sludge Removal Program," *New York Times*, April 16, 1992, p. B3.

45. "Ocean & Medical Waste Dumping, P.L. 100-688," *Legislative History, Senate Report No. 100-431*, pp. 5869-5872.

46. Kevin Flynn, "Sludge Withdrawals Leave City Mired," *Newsday*, Nov. 15, 1991, p. 21.

47. "Oklahoma Places Moratorium on Sludge from Out-of-State," *Sludge*, Vol. 17, No. 9, April 22, 1992.

48. Michael Specter, "Ultimate Alchemy: Sludge to Gold: Big New York Export May Make Desert, and Budget, Bloom," *New York Times*, Jan. 25, 1993, p. B1.

49. Michael Moss, "Officials Seek Probe on Sludge Haulers," *Newsday*, Feb. 4, 1991, p. 21.

50. Kevin Flynn, "Sludge Plan Probe: DA Checks Ties Between Firms and Politicians," *Newsday*, April 15, 1992, p. 23.

51. Kevin Flynn, Tom Curran and Kathleen Kerr, "Mobster: Sludge Firm Tied to Crime Family," *Newsday*, June 4, 1992, p. 110.

52. Selwyn Raab, "Mafia Tale: Looting the Steel of the West Side Highway," *New York Times*, May 9, 1993, Section 1, p. 27.

53. Kevin Flynn and Michael Moss, "Stink Over Sludge: Arizona Says City's Waste Contaminated," *Newsday*, Aug. 2, 1994, p. A08.

54. Ibid.

55. Kevin Flynn, "City Sludge Plan Kept Under Wraps," *Newsday*, Dec. 10, 1991, p. 21.

56. Keith Bagwell, "Sewer Sludge from NYC is Deposited on Farmland," *Arizona Daily Star*, May 22, 1994, p. 1B.

57. Keith Bagwell, "Tainted Sludge Used for Years on Pima Farms," *Arizona Daily Star*, Oct. 2, 1994, p. 1B.

58. Bagwell, "Sewer Sludge from NYC."

59. Keith Bagwell, "Sludge Test Could Result in Cleanup," *Arizona Daily Star*, June 25, 1994, p. 1B.

60. Keith Bagwell, "Sludge is Found to Harbor Germs Far Beyond Limit," *Arizona Daily Star*, July 28, 1995.

61. "Texas County Tempted by Financial Rewards of Dumps," National Public Radio All Things Considered, March 21, 1994, Transcript #1428-6.

62. *Sludge*, Sept. 27, 1994.

63. Maggie Rivas, "W. Texans Fight to Reject Dumping Sites: Climate to Store Nuclear Waste, Sludge Called Ideal," *The Dallas Morning News*, March 20, 1994, p. 45A.

64. "Abraham Angry With TNRCC," *Texas Industry Environmental Advisor*, Vol. 7, No. 4, Feb. 25, 1994.

65. Michael Moss and Kevin Flynn, "Flushing, Texas: Exported City Sludge is Tainted," *Newsday*, Aug. 3, 1994, p. 7.

66. Transcript of TV Nation program, NBC Television, Aug. 2, 1994.
67. Ibid.
68. "EPA Whistleblower, Sony Inc. Named in $33 Million Libel Suit," *BNA Chemical Regulation Daily,* Jan. 6, 1995.
69. "Whistleblower Seeks Special Prosecutor, Alleges Obstruction in Texas Sludge Case," *BNA National Environment Daily,* April 5, 1995.
70. Timothy M. Straub, et al., "Hazards from Pathogenic Microorganisms in Land-Disposed Sewage Sludge," *Reviews of Environmental Contamination and Toxicology,* Vol. 132, (New York: Springer-Verlag, 1993), p. 55-91.
71. Ibid.
72. Letter from Kenneth Dobin to Sandra Messner, Feb. 10, 1994.
73. "Community Organizers: Some Composting Sites Could Be Harming Neighbors' Health," *Sludge,* Vol. 19, No. 7, March 29, 1994.
74. Interview with Ed Rollers.
75. Ed Merriman, "Farmers, Public Warned of Sludge Danger," *Capital Press,* July 19, 1991, p. 3.
76. Statement of Karl Schurr, presented to the Coshocton County Board of Health, Coschocton, OH, Nov. 1992.
77. Gene Logsdon, "Public Acceptance: How Does Society Learn About Sludge Safety?" *BioCycle,* May 1992.
78. "Acceptance Strategy Should Include World Wide Web Sit, Media Relations," *Sludge,* Vol. 20, No. 16, Aug. 1, 1995, p. 127.
79. Letter from J.M. Dryer, Heinz USA, to Jane Shumaker, Nov. 19, 1992.
80. Letter from Chris Meyers, Del Monte, to Alice Gallagher, March 24, 1995.
81. Interview with Rick Jarman.
82. Interview with Brian Baker.

Chapter Nine: Silencing Spring

1. Rachel Carson, *Silent Spring,* (New York: Houghton Mifflin, 1962).
2. Frank Graham, Jr., *Since Silent Spring,* (New York: Houghton Mifflin, 1970), pp. 1-94.
3. "Monsanto Chemical Company published a rebuttal to Rachel Carson's Silent Spring," *PR News Casebook,* (Detroit: Gale Research, 1993), p. 439.
4. Janet Raloff, "Beyond Estrogens," *Science News,* Vol. 148, No. 3, July 15, 1995, pp. 44-46.
5. E. Bruce Harrison, *Going Green: How to Communicate Your Company's Environmental Commitment,* (Homewood, IL: Business One Irwin, 1993).
6. News release from E. Bruce Harrison, April 14, 1994.
7. *O'Dwyer's Directory of Public Relations Firms 1994,* pp. 75-76.
8. *O'Dwyer's Directory of Public Relations Firms 1990,* p. 220.
9. There is no exact figure; this is the authors' best estimate, based on the estimates of PR industry observers.
10. Kevin McCauley, "Going Green Blossoms as PR Trend of the 90s," *O'Dwyer's PR Services Report,* Jan. 1991, p. 1.
11. E. Bruce Harrison, "Managing for Better Green Reputations," *International PR Review,* Vol. 17, No. 3, 1994, p. 25.
12. Rush Limbaugh, *The Way things Ought to Be* (New York: Simon & Schuster, 1992), p. 167.
13. Judi Bari, *Timber Wars* (Monroe, ME: Common Courage Press, 1994), pp. 98, 135, 178.
14. Carl Deal, *The Greenpeace Guide to Anti-Environmental Organizations* (Berkeley, CA: Odian Press, 1993), p. 84.
15. Joe Lyford, Jr., "Trade Uber Alles," *Propaganda Review,* No. 11, 1994, p. 26.
16. Howard Muson, "Winds of Change," *Across the Board,* June, 1994, p. 23.
17. Ibid.
18. Harrison, p. 8.
19. Ron Arnold, "Getting Rich: The Environmental Movement's Income, Salary, Contributor, and Investment Patterns" (The Center for the Defense of Free Enterprise, 1994), p. 7.
20. Harrison, p. 216.
21. Keith Schneider, "For the Environment, Compassion Fatigue," *New York Times,* Nov. 6, 1994.
22. McDonald's news release on PR Newswire, April 11, 1995.
23. Tom Kuntz, "The McLibel Trial," *New York Times,* Aug. 6, 1995, p. E7.
24. Mark Dowie, *Losing Ground: American Environmentalism at the Close of the 20th Century,* (Cambridge: MIT Press, 1995), p. 140.
25. Harrison, p. 277.
26. Jerry Mander, *In the Absence of the Sacred: The Failure of Technology and the Survival of the Indian Nations,* (San Francisco: Sierra Club Books, 1991), p. 131.

27. "S.W.A.T. Team Blitzes the Nation," Monsanto news release, March, 1994.
28. Allen Center and Patrick Jackson, *Public Relations Practices,* 4th edition (Englewood Cliffs, NJ: Prentice Hall, 1990), p. 354.
29. Peter Stisser, "A Deeper Shade of Green," *American Demographics,* March, 1994.
30. Jenni Laidman, *Bay City Times,* Saginaw, MI, Sept. 12, 1994.
31. *The Green Business Letter,* Washington, DC, March 1994, pp. 1, 6-7.
32. Ibid.
33. Gregg Easterbrook, "Forget PCBs, Radon, Alar," *New York Times Magazine,* Sept. 11, 1994.
34. Carl Deal, p. 62-63.
35. Ibid.
36. *Earth Day—The Beginning,* (New York: Arno Press & *New York Times,* 1970), p. xv.
37. Ibid.
38. Arnold, p. 9.
39. Interview with Bruce Anderson.
40. Interview with Gaylord Nelson.
41. Ibid.
42. Interview with Bruce Anderson.
43. Mark Megalli and Andy Friedman, *Masks of Deception: Corporate Front Groups in America* (Essential Information, 1991), pp. 90-93.
44. "Profiles of Top Environmental PR Firms: Shandwick Public Affairs," *O'Dwyer's PR Services Report,* Feb. 1995, p. 41.
45. *O'Dwyer's Directory of PR Firms 1993.*
46. "Profiles of Top Environmental PR Firms: Shandwick Public Affairs," *O'Dwyer's PR Services Report,* Feb. 1995, p. 41.
47. *O'Dwyer's Directory of PR Firms 1993.*
48. Interview with Jerry Klamon.
49. Internal memorandum, Earth Day USA, Sept. 28, 1994.
50. Terry Mollner and James Dixon, "The Earth Day Corporate Team," memo, pp. 7-9.
51. John H. Cushman, Jr., "A Tug-of-war Over Earth Day '95," *New York Times,* Oct. 29, 1994. See also Jack Anderson and Michael Binstein, "Earth Day and Corporate Greenwashing," *Washington Post,* March 27, 1995.
52. "Working Draft—An Environmental Petition to Newt Gingrich," Jan. 1995.
53. "Don't Get Hopes Up With GOP Congress," *O'Dwyer's PR Services Report,* Feb. 1995, p. 6.
54. "GOP Set to Slash, Not Trash, Green Regs, Say PR Execs," *O'Dwyer's PR Services Report,* Feb. 1995, pp. 1, 8.

55. Gregg Easterbrook, *A Moment on the Earth,* (New York: Viking, 1995).
56. Advertisement, *New York Times Book Review,* April 16, 1995, p. 5.
57. Peter Montague, "Rush Limbaugh With Book Learning," *Rachel's Environment & Health Weekly* #437, April 13, 1995.
58. Easterbrook, *A Moment on the Earth,* p. 255.
59. Gregg Easterbrook, "The Good Earth Looks Better," *New York Times,* April 21, 1995.
60. "New Environmental Grass Roots Sprouting," *PR News,* Vol. 51, No. 2, Jan. 9, 1995, p. 1.
61. Stuart Auerbach, "PR Gets Entrenched as a Washington Business," *Washington Post,* February 18, 1995, quoted in Joyce Nelson, "Great Global Greenwash," *Covert Action,* Spring 1993, p. 58.
62. James Lindheim, "Restoring the Image of the Chemical Industry," *Chemistry and Industry,* August 7, 1989, p. 491, quoted in Joyce Nelson, "Great Global Greenwash," p. 57.
63. "A Stealth Campaign by Timber Industry," *Seattle Post-Intelligencer,* Dec. 26, 1993, p. D2.
64. "Edelman Helps 'Wise Use' Group Get Coverage from DC Fest," *O'Dwyer's Washington Report,* Vol. V, No. 12, June 5, 1995.
65. "Profiles of Top Environmental PR Firms," *O'Dwyer's PR Services Report,* Feb. 1995, p. 31.
66. Joyce Nelson, "Dangerous Anti-Environmental PR," sent to authors, 1995.
67. Claude Emery, SHARE Groups in British Columbia, Canada Library of Parliament, Dec. 10, 1991, p. 20.
68. Dean Kuipers, "The Gambler's Summit," *Propaganda Review,* No. 11, 1994, p. 17.
69. *The Greenpeace Guide to Anti-Environmental Organizations,* p. 25.
70. Kuipers, p. 21.
71. David Helvarg, *The War Against The Greens: The "Wise Use" Movement, The New Right and Anti-Environmental Violence,* (San Francisco: Sierra Club Books, 1994), p. 358.

Chapter Ten: The Torturers' Lobby

1. Sheldon Rampton, "Colombia: The Bosnia in Our Own Backyard," *Z Magazine,* March 1994, p. 34.
2. Ibid., pp. 34-35.

3. Barry Siegel, "Spin Doctors to the World," *Los Angeles Times Magazine,* Nov. 24, 1991, p. 18.

4. Kevin McCauley, "Sawyer Miller Ads Battle Drug-Marred Image of Colombia," *O'Dwyer's PR Services,* Aug. 1991, p. 1.

5. Siegel.

6. Ibid.

7. "Juan Valdez, Call Your Office," *Newsweek,* June 20, 1988, p. 53.

8. Siegel.

9. Ana Arana, "The Colombia Connection: What Did Sawyer/Miller Do For Its Money?" *Colombia Journalism Review,* Vol. 31, No. 3, Sept./Oct. 1992, p. 32.

10. McCauley.

11. Rampton, pp. 35-36.

12. Ibid., pp. 37-38.

13. Steven Gutkin, "Is Colombia's Drug War for Real?" *Washington Post,* July 22, 1995.

14. Alex Carey, *Taking the Risk Out of Democracy: Propaganda in the US and Australia,* (Sydney, Australia: University of New South Wales Press, 1995), p. 12.

15. Scott M. Cutlip, *The Unseen Power: Public Relations: A History* (Hillsdale, NJ: Lawrence Erlbaum Assoc., 1994), pp. 143-155.

16. Ibid.

17. Trento, p. 205.

18. John Omicinski, "Capital Insiders Get Millions from Rights-Abusing Countries," Gannett News Service, Dec. 14, 1992.

19. "Agents of Influence," *The National Journal,* Vol. 24, No. 51-52, Dec. 19, 1992, p. 2904.

20. Trento, pp. 209-210.

21. *Haiti: A Look at the Reality,* (Hyattsville, MD: Quixote Center, 1993).

22. Phil Davison, "'Shadow' Plays Dirty Tricks in Haiti," *The Independent,* Nov. 2, 1993, p. 12.

23. Dick Kirschten, "Haitian Headache," *National Journal,* March 13, 1993.

24. Nancy Nusser, "Ex-Dade Politico Helps Haiti's Army," *The Palm Beach Post,* Sept. 3, 1993, p. 1A.

25. Robert C. McCandless, Foreign Agents Registration Act statement, May 20, 1992.

26. James Ridgeway, "Family Business: Haiti's Behind-the-Scenes Warriors Come Out in the Open," *Village Voice,* Oct. 26, 1993, p. 22.

27. Robert C. McCandless, "A Suggested Compromise: To End the Haitian Embargo Stalemate" (attachment to a letter to US Rep. Charles Rangel), Aug. 13, 1992, p. 2.

28. Robert D. Novak, "Why So Hard on Haiti's Military?" *Washington Post,* Oct. 21, 1993.

29. Robert D. Novak, "Allegations About Aristide," *Washington Post,* Oct. 28, 1993.

30. Ridgeway, p. 21.

31. Don Bohning and Christopher Marquis, "Powerful Haitian Clan's Tie to Peace Process Criticized," *Miami Herald,* March 2, 1993, p. 1A.

32. "Haitian Army: Docile Instrument of US Hegemony," *Haiti Info,* Vol. 2, #26, Sept. 23, 1994.

33. Gary Gunderson and Tom Peterson, "What We Think: American Views on Development and US-Third World Relations," *Needs,* June 1987, p. 6. (This citation, along with footnotes 33-37, was quoted previously in Liz Chilsen and Sheldon Rampton, *Friends In Deed: The Story of US-Nicaragua Sister Cities* (Madison, WI: Wisconsin Coordinating Council on Nicaragua, 1988), pp. 91-92.

34. Nick Eberstadt, "The Perversion of Foreign Aid," *Commentary,* June 1985, p. 19.

35. Ibid.

36. Andrew E. Rice and Gordon Donald, Jr., "A Constituency for Foreign Assistance," in *U.S. Foreign Assistance: Investment or Folly?,* ed. by Gerry Feinstein and John Wilhelm (New York: Praeger, 1984), p. 358.

37. Ibid., p. 360.

38. Vincent Kavaloski, "The Alchemy of Love," Foreword to Chilsen and Rampton, *Friends In Deed,* p. ix.

39. John R. MacArthur, *Second Front: Censorship and Propaganda in the Gulf War,* (Berkeley, CA: University of CA Press, 1992), pp. 51-53.

40. Sheldon Rampton, "Soldier Tired of 'Blowing Things Up,' " *Daily Register,* Dec. 31, 1983, p. 1.

41. MacArthur.

42. Ibid.

43. Ibid.

44. Sara Miles, "The Real War: Low-Intensity Conflict in Central America," *NACLA Report on the Americas,* Vol. XX, No. 2, April/May 1986, p. 19.

45. Rudy Maxa, "Managua, Nicaragua, Is a Hell of a Spot," *Washington Post Magazine,* Nov. 13, 1977, p. 5.

46. Karen DeYoung, "Politics by Media in Managua: Self-described 'Flack' Helps US Reporters 'Understand' Somoza," *Washington Post,* Feb. 9, 1978, p. A22.

47. Norman L. Wolfson, "Selling Somoza: The Lost Cause of a PR Man," *National Review,* July 20, 1979.

48. Edgar Chamorro, written affidavit, Sept. 5, 1985.

49. Miles, pp. 30-32.

50. Ibid., p. 34.

51. Ibid., pp. 40, 42.

52. Robert Parry and Peter Kornbluh, "Iran/Contra's Untold Story," *Foreign Policy,* No. 72, Fall 1988, p. 4.

53. Ben Bradlee, Jr., *Guts and Glory: The Rise and Fall of Oliver North,* quoted in "Gelb Fights to Restore USIA Satellite TV Network," *O'Dwyer's PR Services,* Oct. 1989, p. 1.

54. Jack O'Dwyer and Jerry Walker, "PR Played Major Role in Events of Iran-Contra Affair," *O'Dwyer's PR Services,* Jan. 1989, p. 1.

55. Ibid.

56. *New York Times,* Aug. 13, 1985; *Washington Post,* Sept. 3, 1985.

57. O'Dwyer and Walker.

58. Parry and Kornbluh.

59. "Alleged 'White Propaganda' of S/LPD Criticized by Comptroller General," *O'Dwyer's PR Services,* Jan. 1989, p. 42.

60. Parry and Kornbluh, p. 25.

61. Ibid.

62. *Washington Post,* March 1986.

63. Ronald Reagan, televised presidential address, March 16, 1986.

64. Trento, chapter 12.

65. Jack O'Dwyer, "Glenn Souham, Son of PR Exec, is Youthful Victim of Iran-Contra Affair," *O'Dwyer's PR Services,* March 1989, p. 10.

66. Judy Butler, interview with George Vukelich, Jan. 1987.

67. "Gelb Fights to Restore USIA Satellite TV Network," *O'Dwyer's PR Services,* Oct. 1989, p. 1.

68. "Harrison, Who Accused Four PRSA Members, Resigns," *O'Dwyer's PR Services,* May 1990, p. 34. See also "PRSA/DC May Hold Debate on CIA Ethics Case," *O'Dwyer's PR Services,* Aug. 1989.

69. MacArthur.

70. Ibid.

71. Hal D. Steward, "A Public Relations Plan for the US Military in the Middle East," *Public Relations Quarterly,* Winter 1990-91, p. 10.

72. "H&K leads PR charge in behalf of Kuwaiti cause," *O'Dwyer's PR Services Report,* Vol. 5, No. 1, Jan. 1991, p.8.

73. "Citizens for Free Kuwait Files with FARA After a Nine-month Lag," *O'Dwyer's FARA Report,* Vol. 1, No. 9, Oct. 1991, p. 2. See also Arthur E. Rowse, "Flacking for the Emir," *The Progressive,* May, 1991, p. 22.

74. *O'Dwyer's FARA Report,* Vol. 1, No. 9, Oct. 1991, pp. 2.

75. *O'Dwyer's PR Services Report,* Vol. 5, No. 1, Jan. 1991, pp. 8, 10.

76. Ibid., p. 1.

77. Rowse, pp. 21-22.

78. Martin A. Lee & Norman Solomon, *Unreliable Sources: A Guide to Detecting Bias in News Media* (New York: Lyle Stuart, 1991), p. xvii.

79. Transcript, "To Sell A War", pp. 3-4.

80. MacArthur, p. 60.

81. Ibid.

82. Ibid., p.58.

83. Ibid.

84. Ibid., p. 54.

85. *New York Times/CBS News* poll, as reported in *O'Dwyer's PR Services Report,* Jan. 1991, p. 10.

86. "To Sell A War," pp. 4-5.

87. MacArthur, p. 7.

88. Lee & Solomon, p. xix.

89. Herminio Rebollo and Leticia Rodriquez, "Mexico Spent $56 Million to Promote NAFTA in the US," *El Financiero Internacional,* April 19, 1993, p. 10.

90. Christopher Whalen, *The Mexico Report,* Aug. 3, 1994, p. 14. Also telephone interview with Whalen, Aug. 9, 1994.

91. Interview with Carlos Diaz in Burson-Marsteller's offices in Mexico City, Aug. 12, 1994.

92. Jim Cason and David Brooks, "La Situación en México no se Percibe en EU," *La Jornada,* Aug. 13, 1995, p. 8.

93. Luis Javier Garrido, "El Fraude Imperfecto," *La Jornada,* Aug. 26, 1995, p. 14.

94. Richard Simpson, et al., "Report on Low-Intensity Conflict in Marquéz de Comillas," Global Exchange, July 5, 1995.

Chapter Eleven:
All the News that's Fit to Print

1. Ben Bagdikian, *The Media Monopoly,* 4th edition, (Boston: Beacon Press, 1992), p. xxvii.

2. Interview with Ben Bagdikian.

3. Buck Donham, "All the Criticism of Journalism" (internet posting to alt.journalism.criticism), March 3, 1995.

4. Jeff and Marie Blyskal, *PR: How the Public Relations Industry Writes the News,* (New York: William Morrow & Co., 1985), p. 28.
5. Interview with Pam Berns.
6. PR Newswire promotional material, 1994.
7. North American Precis Syndicate promotional material, 1994.
8. RadioUSA promotional material, 1994.
9. Interview with Bob Goldberg, president of Feature Photo Service.
10. Trento, p. 245.
11. David Lieberman, "Fake News," *TV Guide,* Feb. 22-28, 1992, p. 10.
12. George Glazer, "Let's Settle the Question of VNRs," *Public Relations Quarterly,* Spring 1993.
13. Trento, p. 231, 233.
14. Speech by Rotbart at Nov. 1993 PRSA conference.
15. TJFR promotional material.
16. *TJFR Environmental News Reporter,* Feb. 1995.
17. Rowan and Blewitt report to National Dairy Board, July 13, 1989.
18. CARMA report to National Dairy Board, May-Aug. 1989.
19. "12 Reporters Help Shape Pesticides PR Policies," *Environment Writer,* Vol. 6, No. 11, National Safety Council, Washington, DC, Feb. 1995, pp. 1, 4-5.
20. Ibid.
21. Dashka Slater, "Dress Rehearsal for Disaster," *Sierra,* May/June 1994, p. 53.
22. Promotional information, Video Monitoring Services, 1994.
23. Jonathan Rabinovitz, "Computer Network Helps Journalists Find Academic Experts," *New York Times,* May 23, 1994.
24. Howard Kurtz, "Dr. Whelan's Media Operation," *Columbia Journalism Review,* March/April 1990.
25. Ibid. See also Ann Reilly Dowd, "Environmentalists Are on the Run," *Fortune,* Sept. 19, 1994, p. 92.
26. Rhys Roth, *No Sweat News,* Olympia, WA, Fall 1992.
27. David Shaw, "Feeling Bombarded by Bad News," *Los Angeles Times,* Sept. 11, 1994.
28. Samuel S. Epstein, "Evaluation of the National Cancer Program and Proposed Reforms," *American Journal of Independent Medicine,* No. 24, 1993, pp. 102-133.
29. David Steinman, "Brainwashing Greenwashers: Polluting Industries Are Waging a Long-Term Disinformation Campaign to Attack the Environmentalist Agenda," *LA Village View,* Nov. 18-23, 1994, pp. 11-12.
30. *Measures of Progress Against Cancer—Cancer Prevention, Significant Accomplishments 1982–1992,* The National Cancer Institute.
31. Rick Weiss, "How Goes the War on Cancer? Are Cases Going Up? Are Death Rates Going Down?" *Washington Post,* Feb. 14, 1995.
32. *Cancer at a Crossroads: A Report to Congress for the Nation,* National Cancer Advisory Board, Sept. 1994.
33. Blyskal, p. 34.
34. Kim Goldberg, *This Magazine,* Toronto, Aug. 1993.
35. Ben Parfitt, "PR Giants, President's Men, and B.C. Trees," *The Georgia Straight,* Vancouver, BC, Feb. 21-28, 1991, p. 7.
36. Dilenschneider, p. 177.
37. Ronald K.L. Collins, *Dictating Content,* (Washington, DC: Center for the Study of Commercialism, 1992).
38. *National Journal,* Oct. 9, 1993.
39. "Resisting Disclosure," *Political Finance & Lobby Reporter,* Vol. XVI, No. 12, June 28, 1995, p. 12.
40. John Dillon, p.36.
41. Trento, p. xi.
42. John Keane, *The Media and Democracy,* (Cambridge, UK: Polity Press, 1991), p. 63.
43. Robert W. McChesney, "Information Superhighway Robbery," *In These Times,* July 10, 1995, p. 14.
44. Kirk Hallahan, "Public Relations and Circumvention of the Press," *Public Relations Quarterly,* Summer 1994, pp. 17-19.

Chapter Twelve:
Taking Back Your Own Back Yard

1. Pamela Whitney speaking at "Shaping Public Opinion: If You Don't Do It, Somebody Else Will," in Chicago, Dec. 9, 1994.
2. Ibid.
3. Mark Falcoff, "Why Europeans Support the Sandinistas," *Commentary,* Aug. 1987.
4. Leslie Wirpsa, "Poor Seek Ways Out of Nicaraguan Crisis," *National Catholic Reporter,* May 27, 1995, p. 7.
5. Dowie, p. 133.
6. Jane Anne Morris, *Not In My Back Yard: The Handbook,* (San Diego, CA: Silvercat Publications, 1994), p. 185.
7. Dowie, p. 131.
8. Carey, p. 20.
9. Mander, p. 123.
10. *PR News,* June 19, 1995.

Index

ABC, 57, 74, 167, 179, 194
Accuracy in Academia, 141
Accuracy in Media, 141, 165
activists, 3, 12, 30, 31, 38, 46-47, 49, 51-55, 57-63, 66-69, 72, 85, 87, 92, 108, 123, 125-130, 132-134, 141, 199, 200-202, 210
Addington, Bill, 117
advertising, 3-4, 6, 13, 18, 20, 21, 25-30, 40-44, 46, 74, 89, 92, 97-98, 130-131, 138, 145-146, 161-169, 175, 182, 189, 193-194, 196, 207-208, 211
Advocacy Communications Team, 30
Advocacy Institute, 69, 214
Aetna Life and Casualty, 96
agribusiness, 10, 123-124, 131, 135
alcohol industry, 65-66
Alex Carey, 148, 197, 202
Alliance for America, 140
Allison, Ed, 41
Alsop, Dee, 171
Altamira Communications, 15
American Academy of Pediatrics, 58
American Airlines, 207
American Beverage Institute, 66
American Cancer Society, 28, 70
American Civil Liberties Union, 69, 83
American Council of Life Insurance, 93
American Council on Science and Health, 9, 189-190
American Cyanamid, 55
American Energy Alliance, 208
American Express, 89
American Federation of Teachers, 52
American Heart Association, 29
American Lung Association, 29
American Medical Association, 58, 125
American Nuclear Energy Council, 41, 43-44
American Petroleum Institute, 93
American Tobacco Company, 1, 25-26
American Tort Reform Association, 96
Americans Against Unfair Gas Taxes, 93
Americans for Constitutional Freedom, 14
Americas Watch, 144
Ameritech, 68
Amnesty International, 74, 144, 174

Amoco, 142
Anderson, Bruce, 134-135, 137
Animal Health Institute, 57
animal rights, 47-48, 60-64, 74, 127, 212
Animal Rights Reporter, 60, 64
antifreeze poisonings, 197-199
APCO Associates, 87
Archer Daniels Midland, 134-135
ARCO Petroleum, 127, 188
Argentina, 193, 207
Aristide, Jean-Bertrand, 151-154
Aristotle, 15, 66
Arkansas Gazette, 182
Armstrong, Donald, 116
Arnold, Ron, 140-142
Arnot, Bob, 194
Ashland Oil, 68-69
Askari, Emilia, 187
Associated Press, 184
astroturf, *see* grassroots PR
AT&T, 72, 80, 83, 136, 193, 208
atomic energy, 33-46, 54, 83, 121, 163, 199-200
Babbitt, Bruce, 97
Bagdikian, Ben, 181, 193
Bagwell, Keith, 115
Bahrain, 169
Baker, Brian, 122
Baker, Howard, 50-51
Baker, Jim, 179
Baltimore Gas & Electric Company, 46
Barnes, Fred, 194
Barnum, Phineas T., 17-19
Bartlett, Kim, 62
Barton, Melanie, 115
Baucus, Max, 103
Bay City Times, 131
Beckel Cowan PR, 79, 93, 95
Ben & Jerry's Ice Cream, 71-76
Bennett, Robert F., 50-51
Bennett, Wallace, 50
Bentsen, Lloyd, 79
Bernays, Edward, 1, 22-26, 32-34, 202
Berns, Pam, 183
Bernstein, Carl, 51, 180, 194
Beswick, Jane, 200